RIOTS

AND

RELIGION

IN NEWFOUNDLAND

The Clash between Protestants and Catholics
in the Early Settlement of Newfoundland

DAVID DAWE

FLANKER PRESS
ST. JOHN'S
2011

Library and Archives Canada Cataloguing in Publication

Dawe, David
    Riots and religion in Newfoundland : the clash between Protestants and Catholics in the early history of Newfoundland / David Dawe.

Includes bibliographical references and index.
Issued also in an electronic format.
ISBN 978-1-926881-04-1

1. Catholic church--Newfoundland and Labrador--Relations--Protestant churches--History.
2. Protestant churches--Newfoundland and Labrador--Relations--Catholic church--History.
3. Catholics--Newfoundland and Labrador--History. 4. Protestants--Newfoundland and Labrador--History. 5. Newfoundland and Labrador--History. 6. Newfoundland and Labrador--Religion. I. Title.

FC2170.R45D38 2011   971.8   C2011-904780-2

PRINTED IN CANADA

Cover Design: Adam Freake
Edited by Iona Bulgin

FLANKER PRESS
P.O. BOX 2522, STATION C
ST. JOHN'S, NL A1C 6K1 CANADA
TOLL-FREE: 1-866-739-4420
WWW.FLANKERPRESS.COM

Canada 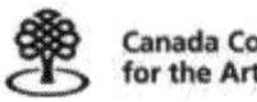 Canada Council for the Arts   Conseil des Art du Canada    Newfoundland Labrador

15 14 13 12 11   2 3 4 5 6 7 8

We acknowledge the financial support of: the Government of Canada through the Book Publishing Industry Development Program (BPIDP); the Canada Council for the Arts which last year invested $20.1 million in writing and publishing throughout Canada; the Government of Newfoundland and Labrador, Department of Tourism, Culture and Recreation.

Table of Contents

FOREWORD

This work is the result of a personal interest that developed into a passion. It began as a term paper in an undergraduate history course at Memorial University in 1980, and was later rejuvenated during a spontaneous trip to the Provincial Archives, then located at the old Colonial Building. Ever since, the conflict between our English and Irish ancestors has captivated me, tempting me to tell the story that most history books have overlooked, diminished, or ignored altogether. This story is such an integral part of who we are, and where we came from, that I knew it had to be told. Although the topic can be somewhat controversial in the minds of some readers, it is still fascinating. I hope you will agree.

I have attempted to reconstruct every scene, including dialogue, as accurately as possible; however, the early records are somewhat stingy on details. For that reason I have exercised literary licence in chapters one through six in order to make the story more complete and enjoyable. Be assured that the facts were not altered, and that nothing was added that absolutely did not, nor could not, have occurred.

I would like to humbly acknowledge several important secondary sources that were used in my research. Patrick O'Flaherty's *Old Newfoundland: A History to 1843*, and *Lost Country*; Gertrude Gunn's *The Political History of Newfoundland 1832 to 1864*; and John Greene's *Between Damnation and Starvation*. Some of the old standbys were also useful, particularly Prowse's *A History of Newfoundland*, with its treasury of footnotes and narratives. Equally important, but probably lesser known to the general reading public, was Keith Matthews's *Lectures on the History of Newfoundland: 1500–1830*, which provided much of the background information regarding English and Irish settlement patterns throughout the province in the seventeenth, eighteenth, and nineteenth centuries. Other secondary sources, all very helpful, are listed in the accompanying bibliography.

The research for primary sources was done mostly in the Provincial Archives, now located at The Rooms, and The Centre for Newfoundland Studies at Memorial University. I wish to extend thanks to the staffs of these two institutions for their valuable assistance and conversation over the years. Larry Dohey of the Archives of the Roman Catholic Archdiocese at The Basilica was also very accommodating in my search for Bishops Fleming and Mullock—the men, not just the clergymen.

I will be forever indebted to my cousin, Karen Dawe, former editor of *The Newfoundland Herald,* who took an interest in my work some years ago and provided me with an opportunity to share my passion with her readers.

My deepest gratitude is extended to my wife and children, who throughout this lengthy process provided me with the constructive criticism and continuous encouragement needed to complete the work.

Dave Dawe
January, 2010

INTRODUCTION

You are to permit a liberty of conscience to all persons, except Papists, so they be contented with a quiet and peaceable enjoyment of the same, not giving offence or scandal to the government.

Instructions to Governors of Newfoundland

1729–1779

Given enough time and patience most Newfoundlanders, if so inclined, could trace their ancestry across the stormy, treacherous North Atlantic to the ancient, mystical lands of England and Ireland. It would be a fascinating walk through time, a journey with many twists and turns, and a destination that would probably raise as many questions as answers, most notably, Why? Why did they leave their homeland all those years ago to settle in the harsh, rugged, yet beautiful land that we today call home? For many, the inspiration behind the move was simple economics. After all, John Cabot had discovered something that would prove to be much more valuable to the English than the New Founde Lande—the rich fishing grounds of the Grand Banks.

Though the English were initially slow to appreciate the potential of their new find, their interest did increase throughout the 1500s and, by the seventeenth century, thousands of West Countrymen had become involved in a fabulous venture known as the "migratory fishery." Returning year after year to these rocky shores, many crews soon realized the value of wintering in the new land for the purpose of preparing their supplies and gear for the next fishing season. Permanent settlement, though not fully sanctioned by the home government until the nineteenth century, despite several honest attempts, evolved sluggishly from the multitude of tiny fishing "rooms" scattered along the coast.

The original "livyers" were hardy, adventurous Englishmen who were willing to leave the Old World behind in order to build hope in the New. Notwithstanding the struggle that eventually developed with the powerful fish merchants back home, to varying degrees and for various reasons these settlers were to remain loyal to the mother country. They were, after all, proud Englishmen.

Our Irish ancestors had a different story.

At first the Irish came as indentured servants to English planters involved in the fishery. However, as the years passed more and more came simply to escape the woeful conditions of their homeland under English rule. On arrival most were in a state of destitution. Besides being poor, they were uneducated and undernourished, with little to contribute to a flourishing industry and a slowly growing colony.

The story of the English and Irish in Newfoundland is generally *not* one of peace and harmony. We could hardly expect that it would be any different, when we consider the lengthy and bitter struggle in the Old Country. For generations the Irish had suffered defeat and humiliation at the hands of English invaders. Not surprisingly, their hatred for the English was carried to the New World, where it festered in a society not totally unlike that of their homeland. Since most Irish were Roman Catholic, the distrust and animosity between them and the early English was in no way alleviated by the existence of strong anti-Catholic laws. The records contain many cases where an Irish settler had his land confiscated and property destroyed for the crime of allowing Mass to be said in his home.

It is little wonder that the inevitable clash between these two ethnic groups would be a prolonged and nasty affair. Though the conflict did not peak until after the granting of representative government in 1832, when religious strife became amplified by political discordance, ugly examples of sectarianism had manifested in the colony long before that. During d'Iberville's terrible campaign of 1696, for example, many Irish were known to have collaborated with the French, a treachery more easily understood when we recall that it had been but a few years since King William had crossed the Boyne. If the priest Abbé Baudoin, who accompanied d'Iberville, was correct, we could hardly expect the Irish to have remained loyal to their masters. In his journal, Baudoin wrote, "The English treat their Irish servants like slaves."

The raid was devastating to English planters all along the Avalon from Ferryland to Heart's Content, and became particularly brutal when the French commander allowed his Indian allies to scalp a captured settler. If the English had felt that the Irish were not particularly trustworthy before, then 1696 likely confirmed their suspicions.

In the following years a criminal element that was largely Irish in configuration developed within Newfoundland society. Though criminal activity was by no means exclusive to the Irish population, according to period records most convicted felons seem to have been members of that ethnic group. This curious statistic was probably as much a reflection of the prejudices that infested the various judicial offices of the time as it was a statement of the *type* of Irishman that inhabited Newfoundland.

One particularly heinous crime committed by a gang of Irishmen and one Irishwoman in 1754 certainly did nothing to diminish English hostilities. This was the brutal robbery and murder of William Keen, a prominent merchant and one of the wealthiest men on the island. Over the years Keen had held various positions in St. John's, including that of magistrate, a role that inevitably brought him into conflict with some of the old town's most undesirable elements, including the rowdy soldiers stationed there for the citizens' protection.

Edmund McGuire, an Irishman in Captain Christopher Aldridge's company of troops, was very familiar with Magistrate Keen's court. A charge of larceny had been laid against McGuire on at least one occasion, and, in September, 1754, he waited to reappear for the more serious offence of assaulting a constable the previous winter.[1]

His earlier convictions, plus the extreme likelihood of a harsh sentence for the alleged assault, may have motivated McGuire to commit the crime which was to lead to his rather ghastly demise.

The story of the English and Irish in Newfoundland begins here, a period when the migratory fishery was still strong but rapidly being displaced due to a continued growth in the resident population. Coin-

---

1. McGuire and another soldier named Hurley had beaten Constable John Worth so severely that he had to beg for his life.

cidently, the mid-1700s was also a period of significant increase in the number of Irish immigrants coming to Newfoundland, a fact which did not go unnoticed by wary English authorities. The murder of William Keen on the night of September 29, 1754, would have extremely serious repercussions throughout the island for the already disadvantaged Irish settlers.

Chapter 1

The Murder of Magistrate William Keen

You are therefore hereby required and directed to repair on board His Majesty's Ship Penzance *at eleven o'clock this morning and there take under your charge Edmund McGuire and Matthew Halluran, and to see the said sentence executed in the manner following. At twelve o'clock this noon you are to cause the said Edmund McGuire and Matthew Halluran to be hanged by their necks on the gibbett erected on the wharf of Mr. William Keen until they are dead and then their bodies to be taken down and hung in chains in the place appointed for that purpose.*

Warrant from Governor Bonfoy to William Thomas, Sheriff

October 10, 1754

It probably came as no surprise that Edmund McGuire was not the only person with sinister plans for Magistrate Keen during the early fall of 1754. Two others who demonstrated no favourable opinion of Keen were Eleanor Power and her husband, Robert. It is believed that Mrs. Power had previously been employed by Keen, and that the scheme to rob him was born during her servitude. The Powers had assembled a band of brigands that included McGuire, along with several others, three of whom were also soldiers stationed at Fort William.

On the night of September 29, 1754, the gang hid in the woods behind the judge's house in Quidi Vidi, devising the best means by which to carry out their plan. Concern about the loyalty of several of those present impelled Eleanor, who came to the event disguised as a man, to produce a Bible so that all might swear allegiance to the others and vow never to tell the truth of this night. By the pale light of a flickering candle each of the ten swore an oath and then kissed the Holy Book.

One of the gang who had been feeling apprehensive was Nicholas

1

Tobin. On October 7, eight days after the crime, either his conscience or his nerves would get the better of him and he would give a complete confession before Magistrate Michael Gill. His deposition provides many of the details of the robbery and murder of William Keen.

Following the strange ceremony in the woods, four of the gang, armed with muskets, positioned themselves around the house to warn of anyone's approach. Eleanor and the remaining members pried open the front door as quietly as possible, then, by the dim light of a candle, crept inside. In no time they retrieved a small wooden chest and some silver cutlery from the dining room. Pleased with the swiftness of their operation, the gang skulked into the woods, eager to lay their hands on the contents of the chest, and to make good their escape. To everyone's surprise, however, when McGuire smashed open the lid with a hatchet, instead of gold coin they found a chest full of liquor bottles.

Angered and disappointed, some of the group immediately suggested re-entering and searching the house. But there was uncertainty and fear among others, who felt that it was pure folly to go back. Even Eleanor, the instigator of the plot, believed that they had been lucky to get in and out without being discovered, but to attempt a second entry was to invite misfortune. Not wanting to take unnecessary chances, Eleanor and Lawrence Lamley then left.

Two others, Nicholas Tobin and a soldier named Dennis Hawkins, influenced by the departure of the first two, also voiced their objections to re-entering the house. However, Edmund McGuire and a third soldier, John Munhall, would tolerate no more desertions. Munhall grabbed Tobin and shook him violently, as McGuire pointed his musket at the two recreants, reminding them of their oath. Seething with anger, McGuire threatened to kill both of them if they attempted to leave, and declared that he should have killed Lamley and the woman. Fearing that the enraged soldiers might follow through on this threat, Robert Power then attempted to prove his complete loyalty to the scheme by suggesting that they might have to kill the magistrate in order to get his money. The possibility was obvious to Munhall, who snatched up one of the liquor bottles and ordered Tobin to drink a dram.

With all signs of mutiny temporarily in abeyance, the eight

remaining conspirators returned to the Keen house, a darker evil now their intent. This time McGuire, Halluran, Munhall, and the fourth soldier, a lad named John Moody, entered the house together. The other four remained outside on watch. McGuire, now the apparent leader, immediately headed upstairs with a musket in one hand, and a candle in the other, followed by Halluran, who was armed with the rusty blade of an old scythe he had found outside.

The candle barely lit the stairwell as the two mounted the steps, inching their way closer to their murderous design. The flickering flame cast weird shadows on the walls and ceiling, and the floorboards creaked underfoot. After an imagined eternity the two men stood outside William Keen's bedroom. Peering into the dark, they could barely discern his form beneath the blankets, but no trunk or strongbox was visible. Halluran whispered that they look under the bed, for it would be just like the old bugger to sleep on top of his money.

Creeping into the room, they approached the bed from opposite sides, and Halluran cautiously lowered himself to his knees. Under the bed was indeed a wooden box. At the most inappropriate moment, however, Halluran hastily snatched up the treasure, bumping the box loudly against one of the posts. Instantly, Keen awakened and, upon seeing the two armed intruders, began screaming at the top of his lungs: "Murder! Murder!"

Unwilling to be denied the wealth in their hands, the two Irishmen pulled the blankets over Keen's head, immobilizing him. Keen was wrestling for his life, and, during the struggle, knocked the candle out of McGuire's hand onto the floor, extinguishing it. Fearful that the alarm had already been raised, in the darkness Halluran plunged his weapon twice through Keen's body. Blood spattered over the two attackers but, to ensure that the deed was done, McGuire lifted his musket and slammed it down on Keen's head.[1]

Yet the murderers were about to find that they had been duped by the judge once again, for the box concealed nothing more than

---

1. Some sources claim that Keen actually lived for another two weeks after the attack. This is an unlikely scenario because of the date of the trial against the conspirators.

shoe buckles. Disgusted, McGuire grabbed the pitiful loot and fled the house with Halluran close behind.

A little more than a week later, aided by Tobin's confession, the conspirators were rounded up. For security reasons, the four miscreant soldiers were held in the blockhouse of the fort, while the civilian outlaws were thrown into the brig of the HMS *Penzance*, a man-of-war anchored in St. John's harbour. For turning king's evidence, Nicholas Tobin was granted a full pardon. The trial for the remaining nine began and ended on October 8. Within one half-hour after the judge had directed them, the jurors returned their verdict: guilty of the felony and murder charges.

Justice was swift and almost as brutal as the crime itself. All nine were sentenced to be hanged, but for McGuire, Halluran, Robert Power, and his wife, Eleanor, Magistrate Gill declared that they also be "hanged in chains."[2]

Later, upon scrutinizing the evidence, Governor Bonfoy saw fit to respite the execution of five of the gang, but not before McGuire, Halluran, and the two Powers had been executed. Ironically, or some might say appropriately, the gallows had been erected on the wharf of the late Magistrate Keen. There was no doubt that the old judge had tried his last case.

The intent of Eleanor Power and her little band has never been made clear. Had they simply planned to rob William Keen, or had murder been a part of their sinister design from the beginning? There is evidence to suggest that others within the Irish community knew of the plan to *murder* the judge, but withheld this information from the authorities. This revelation followed the trial, and resulted in an outbreak of widespread paranoia among the English, many of whom believed that this crime was but the beginning of a local Irish uprising. Governor Bonfoy reacted to this fear by initiating the cruellest anti-Irish campaign Newfoundland was ever to experience. For relatively

---

2. "Hanging in chains," or gibbeting, meant that the body of the executed criminal was tarred, wrapped in chains, and left hanging from a wooden gallows for months or even years. The gruesome spectacle of a rotting corpse was meant to deter other would-be criminals.

minor crimes, property was seized, severe punishments meted out, and many Irish settlers banished from the island with nothing but the clothes on their backs. Although there were criminals within their numbers, most local Irish were peaceable, law-abiding citizens, who wanted nothing to do with robbery and murder.

In 1755, Governor Dorrill, Bonfoy's successor, continued the unrestrained persecution of Irish Catholics. Having learned that a "renegade priest" was in Conception Bay, Dorrill sent this message to the magistrates at Harbour Grace:

> *Whereas I am informed that a Roman Catholic priest is at this time at Harbour Grace, and that he publicly read Mass, which is contrary to the law, and against the peace of our Sovereign Lord the King, you are hereby required and directed on receipt of this, to cause the said priest to be taken into custody and round to this place. In this you are not to fail.*

Concern over Irish aggression was further heightened in 1756, when war again broke out between England and France. This concern was apparently substantiated when the French attacked and captured St. John's in 1762 with a force of 750 soldiers, 161 of whom were Irish. During this brief occupation there were numerous accounts of pillage and rape, some of the worst examples allegedly being perpetrated by Irishmen, thus "verifying" what the English had feared.

When peace returned in 1763 there was little chance that the English in Newfoundland would willingly forgive and forget the atrocities that had been committed. The prejudices and distrust of the pre-war years likely intensified after the siege of St. John's.

Dramatic liberal changes beyond the control of local authorities would soon occur. A new "enlightenment" was dawning in the mother country. Eleven years after the Treaty of Paris had ended the Seven Years War, new legislation guaranteed French Canadian Catholics the right to worship freely in their own faith and hold public office.[3]

Although the real reason for English generosity at this time may

---

3. This was the Quebec Act of 1774.

have been to persuade Quebecers not to join with their rebellious neighbours to the south, the seeds of liberalism had been planted. By 1779 Newfoundland's Catholics were also afforded the right to free worship. It would be another five years, though, before the first priest arrived. Father James Louis O'Donel was an Irish Franciscan with a love of his religion and a desire to live in harmony with his English neighbours.

But old ways die hard. Although Irish Catholics now worshipped as they wished, most were still considered to belong to the "lower orders" of society, and enjoyed few of the same privileges as their English counterparts. Any change in this status was not coming easily.[4]

The arrival of Father O'Donel in 1784 tended to the spiritual needs of many Irish Catholics, but it was the appearance of a different character that kindled their admiration. In a relatively short time this dashing figure would become the champion of the oppressed and underprivileged, the folk hero of whom tales were spun while listeners gathered around a roaring mid-winter fire. Though no doubt the stories have been greatly exaggerated over the years, and evidence supports that this "hero" was little more than a clever highwayman in charge of a band of thieves, the legend of Peter Kerrivan lives, even today, along the Avalon's southern shore.

---

4. "Lower orders" was the term generally used to refer to the lower class of society. During the eighteenth and early nineteenth centuries, a greater portion of the lower orders was composed of Irish.

CHAPTER 2

PETER KERRIVAN AND THE SOCIETY OF MASTERLESS MEN

Gentlemen,
Having considered your letter of the 1st, and the several papers accompa-
nying it, which contain an account of your proceedings relative to the
Irish convicts . . . until such time as proper Steps can be taken to send
them out of the Country, I am to acquaint you that altho' there does not
appear to be any Charge made against them so as to authorize their being
remitted to Prison, yet, as the safety of the Place was at stake, I think you
acted very prudently in complying with the desire of the Inhabitants, and
thereby prevented many irregularities in the Fishery, which would have
been the consequence of suffering such a Banditti to go at large about the
Island.

Governor Mark Milbanke
September 10, 1789

Gentle waves lapped at the shoreline, belying the sombre mood of the crowd gathered to watch the event taking place. From the English warship anchored in Ferryland harbour the steady beat of a military drum sounded, interrupted occasionally by the shouts of an officer on board. Movement on the deck of the vessel caused a slight but noticeable stir among the spectators on shore, as many jostled for a better view. Seconds later four prisoners could be seen upon the quarterdeck, surrounded by heavily armed guards who paraded them before a small group of officers. Dressed in tattered clothing, their faces dirty and unshaven, their shoulder-length hair tangled and unkempt, the four were a motley group. Up close they appeared to be wild and uncivilized men. To the local people, however, these prisoners became fondly known as the "Irish youngsters," a term used to refer to any young Irishman indentured to an English planter. The four had been captured by a marine patrol sent into the woods behind

Ferryland to search for the infamous Peter Kerrivan and his Society of Masterless Men. The four prisoners were said to be recent recruits of the gang.

Once in custody they had been given a lopsided trial by frustrated authorities desperately wanting to set an example for others who might wish to join Kerrivan. A guilty verdict had seemed predetermined. Now, standing defiantly before Captain Edward Pellew of His Majesty's frigate *Winchelsea*, the four young Irishmen would soon pay the ultimate price for their brief adventure with the lawless.[1]

Pellew spoke with a voice loud enough that those on shore would hear, and heed his words: "You men have been found guilty in a court of law of numerous acts of sedition and civil disobedience. A sentence of death has been decreed, for which we here today have assembled to witness. Do any of you have any final words or requests, before we carry on with the business?"

Pellew tapped the hilt of his sword impatiently, and scornfully glared at the prisoners before him. He expected expressions of remorse, or maybe a plea for mercy. But the silence was broken only by his tapping, and the creaking of the ship's rigging.

Finally, with a tone of exasperation, Pellew spoke again: "Very well, then! Let's get on with it, shall we, gentlemen."

One at a time, each of the prisoners shuffled forward amidship, where he was ordered to stand in the open gangway. One of four nooses that hung from a yardarm high above the deck was placed around his neck and, with ceremonial indifference, he was pushed off.

Following each execution a moan of barely suppressed anger and horror arose from those onshore. As the last body swung out from the ship's side, still convulsing as it was hoisted to join the three already swinging above, a voice shouted, "Erin go braugh!" followed by a loud cheer of defiance that echoed across the water.

* * * * *

---

1. Edward Pellew was destined to become one of Britain's greatest naval captains during the Napoleonic Wars.

This scene is partly fictional, yet based on the evidence provided in the records. Although four young Irishmen, members of Peter Kerrivan's Society of Masterless Men, were caught by a squad of British marines and executed aboard a Royal Navy frigate in Ferryland harbour, many details of the story remain elusive. We know that Captain Pellew and his ship had been ordered to Ferryland in October, 1788, by Governor Elliot, to spend the ensuing winter there. This action was due to the riots which had plagued that community during the previous winter, as well as a subsequent petition from local merchants for military protection. In September, 1789, a letter written by the new governor, Mark Milbanke, tells of the peace and quietness which prevailed at Ferryland throughout the year following Pellew's assignment, and attributed this to the captain's efforts.

Though we might speculate that Pellew had laid down the heavy hand of military justice often during his tenure in Ferryland, we do not know if he was responsible for hanging the four Irish youngsters. In fact, we are not certain that they were even executed during the time Pellew was in Ferryland. Pellew, however, later appears as a member of the Ferryland Surrogate Court, in 1791. On March 24 of that year 137 Irishmen were convicted of "riotous and unlawful assembly" for the 1788 disturbances, and were penalized with fines and/or deportation. Many of these men were convicted *in absentia*, and court documents for the proceedings bear the notation, "Sentence to be executed if they return." Some of those absent from court may have been members of the Masterless Men. One of those convicted in 1791 was Thomas Kerrivan, who was fined £7, sentenced to be lashed thirty-nine times, and ordered to be sent "home" to Ireland. This Kerrivan may have been related to the leader of the outlaw band.

For years many have wondered about the existence of this so-called Society of Masterless Men. Who were they? Where did they come from? How did they live? Most, apparently, had been indentured servants who had run away from their masters—thus the significance of the gang's name. During the seventeenth and eighteenth centuries, planters in the Newfoundland fishery often had indentured servants, usually Irishmen, who were brought to the New World with the agreement that they would work for the planter, their "master," for a set period of time. On the expiration of that time the servant was set "free," and sometimes given money or goods earlier agreed on, so that he or she could start a new life.

Many planters treated their servants as slaves, as Baudoin had noted in his journal almost 100 years earlier. Frequent lashings constantly reminded the servant of his or her station. Numerous planters cheated their way out of having to pay the earlier negotiated remittance. As a result, many servants ran away from their masters rather than having to cope with the torturous life they had unknowingly agreed to.

Other members of Kerrivan's Masterless Men were deserters from the Royal Navy. Their charismatic leader was an Irishman who had been pressed into the navy while just a lad.[2]

In 1750 Peter and several of his companions had slipped away from their ship while it was anchored in a port on Newfoundland's Avalon Peninsula, and had fled deep into the wilderness to avoid inevitable search parties. They established a hideout on the Butter Pot, a 1,000-foot peak well inland from Ferryland, and learned to live by hunting, gathering edible plants and berries, and stealing from nearby communities. Before long, they had developed a small but lucrative black market with local fishermen, trading furs and wild meat for gunpowder, shot, and other necessities.

In the late eighteenth century, an extremely difficult period for the Irish in Newfoundland, the campaign against Irish Catholicism undoubtedly contributed to the rapid growth of Kerrivan's little band, which quickly gained a reputation for its bold raids upon southern shore merchants.

With the passage of time, tales of the gang's exploits became

---

2. Life aboard a naval vessel in the age of sail was quite harsh. In addition to the obvious hazards of warfare, the food was usually bad, there were lengthy periods at sea, and the lash was used frequently by cruel officers. As it was sometimes difficult to find sailors willing to spend their lives in these difficult conditions, naval captains would order "press gangs" ashore to force, even kidnap, men to fill their crews. Thus the term "pressed into the navy."

common knowledge and, with each narrative, more exaggerated. Through a combination of fact and fiction, Peter Kerrivan and the Society of Masterless Men became legends in their own time, heroes to a class of people who were constantly being trampled by the rich and powerful. Kerrivan's admirers created the fallacious image of a New World Robin Hood. There is little evidence that Peter robbed from the rich and gave to the poor, but there is plenty of evidence that local sympathizers aided the Masterless Men, not only by illegal trading, but also by acting as their spies.

Even though at least three expeditions were sent by the British navy to find and execute all of the Masterless Men living in the Butter Pot area, the only one with any success was the one which captured the four Irish youngsters. The gang likely had prior knowledge of each military excursion launched against them, and each time they eluded the authorities by skilful use of trails and false leads constructed for such a purpose. After three attempts, the British navy let well enough alone, probably due to the overall cost in man-hours, frustration with the lack of any tangible success, and the realization that they were fighting a lost cause against a partisan group with much local support. After the third military failure, the outlaw problem became a matter for civil authorities.

The British assessment of a strong support group within the communities for the Masterless Men was correct. Several members, including Peter Kerrivan, even sought courtship and marriage with local girls. Because of the gang's status amongst the Irish population, some of the relationships were likely approved by the parents of these young women. In most cases, the wives moved back to the Butter Pot to remain with their husbands and raise their families there. This resulted in a proliferation of the outlaw community, which lived freely for at least another generation.

One interesting yet controversial feature of the tale of the Masterless Men is the supposed contact between them and the Beothuks. During the late 1700s an English planter from Ferryland named Robert Carter supposedly shot and killed three Indians who appeared on the hills just west of the town. If this report was true, it may prove that natives were still living on the Avalon Peninsula during the early years of the Masterless Men, and that there was contact between the two groups. Local folktales suggest that some Beothuks joined the gang as a means of personal survival once they realized that their tribe was rapidly dying off. A great deal of conjecture surrounds this part of the Kerrivan legend, however, since most historians say that the Beothuks had left the Avalon well before the end of the eighteenth century.

Coincidently, by the early nineteenth century, around the same time that the Beothuks were fading from a land which had been theirs for so long, the Masterless Men were also declining in number. The latter's main source of recruits had always been servants who had run away from cruel masters, but by the early 1800s times had changed. Fishermen were now given legal rights, thus providing an opportunity for "free" servants to eke out a livelihood on their own. Permanent settlement was finally gaining recognition in a colony which, for centuries, had been viewed by the home government in England as little more than a seasonal fishing station for West Country merchants. In 1783, Governor John Campbell partially ended the dark days of Catholicism in Newfoundland by granting permission for a chapel to be built in St. John's. The following year Father James O'Donel arrived, and by 1790 authorized clergy were placed in three other communities, including Ferryland. As well as ministering to the spiritual needs of the populace, O'Donel likely exerted his peaceful and law-abiding influence.

In addition to legal and clerical advancements, a general upswing in Newfoundland's economy as a result of the Napoleonic Wars, and later the War of 1812, became evident in this period. Salt fish produced in Newfoundland was a staple food for the British army and navy, providing a steady market for the merchants. These improvements gave men incentive to remain in settlements and make an honest living. The life of the outlaw had begun to look less attractive, even to the Masterless Men. Around 1820, the last of the band had either returned to civilized society or died off.

Perhaps to his credit, but certainly to the admiration of many,

Peter Kerrivan refused to leave the wilderness that had been his home and sanctuary for so long. He survived to a ripe old age, and died upon the Butter Pot on some unknown date, leaving behind an adventurous spirit that lives today in the hearts of his many descendants.

In 1793, during what was probably the height of Kerrivan's career, war between England and France had broken out again. Though prosperous times were just ahead, in 1793 Newfoundland experienced great difficulty: the fishery was in recession, powerful merchants in the home country were renewing their efforts to maintain control of the local economy, and the Irish problem persisted. Although prohibition of the Catholic religion had been lifted fourteen years earlier, the plight of most Irish would soon be significantly altered. O'Donel had worked tirelessly since his arrival building churches and lobbying for more priests to minister to the needs of Newfoundland's Catholics, a fairly successful campaign that most Protestants eyed with envy and suspicion. Ironically, O'Donel would prove himself a valuable ally to the authorities around the turn of the century, even to the point of saving the colony from armed insurrection at the hands of his fellow Irish.

CHAPTER 3
THE UPRISING OF THE UNITED IRISH SOCIETY

Oh Paddy dear and did you hear the news that's going round,
The shamrock is forbidden by law to grow on Irish ground.
No more St. Patrick's Day we'll keep, his colours can't be seen,
For there's a cruel law against the wearing of the green.

"The Wearing of the Green"
Irish ballad

Guard duty on Signal Hill was never a popular assignment for soldiers stationed in St. John's. It was cold, windy, lonely, and monotonous. The long hours without comfort or companionship not only exhausted the men physically, it gave them far too much time to think. This was particularly worrisome for officers of the Newfoundland Regiment in the year 1800. Skinner's Fencibles, as the unit was commonly known, was composed largely of Irish immigrants or their descendants and, at a time when there was great unrest in the homeland, Irishmen on this side of the Atlantic were uniting with their fellow countrymen in a spirited cause that was ultimately destined to fail.

General John Skerret was in command of the regiment at this time. He was detested by his men for being a strict disciplinarian, but particularly because of his involvement in the suppression of Irish rebels during the bloody uprising of 1798. All had heard of the death of Father Michael Murphy, killed by Skerret's gunners while he lead his men at the Battle of Arklow, a martyr for the cause. Now, Irish fugitives were being discovered among the inhabitants of St. John's, having fled their homeland in the wake of the defeat of the United Irish.[1]

In fact, not long after his arrival in Newfoundland a year earlier,

---

1. The United Irish Society (UIS), formed in 1791, was dedicated to the overthrow of English rule in Ireland.

Skerret had learned of the presence of several Unitedmen he claimed to have ordered deported from Ireland.

Though Skerret may have been a tyrant, he was no fool, and immediately sought the aid of the Roman Catholic bishop, James Louis O'Donel, knowing of O'Donel's abhorrence for mob violence. Skerret soon learned that he had reasons to doubt the loyalty of the men under his command.[2]

His policy of firm discipline in response to a threat may have been typical of military leaders of the day, but it demonstrated an unfortunate apathy towards an already disgruntled regiment. In effect, Skerret's actions were to inadvertently cause the mutinous mood of soldiers to spread, forcing the hand of those who may have remained loyal.

* * * * *

After 300 years of European occupation the port of St. John's still had few amenities by the turn of the nineteenth century. Narrow, rutted streets, not much more than pathways were lined by unpainted, nondescript buildings. Hogs, dogs, fowls, and rats wandered the alleyways, vying for the same morsels of rotting sustenance that lay about the stinking ditches. In the east end, fish flakes on tall spruce poles hid the moving mass of offal that gave the place its repulsive name, Maggoty Cove. The stench of fish permeated everything. Rough and vulgar sailors from both sides of the Atlantic claimed this ground, mixed with equally rough and vulgar women who were willing to trade sex for money or liquor.

There were signs of decency and progress amid all the filth and depravity, however. Both the Church of England and the Roman Catholic Church had constructed houses of worship, relatively small buildings at this point, but each with its own promise of growth. Bishop

---

2. Two years earlier Sergeant James Dailey of the Newfoundland Regiment had planned a joint mutiny between the soldiers at Fort William and the sailors aboard HMS *Latona* anchored in the harbour. Though the conspiracy ended in failure, the threat of revolution remained long after harsh discipline had been dispensed.

O'Donel had worked particularly hard to turn the lost souls among his flock back to the path of righteousness. There was even talk of schools for the education of the young, with missionaries from the Society for the Propagation of the Gospel (SPG) speaking the loudest. Law, of a sorts, had existed for many years, though no real courthouse could be found amid the countless taverns. Fort Townshend, heavily armed and imposing, crowned the skyline above the cluster of buildings below, its image reminiscent of an earlier age when feudal lords ruled over their own fiefdoms. To the east stood the much older but still operative Fort William. At least in the spring of 1800 the citizenry of St. John's should have had little cause to worry when it came to foreign invasion. One could hardly have expected that the actual threat would come from within the ranks of the Newfoundland Regiment.

Grumblings of discontent were not unfamiliar to officers of His Majesty's military during this period. Everything from excessive drill to inadequate rations generated its share of complaints. But the word around the officers' mess in the spring of 1800 was much more serious than grievances over spoiled food.[3]

Rumours were being repeated about attempts by the United Irish Society (UIS) to enlist Irish soldiers from the regiment, and to join as many as 400 citizens to overthrow the military and take control of the town. The officers had learned that Governor Waldegrave may have been aware of the seditious intent of the Irish soldiers as early as the previous summer. Indeed, these rumours of mutiny and treason were soon confirmed for Skerret by a most unlikely source.

Sometime in early April, Bishop O'Donel called on the general with information he supposedly had gained from the confession of one of his parishioners.[4]

---

3. In 1798 the morale had dropped significantly, due in large part to the discovery that much of the salt beef and flour stored for the garrison's winter use was rotten beyond human consumption.

4. Historians debate the origin of O'Donel's information. It was Pedley, writing in 1863, who claimed that the bishop had heard of the scheme through confession. (Fitzgerald, John. "The United Uprising in Newfoundland, 1800," Newfoundland and Labrador Heritage website, 2001.)

Skerret thanked the bishop for his invaluable assistance, and moved to quash yet another rebellion, a mission that he probably relished in light of the enthusiasm with which he had performed the task in 1798.[5]

In the western sky the fading sunlight left behind a spectacular blend of yellow and red. Ships in the harbour rode peacefully on the swell of the incoming tide. Whiffs of smoke lifted from chimneys all over town. A gentle breeze stirred the trees ever so slightly.

In a lonely guardhouse atop Signal Hill, Sergeant Kelly waited. He paid no attention to the bucolic scene around him, his thoughts instead reviewing the plan, seeking reassurance of inevitable success. Though his demeanour betrayed no anxiety or misgivings about the cause, Kelly could not deny his concern about the possibility that Skerret and his officers were aware of the plot. Why else did the general order continuous drill last Sunday, the very day the mutiny was to begin? And what about this damned function that Colonel Skinner was presently hosting inside his quarters at Fort William? Coincidences? Maybe.

Kelly shook off his uneasiness, determined that this night would make all patriots in old Ireland proud. Tonight's work would revenge the crushing defeats of '98, the Boyne, and all others. Unitedmen would toast Tandy in that bastard Skerret's quarters before morning.[6]

Elsewhere in St. John's, James Murphy attempted to spread the order to all civilian members of the United brotherhood. At 11:00 p.m. soldiers from Signal Hill, as well as both forts, would rendezvous at the powder shed behind Fort Townshend. A surprise assault should quickly subdue any military resistance, essentially leaving the entire town in the hands of the UIS. Details of the actual subjugation of the military were apparently unnecessary, but it was hoped that large numbers of Irish within the regiment would not resist once it started.

---

5. Upon his retirement, O'Donel would receive a hefty pension from the British government, largely due to his role in informing the authorities of this uprising.

6. Napper Tandy was one of the leaders of the UIS uprising of 1798 in Ireland.

Covert signals were relayed throughout the town: a coded knock on a windowpane, a coloured rag tied to a tree, a discerning wink between passers-by. All designed to alert the brotherhood that the plan was afoot. As discreetly as possible, the members collected whatever weapons were available, then waited. All over town Englishmen and their families prepared for bed, completely unaware of the treachery unfolding in their very midst.

The western sky had darkened significantly and, from his vantage point high above Fort William, Sergeant Kelly could barely make out the line of horse-drawn carriages in front of Colonel Skinner's quarters. Though the signs were not good, there was no turning back now. Should the plan be delayed even one more night, the likelihood of success would be considerably diminished. It had to be tonight, and it had to succeed.

Sometime after 10:00 p.m., Kelly saw band of men emerge from the nearby woods. In spite of the darkness, he needed no signal to know who they were. There were twelve in the group, a number which pleased Kelly and lifted his confidence significantly, for it meant that virtually every man on guard duty atop Signal Hill had abandoned his post. With Kelly taking the lead, the band of deserters headed for their rendezvous. Unknown to the mutineers, however, their desertion had already been discovered by vigilant officers, who were about to spread the alarm.

By the assigned time of 11:00 p.m., Kelly and his followers had reached the powder shed and had been joined by six men from the detachment of Royal Artillery. But something was terribly wrong. A commotion was taking place far behind, and Kelly could not be sure what it meant.

Suddenly, several shots rang out from the vicinity of Fort William. Shouts, curses, the beating of drums, then, just as suddenly, silence. Anger and fear quickly overcame the men behind the shed. Although the element of surprise was obviously gone, Kelly still had no idea what had really happened. Were large numbers of his countrymen rising up? Was English blood being spilled for the many injustices committed upon the Irish? Or were the months of planning and anticipation about to be one more exercise in futility?

An eternity dragged by before Kelly detected movement. Scores of figures appeared at the eastern edge of the Barrens but, due to the darkness, it was practically impossible to tell if they were friend or foe. Their gait was swift and purposeful, like men who knew where they were headed, suggesting they might be Irishmen bound for the powder shed.

The truth was, these were loyal soldiers who had intercepted about thirty deserters, Unitedmen all. Their identity was not revealed to Kelly's band until it was too late, when from the darkened figures a voice of authority shouted for the mutineers to drop their weapons and surrender. The UIS uprising in Newfoundland was over before it had a chance to begin. The situation was not lost on Kelly and many of his followers, but some preferred to answer the order with gunfire. Several rounds from Kelly's men were answered by a heavy volley that quickly proved the futility of further resistance. The deadly consequences of capture were known to all, and thoughts of insurrection were suddenly replaced by those of flight. As musket balls whined overhead, the nineteen rebels beat a hasty retreat, with dozens of their former comrades in close pursuit.

In the days following the failed uprising, tensions continued to run high throughout the town and the regiment. For the English residents, the United conspiracy gave them cause to doubt the level of protection under which they lived. But, more significantly, it verified their distrust of their Irish neighbours.

Their fears may have been alleviated somewhat by the capture of most of the nineteen fugitives over the next fortnight. Hungry and exhausted, several men were caught after they had returned to St. John's searching for a safe haven. One of these was discovered by Captain William Haley hiding out in the loft of the Roman Catholic chapel.[7]

Of the original nineteen, the only two never found were the alleged leaders, Kelly and Murphy. As many as five of the captives may have turned king's evidence against their co-conspirators, for

---

7. The Bally Haley golf course in St. John's is named for Captain Haley.

they were never court-martialled, thus leaving twelve men to be tried for their pitiful act of treason.[8]

The trial was brief, the verdict predictable, the sentence harsh. Even Bishop O'Donel could find little cause for mercy:

I have a vast heap of trouble on my hands as I must very soon be preparing no small number of the Newfoundland Regiment for death. Those villains who formed a plot to take and plunder the town, were strictly bound together with the infamous link of the United Irishmen's oath.

Five of the convicted mutineers were sentenced to hang, the remaining seven to be transported to Halifax for execution by firing squad.[9]

Due to the local sheriff's concern that an attempt might be made to rescue the condemned men, Skerrett ordered the sentence against

---

8. The numbers are not consistent. Both Aiden O'Hara and John FitzGerald, in recent articles, claim that eight men were sentenced to be shot. However, in a letter to Governor Waldegrave on July 2, 1800, Jonathan Ogden stated that there were seven. I am inclined to favour Ogden's letter. (Fitzgerald, John. "The United Uprising in Newfoundland, 1800," Newfoundland and Labrador Heritage website, 2001.)

9. Various sources tell of different punishments being meted out to those who were not hanged at St. John's. John FitzGerald says that three of them were executed in Halifax, while the *Encyclopedia of Newfoundland and Labrador* says that the men faced life imprisonment. Again I refer to the letter from Ogden to Waldegrave which states, "General Skerret ordered a general court martial upon twelve of those taken, five of whom were sentenced to be hanged, and seven to be shot; the former were executed upon the gallows erected upon the spot where they met at the powder shed, the other seven were sent to Halifax, to be further dealt with as His Royal Highness should think proper." FitzGerald seems to be partially correct, though, as there is evidence that the Duke of Kent was going to remit the death sentences of all but three who had been sent to Halifax. Garret FitzGerald, Pierce Ivory, and Edward Power did hang, for they had somehow commandeered the vessel which was transporting them, but were overtaken and recaptured shortly thereafter. (Fitzgerald, John. "The United Uprising in Newfoundland, 1800," Newfoundland and Labrador Heritage website, 2001.)

the first five to be carried out swiftly. A gallows was therefore erected behind the powder shed, the site of the ill-fated rendezvous, a decision no doubt intended to insult as well as deter.

No records reveal how these five Irishmen behaved during their final moments. Quite likely they bore many emotions as they climbed those fatal steps: fear, anger, sorrow, and, possibly, no small measure of defiance. But General Skerret had the final word in this round of English/Irish dissension. The five bodies of his traitorous underlings were ordered to remain hanging in chains until he saw fit to have them removed. While the sight of putrefying corpses slowly twisting in the wind might have been more than enough to scare the daylights out of most men, evidence shows that it did not end anti-English sentiment among the Irish Catholics in St. John's. Without exaggeration, 1800 was merely a preview of the approaching years of torment and strife.

The remainder of Sergeant Kelly's band was shipped to Halifax for their appointment with the firing squad. To dissolve any further sentiments of mutiny within the Newfoundland Regiment, the Duke of Kent, commander of all British military in North America, ordered it also transferred to Halifax, where it would be removed from any undesirable Irish influence.

The story of the United Irish uprising in Newfoundland does not end there, however. Knowing the contempt Skerret held for traitors, and his unrelenting distrust of the Irish, we can correctly assume that his determination to round up all Unitedmen living in Newfoundland continued well beyond the events of 1800. A letter to the Duke of Kent the following summer clearly indicates his persistent fears:

> *The management of this conspiracy appears to have been under the direction of the same united men in town, and is of greater extent than I at first viewed. If I was at this moment empowered to declare martial law, I would say that the standard of rebellion was erected on this island.*

With these words Skerret expressed his belief that there were

UIS men living in many outports outside St. John's, especially along the southern shore, where the Irish vastly outnumbered the English. Proof of Skerret's determination to protect loyal English subjects, and to deter further acts of sedition, can be seen in his reinforcement of the garrison at Placentia, a town made up almost entirely of Irish Roman Catholics living under the influence of an Irish patriot named Pearce Sweetman.[10]

In fact, in 1805 Skerret was still sending letters to his superiors expressing strong doubts about the loyalty of the men under his command within the colony.

The attempted rebellion in St. John's in 1800 was a reaffirmation of sorts, for English residents had never learned to trust the Irish living among them. Ironically, they owed amends to Bishop O'Donel, an Irishman who was equally distrustful of "the maddened scum"[11] who aroused the naturally rebellious spirit of many of his countrymen. For several more years O'Donel ruled over his flock, working hard to instill peace and goodwill between them and their English neighbours.

O'Donel's pacifying nature served the English well in the years following the uprising of 1800. It was just as well, since increasingly prosperous times were ahead for all settlers in Newfoundland, and it would not do to have civil and military unrest disrupting them. The war with France, which overlapped with a war against the United States in 1812–14, was the catalyst for terrific economic growth. Not only were legal fish markets virtually monopolized by the Newfoundland trade, but also the brokers who ran black markets inside France and Spain grew to depend almost entirely on their erstwhile competitor.

Though official English policy continued to discourage permanent settlement, in the hope that when peace returned so too would the migratory fishery, the truth was that Newfoundland's population was growing and diversifying. In the early decades of the nineteenth century

---

10. Sweetman, an Irish merchant with premises in Placentia, was supposedly involved in the planning of the attack upon Ross during the UIS uprising in Ireland in 1798.

11. O'Donel's own words in a letter to the Catholic bishop of Quebec.

St. John's had numerous tradesmen, including carpenters, masons, and tailors, who were followed in 1807 by the first newspaperman, John Ryan. This last arrival, nearly coinciding with the appearance of the reformer Dr. William Carson, were, in the opinion of one historian, two of the most significant events to herald a new era in Newfoundland history.[12] Finally, after 300 years, Newfoundland was showing signs of becoming a *real* colony, despite the best efforts of influential West Country merchants and their powerful friends in Parliament.

News of Newfoundland's increasing prosperity soon spread to Europe, and instigated an influx of Irish immigrants to the island. Many of these newcomers may have been of an even less peaceable manner than their predecessors, though, particularly in the wake of the recent uprisings in Ireland.[13]

But for several years the control exercised by Bishop O'Donel and his successor, Patrick Lambert, kept most local Irish on the right side of the law.[14]

Between 1800 and 1816 Newfoundland's population tripled, due mostly to the large numbers of Irish who flocked to our shores seeking that which was denied them in their homeland—the opportunity to earn a good living.[15] Among those was young Patrick Morris, whose voice of reform, some would later say agitation, would ring loudly with that of Carson and others in the years ahead.

As long as times were good, there was little trouble. Work was abundant and wages were high, so there was hardly any need to beat the drum of political change, despite the obvious disparity between the wealthy and the working class, and the English and the

---

12. Patrick O'Flaherty, *Old Newfoundland: A History to 1843*, (St. John's, NL: Long Beach Press, 1999), 117–18.

13. Ibid., pp 122–23.

14. O'Donel resigned in 1807 because of declining health. He died in Ireland in 1811.

15. For more information on the Irish immigration to Newfoundland, see Keith Matthews, *Lectures on the History of Newfoundland: 1500–1830* (St. John's, NL: Breakwater Books, 1988).

Irish. And yet, men like Carson and Morris may have already been planning the future.

The first signs of economic slowdown became evident in 1814 after Spain imposed a set of tariffs on cod imported from Newfoundland, delivering a crippling blow to the fishery.[16]

With the sudden ruination of many planters and merchants came unemployment, and lots of it. The following year saw wages that were considerably lower, for anyone who was fortunate enough to find work. But the stream of Irish immigrants continued. Flooding the streets, they wandered, aimless and distraught, joining the hordes of the already impoverished, their dreams of a better life crushed. Crime increased drastically, for even law-abiding citizens had to eat. Though destitution was not an Irish monopoly during this time, the greatest percentage of the poor were from that ethnic group. It may have been only natural for implanted English settlers to eye these newly arrived Hibernians with more than a little distrust, and no small amount of contempt.

Within a very short period, the peaceful coexistence that Bishop O'Donel had struggled to achieve was to be literally incinerated, and the next few years some of the most depressing and tragic in Newfoundland's history.

---

16. See Shannon Ryan's analysis in *Newfoundland-Spanish Saltfish Trade: 1814–1914* (St. John's, NL: Harry Cuff Publications, 1983).

CHAPTER 4
THE WINTER OF THE RALS: PART ONE

According to the Dictionary of Newfoundland English, *the term "ral," in common usage in the early nineteenth century, was synonymous with "rowdy" or "hooligan."*

A savage wind howled through the evergreen trees, causing them to bend and shake in a most frightful manner. Painfully cold snowflakes swirled about, blinding the three men who slogged pathetically through the huge drifts, their heads bent into the wind and their hands clasping their collars tightly about their necks. Darkness had fallen an hour earlier, making it impossible to find the trail in the midst of what was turning out to be another of Nature's furies.

It was January 19, 1817, and already the island of Newfoundland had been nearly devastated by one storm after another, adding almost insufferable misery to a colony that was facing starvation after two utterly dismal fishing seasons. Both St. John's newspapers, *The Royal Gazette* and *The Mercantile Journal,* over the past several months had been full of notices of insolvency. It seemed that every reputable businessman in the capital city and the larger outports had gone bankrupt.

A few short years before, Newfoundland had experienced an economic boom that was the envy of the entire British empire. With the mother country at war against Napoleon in Europe and Uncle Sam in North America, Newfoundland merchants could basically name their price for the valuable salt cod needed to feed Britain's fighting men. The old colony had become so attractive that, during the years 1814 and 1815, 11,000 Irish had immigrated to St. John's, each in search of the wealth to be made in the fishery.

Ironically, the coming of peace to the outside world meant the end of prosperity for Newfoundland. The price of cod plummeted as traditional markets were swallowed up by nations that had been previously too busy fighting. By the winter of 1815 so many merchants had shut their doors permanently that there were hardly enough operable businesses to bring in adequate provisions.

Between 1815 and 1817 the prospects had worsened. As if man alone could not do enough to trample the crippled colony, Fate had also decided to try her hand. On February 12, 1816, a terrific fire in the capital city levelled 120 dwellings and several important businesses, leaving about 1,000 people homeless, cold now as well as hungry. By the winter of 1817 Newfoundland residents had already witnessed tremendously difficult times. Yet, little did they know of the terrible anguish they were about to face.

January 19, 1817, was not a fit night to be abroad anywhere, let alone miles into the wilderness. But Captain David Buchan of the Royal Navy and his two companions were on an urgent mission. Unceasing hardship had finally caused a transformation within the beleaguered population of Newfoundland, and lawlessness was rampant. Bands of half-starved, half-crazed citizens roamed the settlements, begging for food during the day, and looting everything in sight by night. Civil unrest had broken out in several communities, the latest in Bay of Bulls, a small fishing community about twenty miles south of St. John's.

On Friday, January 17, the brig *Guysborough* from Halifax had put in to Bay of Bulls, loaded with bread and flour for the starving residents. Six armed men, supported by an angry mob, seized the vessel and demanded the cargo be given to them. Later that night Magistrate Peter Carter from St. John's arrived in the community, followed by a contingent of soldiers from Fort Townshend and a number of seamen from Buchan's ship, HMS *Pike*. An armed standoff ensued the next day.

Owing to unforeseen circumstances, Captain Buchan and his companions, a lieutenant named Bishop, and a local man acting as guide, were unable to leave the capital city until two days after the *Guysborough* had been seized. Several miles into their journey the weather had rapidly worsened until by the time they were halfway to Bay of Bulls the three men struggled through waist-high drifts, the trail had disappeared completely, and they were lost.

Any possibility of reaching their destination that night gone, Buchan ordered the guide to head for the nearest settlement, Petty Harbour. They could find shelter there and, in the morning, continue their trip, hopefully with the storm abated.

The pitiless wind and snow confused the men's senses, each gust causing trees and boulders to appear and disappear like ghostly apparitions. Every step forward was a step into the unknown. The guns and provisions they carried grew heavier, becoming a burden that sank the men into the snow and sapped their energy. The excruciating cold penetrated to their bones, making any movement a painful task, and slowed their progress further. Hours of tormented searching failed to reveal the trail to lead them out of the woods. But just when their prayers seemed unheard and death in the frozen wilderness a dreadful likelihood, dawn broke and the storm gradually diminished. The three men were half a mile from Petty Harbour, cold, hungry, and utterly fatigued.

To their great relief, they soon discovered that the crisis in Bay of Bulls had ended. Four ringleaders had been apprehended by the military and would soon be in a St. John's jail. Oddly enough, the storm which had nearly killed Buchan was also responsible for allowing the *Guysborough* to escape from her captors and slip out of the harbour.

The brave Captain Buchan returned to St. John's, but his valuable services were required often over the ensuing months in communities throughout the colony. Only days later, reports trickled in from Carbonear, where a riot had erupted on January 25. A mob of about 150 people had raided the mercantile premises of John Elson, stealing, of all things, flour. From there the crowd had moved on to Gosse and Company, where they grew more violent and plundered everything in the storehouse. According to Elson, this act was committed primarily by "a banditti of persons living in tilts on the borders of the woods at the south side of the harbour, the majority Irish." Many, if not most, were recent immigrants with no real ties to the community, a group that had been eyed with suspicion since their arrival.

No single group, however, possessed a monopoly on violence during this horrible winter. Many who had been prosperous during the good years now had to turn to whatever means possible to survive. One observer tells how "The streets are now filled with beggars of the lower order by day, and then of the middle class of society by night."

Violence and mayhem were not restricted to one or two communities. St. John's, Carbonear, Harbour Grace, Brigus, Renews, Bay of Bulls, and Holyrood were all staggered by a continuous state of alarm. In many of these places citizens who still owned anything worth protecting, and who could be "entrusted with a flintlock," began organizing vigilante committees.

Throughout the winter months a lawless band of about 100 men roamed the streets of St. John's "assaulting and pilfering at will." In March a schooner bound for Placentia Bay was boarded by these ruffians, who intended to seize her cargo of bread. This act of piracy was foiled the next day, however, when the authorities captured the leaders of the mob and tossed them in jail. The remainder of the gang became so incensed and determined to free their comrades that a force of forty armed men were ordered to guard the prisoners for several days.

Meanwhile, in Harbour Grace mob rule had escalated when several schooners that had been preparing for the coming seal hunt were recklessly attacked and damaged so badly that they were unable to head to the Front. This inexcusable act was partly responsible for the dismal number of seals returned in the spring, at a time when most Newfoundlanders hoped that this relatively new industry might help alleviate some of their distress.

The hardships endured by the people of Newfoundland lessened only slightly with the end of winter. The terribly depressed fishing industry continued to produce hundreds of unemployed men who walked the streets with criminal intent. Those not involved in illicit activities only managed to survive through the charity of volunteers. All too soon, what could barely be called a fishing season came to an end, and the cold autumn air again announced another winter. The poor, demoralized citizens of Britain's oldest colony would experience a season that was unequalled by any other for its suffering and destitution. In view of the tribulations already witnessed, many would not have thought it possible.

CHAPTER 5
THE WINTER OF THE RALS: PART TWO

Sir - The brig Messenger, *of which you are master, having been chartered for the purpose of conveying a cargo of provisions to the suffering inhabitants of the town of St. John's in Newfoundland; we desire that you will proceed with all possible diligence to that place, and that, on your arrival, you will wait on His Excellency Francis Pickmore, commander in chief in and over the island, and request that he have the goodness to receive the cargo now laden on board your vessel, and dispose of the same in the manner pointed out in our respects of this date, and which we herewith commit to your charge.*

Instructions to Captain George Peterson
Boston, December 27, 1817

Candles and smelly cod oil lamps emitted a pale, ghostly light from the many public houses along Water Street. A northerly wind carried the bite of an early frost, confirming what many citizens had feared. The approaching winter would be just as long as the last, and, in all likelihood, just as cold.

The usual noises disturbed the night. Drunken soldiers and sailors, accompanied by equally intoxicated ladies of the evening, stumbled from one tavern to the next, laughing, shouting obscenities, and fighting among themselves. From somewhere came the loud crash of shattered glass, immediately followed by a barmaid's terrified screams and the thunderous curses of an irate tavern owner. A single pistol shot in the distance caused only a momentary interruption in the revelry. Gunfire at almost any time of the day or night had become fairly commonplace by November, 1817. It often meant nothing more than the death of a stray dog, or maybe even one of the huge rats that occupied every storehouse along the waterfront. But in recent months a pistol shot could just as likely mean the vigilante committee was pursuing yet another of the rals.

By 10:00 p.m. most "respectable" citizens were in their beds, secure in the belief that they were safe from the scoundrels who took over the town at night. Many, however, were not flippant about their immunity, and slept with a loaded weapon within easy reach. Those who were still awake could probably hear the distant call of the town crier, whose unlikely message brought some relief: "Ten o'clock, and all's well."

In a few short moments the crier's declaration was falsified. Some inebriated revellers walking between taverns realized a sharp increase in the cold wind as it funnelled through the narrow streets. Those who were more alert noticed something else: thick smoke rising from the eaves of a vacant house and billowing into Water Street.

"Fire! Fire!"

The ominous cry had an immediate and terrifying effect. The disastrous conflagration of 1816 was still a fresh memory for the people of this city, and everyone knew well the devastating possibilities of a windy night such as this. Dozens of men and women poured into the street, running in all directions. Within minutes tall flames burst through the roof of the house, and hundreds of blazing embers exploded into the sky, to land on nearby buildings like tiny incendiary bombs. Tarred roofs were ideal fuel and, before long, other fires were ignited, stoked by the ever-increasing wind.

Although the destruction of private homes was the immediate concern, the distinct possibility that this fire might spread to the large storehouses lying in its path was a frightful thought. These premises, owned by the city's most powerful merchants, contained the provisions, including food, necessary to get the colony through the winter months when the shoreline was often frozen and no vessels could get in or out. If these buildings were destroyed by the fire, then the entire colony would face the likelihood of starvation.

Hundreds of volunteers, accompanied by soldiers from the two forts, and sailors from ships in the harbour, were soon in the midst of the roaring fury, desperately fighting to contain the blaze. Despite their best efforts, one house after another was swiftly consumed, and the fire inevitably advanced to the storehouses on the south side of the street.

About this time a shocking discovery was made by those struggling to save their homes and everything they possessed. Dozens of men and women stood idly by, watching curiously, even gleefully, as the destruction continued, not offering the least assistance. The manager of Pivie, Nicol, and Forsyth, a firm which was to be completely lost, later had this to say:

To the great disgrace of the lower orders of the community, instead of aiding us in stopping the destructive element, they absolutely retired to a short distance from the fire, and were observed to exhult [sic] openly at the great misfortune which had befallen more than half of the inhabitants of respectability in this town; and they refused to work, notwithstanding repeated remonstrances, entreaties, and offers of reward which we, in common with our neighbours, made them. Such a savage conduct we suppose, was scarcely ever before equaled.

The inferno raged for six hours until about 4:00 a.m., levelling everything on Water Street as far west as the Governor's Wharf (in the area of the present-day courthouse steps), and as far east as the old Ordnance Wharf. In addition to Water Street, Holloway and Gambier Streets were also completely destroyed, as well as a considerable extent of Duckworth Street. Upwards of 130 houses had burned, along with wharves and numerous important storehouses containing the precious winter provisions. The total value of lost property was later estimated to be between £400,000 to £500,000.

The unfortunate Francis Pickmore, the first governor ordered to winter in the colony, imposed an embargo on all shipping until the full extent of the loss could be determined. He also requested aid from Halifax in the form of bread and flour. Yet, if he thought his troubles were harsh enough already, it was probably just as well that neither he nor the citizens of St. John's could foretell the events of November 21.

On that night, just two weeks after the first fire, sailors doing night watch aboard a warship in the harbour noticed a telltale red glow above the premises of Huie and Reed. The alarm was sounded and the army and navy went swiftly to work in a repeat performance, as still another tragedy was about to be played out. Once more, little could be done, as the savage flames spanned the narrow streets and alleyways, leaping from one building to the next. To the complete disgust of those fighting the fire, there was again the presence of many people who not only refused to lend assistance but who commenced to loot homes and businesses alike. This distraction greatly hindered all attempts to quench the flames, as citizens now struggled on two fronts to save what they owned. Daylight the following morning revealed the charred skeletons and smouldering ruins that had been the city of St. John's. A tremendous number of homeless people, nearly 2,000 in all, both emotionally and physically drained, now wandered about, searching the ashes for some small comfort.

The opening words of a letter sent by Governor Pickmore to the Colonial Secretary in London reflected the utter demoralization felt by all:

My Lord, I have to perform the painful duty of reporting to Your Lordship a calamity similar to that which befell this town on the 7th instant.

The Grand Jury which later looked into the causes of both fires was even more passionate in its report:

Calamities so extensive would have been in our most prosperous times productive of severe distress, but on retrospecting to our situation for the last three years, during which period we have alternately suffered by fire, by famine, by lawless outrage, and numerous mercantile failures, which have greatly injured the commercial reputation of the town, the recent conflagration seemed only wanting to consummate our misfortune.

With so many homeless now joining the ranks of those already prowling the streets of St. John's, the number of assaults rapidly increased, along with the degree of pillage. Due to the recent fires, there was not enough food and clothing to go around, and the additional stress on the operable charities was extreme.

By early December Pickmore had to make a difficult decision. As a result of the continuous looting and severe lack of provisions, he ordered that many of the poor homeless immigrants be deported. The majority were sent back to Ireland; others were given passage to either Nova Scotia or the United States.

As Christmas approached, the dreadful cold that had frozen much of the shoreline, also took its toll in human lives. Numerous bodies were found daily, frozen to death in the pitiful shelters they had fashioned out of the scorched wood left by the fires. But it wasn't only the poor who were cold. Governor Pickmore himself complained of the terrible drafty conditions that existed at his residence inside Fort Townshend and wrote home of his intentions to have a more suitable dwelling constructed sometime in the future.

News of the horrific state of affairs that prevailed in Newfoundland slowly reached distant ears. On December 27 the Newfoundland Welfare Committee was organized in Boston, Massachusetts, to raise funds and provisions to aid the poor suffering colony. Likewise, philanthropists in Halifax, London, and as far away as Bermuda, also collected relief packages.

On January 1, 1818, a discovery was made which completely shocked and infuriated nearly the entire population. A deliberate attempt to set fire to the home of a store owner in Maggoty Cove in the east end of the city went afoul, even though the culprits managed to escape. Pickmore immediately issued a proclamation offering the sum of £400 for the capture or information leading to the capture of "some persons of diabolical dispositions." An additional £1,000 was offered by a group of merchants and principal inhabitants of the city. This arson plot left little doubt in the minds of many, including that of Pickmore, that the great fires of November had also been intentionally set.

Despite the sizeable reward being offered, no reliable information was forthcoming, and the would-be arsonists continued to elude authorities. Whereas most "respectable" citizens were prepared to blame some of the lower orders, specifically the multitude of homeless and unemployed Irish, one year later a visiting naval captain named William Eliot proposed a different, and very disturbing theory.

It is whispered amongst the better-informed of this island that some of the mercantile community have most opportunely escaped bankruptcy by what might almost be termed a providential conflagration.

The insinuation was extremely serious, to say the least, but since no individual was ever brought to trial for being connected to the fires of 1817, it could never be proven.

Some good news finally arrived on January 16 when the brig *Messenger* sailed into St. John's harbour from Boston. The charitable people of that city had loaded the little vessel with "174 barrels of flour, 11 tierces of rice, 125 barrels of Indian meal, 27 barrels and 963 bags of bread."[1]

The unlimited gratitude felt by the citizens of St. John's was eloquently expressed in *The Mercantile Journal* of January 23:

It is impossible to contemplate this timely and extraordinary act of generosity and not feel sentiments of gratitude and affection for men almost strangers to us, and the citizens of a foreign government. And when we remember that it was but yesterday, as it were, we were emerged from a state of warfare with these very men, we may reasonably conclude that the sentiments impressed by their benevolence, must rest upon a durable foundation.

Two weeks after the arrival of the *Messenger* the schooner *Assistance* left Halifax, loaded with lumber and beef, also bound on a mission of mercy. After three days' sail, she got stuck in the ice near Cape St. Mary's. In spite of numerous attempts by the crew to free the stricken vessel, there was nothing left to do but wait for the ice to loosen up on its own.

The death toll in Newfoundland grew steadily during the month of January and into February as the harsh winter continued. One storm

---

1. A tierce was an old English unit of measurement equal to about 159 litres. The term may also refer to the barrel which held the equivalent of this measurement.

after another battered the land and its starving inhabitants until it seemed that God himself had turned his back on the place. When they weren't being buried by snow, the people were freezing to death in the bitter cold. And when they weren't freezing to death, they were being attacked and robbed by gangs of rals, who, like the weather, seemed to be an ever-present pestilence. The vigilante committees barely managed to contain these outlaw bands, and it took men like Captain Buchan to maintain some sense of hope throughout these desperate times. As he had done the previous year, Buchan travelled from one community to the next, lending whatever aid was within his power, including his able leadership in matters of civil authority.

When it seemed that things could get no worse, word came down from Fort Townshend on February 27 that Governor Pickmore had died at 6:00 the previous evening. The terrible drafty conditions of his residence inside the fort had finally caused him to catch a bad cold that, within two weeks, left him a corpse. The official cause of death: a "bronchial congestion."

An elaborate funeral service and procession was held for the governor on the morning of Tuesday, March 3, following which his body remained interred in a vault in the Anglican church. The senior naval commander on station, Captain John Bowker of HMS *Sir Francis Drake*, took over the governor's duties temporarily. His first order was for the men of his ship and two others in the harbour to cut a channel through the ice so that the remains of the late Francis Pickmore could be transported back to England. It took three weeks to complete the channel, which was eventually over 2,800 yards long and extended well beyond the Narrows, through ice that was three to five feet thick. When Pickmore left Newfoundland for the last time, his body was preserved in a puncheon of rum.[2]

By mid-March, 1818, there was finally a general improvement in

---

2. A similar channel had been cut a month earlier to allow the brig *Messenger* to leave, along with several other vessels that had also been stranded in St. John's harbour. *The Mercantile Journal* reported on February 13 that this channel was frozen over the very next day, solid enough "to bear a number of persons, so severe was the cold."

the conditions on the island. The first sign of hope was evidenced in the number of seals being taken by landsmen, and in the departure of several large schooners for the Front. The hunt provided meat that was sorely needed by the famished population, as well as oil and pelts to help merchant houses claw their way back from the brink of economic collapse. Even the weather conditions demonstrated that God had not turned his back on the old colony after all. As the sun's rays grew stronger, and the great band of ice that for months had strangled the island gradually shifted, an increasing number of vessels could finally leave port. More importantly, more vessels carrying supplies could finally get in.[3]

These improvements also meant that one incessant plague on the colony dwindled almost entirely out of existence: the gangs of hardened men known as the rals. It isn't certain what happened to these desperate criminals, but it is likely that most either returned to respectable living or were driven from the island. Some undoubtedly continued their delinquent behaviour, but in all likelihood they too were eventually brought to justice.

Another sign of hope for the colony was the late arrival of the schooner *Assistance*, on March 18. She and her crew had been frozen in the ice off Cape St. Mary's ever since February 6. This aid from Halifax was one more example of the benevolence of men and women towards others in times of need, and provided a spiritual as well as a physical boost to the beleaguered people of Newfoundland.

---

3. The extremely cold winter of 1817 has been attributed to the volcanic eruption of Mount Tambora in the East Indies, which threw fifty cubic miles of volcanic ash into the atmosphere, disrupting weather patterns worldwide. (Decker, Robert. "Four Worst Eruptions in History," Encyclopaedia Britannica online.)

Chapter 6
The Butler/Landergan Affair

We beg leave, Sir, to remind you of the forlorn and desolate condition of the poor young man whom you are going to dispossess of the only little property which would make the rest of his life agreeable, and left to him by his Uncle just before he was going to appear before that God to whom we must all render an account of our actions, good or bad.
Anonymous letter sent to Magistrate William Piercy of Brigus

The severe economic depression which struck the island of Newfoundland in the wake of the Napoleonic Wars and the War of 1812 fostered an atmosphere of reform within a growing segment of its population. Some public figures blamed the economic problems on the lack of a local legislature, promoting the radical idea that Newfoundland should be allowed to govern itself. The soon-to-be champion of the reform movement, Dr. William Carson, had already begun publishing pamphlets that criticized England's ancient policies towards his newly adopted home, in particular those which favoured the interests of West Country merchants, when a seemingly insignificant affair afforded him an opportunity to sound the rallying cry, one which would create many allies as well as many enemies.

Since 1792, surrogate courts, presided over by individuals who often demonstrated strong partisan inclinations, had administered a crude interpretation of the law to most outports along Newfoundland's east coast. The excessive actions of one of these courts drew the ire of Dr. Carson and his ideological colleagues, and may be the actual starting point of the movement towards self-government in Newfoundland.[1]

---

1. Governor James Gambier may actually have been the first to suggest this novel idea in 1804, but the home government paid little heed to the suggestion.

* * * * *

Rain poured straight from the heavens on the little outport of Cupids on this May morning, turning the narrow roadway into a muddy mess, and soaking the clothing of the two figures that trudged between picket fences and unpainted clapboard houses. In several small fields cows and sheep huddled together for warmth and protection. In the distance a dog barked, breaking the monotonous drumming of the rain and the sucking noise of the strangers' boots in the mud.

The men turned up a narrow lane that led to a small, grey homestead, from the chimney of which lifted the lazy smoke of a kitchen fire. Tattered fragments of cloth hung in both little windows that faced the harbour, one window presently being occupied by the dirty but smiling face of a small child.

Just as the two strangers reached the front step, the rickety wooden door opened, and a short, slovenly woman appeared, her hands clinging tightly to her filthy apron. She assumed a position in the middle of the doorway which immediately denied the two men any right to proceed further, and eyed them with hostility.

After a moment of awkward silence, the taller of the two men spoke.

"Is your husband, James Landergan, at home, Mam?"[2]

"No, he is not," was the terse reply. This was followed by another moment of silence.

"Well then, I'm Michael Kelly, Mam, and this is Constable Moors . . ."

"I knows who ye are, and I knows why ye're here!"

Kelly was taken aback by the woman's brashness, but he had little patience for insolence and disrespect towards himself or his position. He reached beneath his soaking greatcoat and pulled out a wad of official-looking papers.

"Well then, you must also know that we're here to take legal possession of this property as representatives of His Majesty's Court."

---

2. Often spelled as "Landrigan" or "Lundrigan".

This statement brought no response from Mrs. Landergan except for a piercing gaze that caused Kelly to shift uncomfortably from one foot to the other, and drew a short cough from Moors, who had been content to remain standing slightly behind his companion. From somewhere outside the officers' range of vision a second child had begun to cry.

"Mam, whereas judgment has been passed against your husband for his refusal to appear before Magistrate Carrington in March of this year, I must ask that you step aside . . ."

Before Kelly could finish, a rusty, weather-beaten old musket appeared from underneath Mrs. Landergan's apron, and was pointed directly at the officer's face.

"If ye don't get off this property now, I'm goin' to blow ye back to wherever it is ye came from."

For several seconds Kelly and Moors stared in disbelief at the woman and the gun, uncertain of their next action. Mrs. Landergan's resolve, however, was unwavering, the musket still pointed as Kelly backed off the step and motioned for Moors to follow.

James Landergan was typical of many Newfoundland fishermen who had fallen into debt during this difficult period. With the return of foreign competition many valuable cod markets had shrunk, or disappeared altogether, throwing scores of Newfoundlanders out of work, and bankrupting dozens of planters and merchants. Being a first-generation Irishman made things more difficult for Landergan, since the authorities passing judgment were all Englishmen with vivid recollections of 1800 and 1817.

Unable to repay an obligation of £15 to his supplier, Graham and McNicoll, following the weak fishing season of 1818, Landergan had been served a writ to appear in court, but never showed up. The reconstructed scene above is probably a close simulation of the actual arrival of the two constables at the Irishman's house. However, Landergan was not visited again until one year later, when another surrogate court, this one presided over by the Anglican minister, John Leigh, and the estimable Captain Buchan, served him another writ to appear.

By now the Irishman's predicament had become common knowledge in and around Cupids. Whether from actual friendship or plain empathy, a number of individuals had drawn up a letter threatening the authorities with retaliation should they proceed with any action against Landergan. It was sent anonymously to Magistrate William Piercy in Brigus:

> *Sir, there are numbers of people who have taken the case into consideration and behold the afflictions of the young man whom you are going to distress that have resolved to make an example of you or your property the very first opportunity, and know Mr. Piercy they are as able to do it as say it . . . You have a family growing up and take care of them. They are born but not dead.*

Governor Hamilton was quick to offer a full pardon to anyone involved in this threat who would snitch on their friends. The offer was never taken up, though, and again Landergan refused to accompany the constables when they came to his door. Even when they warned him that on their next visit they would be accompanied by a squad of marines, Landergan brazenly replied: "Well, I hope they have a damn good time of it then."

Later that same night, July 5, 1820, Constables Michael Kelly and William Keeting did return with the marines, as promised, apprehended Landergan without resistance, and brought him on board Buchan's ship, the *Grasshopper*, where he spent the night confined under close guard.

The scene the following day was a tense one, as throngs of men, women, and children anxiously milled about the dwelling house in Port de Grave where court was being held, faces pressed to the windows for a look at the proceedings inside. Offering little in his own defence, "his manner very becoming," Landergan was sentenced to be lashed thirty-six times with the cat-o'-nine-tails for his contempt of court and had to forfeit his property to Graham and McNicoll as repayment of the outstanding debt.

Landergan was immediately hauled from the court and, before

a crowd of onlookers, some simply curious, others incensed with the entire affair, was bound to a nearby fish flake. The bosun's mate from **HMS** *Grasshopper* then commenced the ordered punishment. After just fourteen lashes, the prisoner collapsed in an epileptic seizure and had to be cut down and carried back inside, to be attended by Dr. Richard Shea.[3]

Even the merely curious could not help but feel sympathy for the poor man's fate.

One day later, in Harbour Main, the same court convicted another indebted Irish fisherman, Phillip Butler, of an almost identical offence. He too was sentenced to be lashed.

These proceedings were too much for the liberal minded, and immediately several prominent personalities, notably William Carson and Patrick Morris, recognized the opportunity this provided. Enlisting the aid of newspaper editor Lewis Ryan and a recently arrived lawyer from Exeter, William Dawe, they filed actions of trespass and false imprisonment against Leigh and Buchan. The central question in the case, according to Chief Justice Forbes, was whether or not the surrogate court had a right to punish for contempt.

The eventual acquittal of Leigh and Buchan was not actually a loss for the reform movement. In fact, as one historian claims, "The whipped fishermen became symbols. Losing in court only added to their symbolic value."[4]

Even Forbes condemned the actions of Leigh and Buchan, castigating "a mode of proceeding which disuse had rendered obsolete in England, and which in every view of the present case, was particularly harsh and uncalled for."

The entire experience apparently weighed heavily on John Leigh's conscience, for he was a man not ordinarily predisposed to harsh conduct. After all, both he and Buchan were well known for their philanthropy, as well as their concern for Newfoundland's

---

3. The court had earlier been notified that Landergan was prone to "the falling sickness."

4. O'Flaherty, *Old Newfoundland*, 132.

native people, the Beothuks. Aware now of the destitution and hardship that he had caused to Mr. Landergan, Leigh bought his property back from Graham and McNicoll and returned it to its rightful owner.

CHAPTER 7

A FLAME NOT EASILY SUBDUED

A lengthy period of transition followed the Butler/Landergan affair. Local merchants, who had grown in both wealth and influence, began to flirt with the idea of an independent legislature. As if trying to appease these "reformers," the British parliament finally granted true colonial status to Newfoundland in 1824, 327 years after Cabot's landing. But this was merely a classic example of "too little, too late." The wave of reform quickly gathered momentum, with supporters from all classes, ethnic groups, and religions, whose reasons for wanting change differed greatly from one to the other.

The Protestant English wanted more control of the island's political and economic future, while at the same time maintaining close ties with the mother country. Within this group, many influential merchants simply wanted more wealth, and their lack of conviction would later contribute to serious divisions within the franchise. Nevertheless, from their eyes it could have been no small irritation to see their West Country counterparts still monopolizing the favours of British parliamentarians, despite the demise of the migratory fishery.

For the Irish even more was at stake. They wanted to be free from the bonds of deprivation and granted a fairer distribution of government patronage, as they were now about 50 percent of the population. Though Roman Catholics had been free to practice their faith since 1779, they were still far from being totally emancipated. Few Catholics occupied public positions, since to do so meant they would have to swear an oath that basically refuted part of the Catholic doctrine. This oath was not specific to Newfoundland, though, for Catholics in England followed the same procedure. Thus, when the Catholic Relief Bill was finally passed by England's parliament, there was joyous celebrating in Newfoundland. Because of some interpretational glitch, the Relief Bill did not include Newfoundland; this meant that Catholics there had to wait another three years before gaining the rights enjoyed by other Newfoundlanders.

In response to this rebuff, protests, petitions, and outrage became common, with the new Roman Catholic bishop, Michael Anthony Fleming, rallying his flock to the drumbeat of Irish patriotism. Though there was support for his cause among many enlightened Protestant citizens, his fervour worried others, especially Governor Cochrane, who made this observation about the relationship then existing between Newfoundland's Catholics and Protestants: "A perfect harmony, or should I rather say *tranquility*, exists between them. Yet I am persuaded . . . that a spark could ignite a flame not easily subdued." His prophetic statement would prove to be accurate.

Due in no small part to the tenuous position of Roman Catholics in Newfoundland, it is not surprising that they would lead the movement towards an independent legislature. They obviously had more to gain. Men such as Patrick Morris, and the bold young John Kent, both Irish-born immigrants, delivered speeches for the cause. There were also influential Protestants on their side: for example, William Carson, and William Dawe, the lawyer who had represented Landergan and Butler. Even the soon-to-be-despised Henry Winton, owner/editor of the popular newspaper *The Public Ledger*, sounded the cry.

Change was inevitable, for a powerful wave of liberalism had swept across England following the Napoleonic Wars, allowing Newfoundland's reform delegates to be met with a sympathetic ear on their visits to London. The impetuous promise never to ask the English House of Commons for "another farthing" should Newfoundland be granted a legislature likely excited many English members.

Not everyone in the mother country, or even Newfoundland, believed in self-government for the "cod fishers." Many West Country families with strong financial connections to the island feared that an independent legislature would mean, among other things, higher taxation.

The fragile peace that had existed for several years between the two major ethnic groups was punctured by signs of unrest. Riots had broken out in Brigus, Carbonear, and Harbour Grace in the wake of another terrible fishing season and more mercantile bankruptcies. The "lower orders" were "insubordinate," committing almost daily acts of vandalism upon their "betters." This was paired, according to Phillip Henry Gosse, with "an habitual dread of the Irish as a class which was more oppressively felt than openly expressed."[1]

Past experiences were not so distant as to be totally forgiven by either party. Though full Catholic emancipation was an ideal endorsed by the learned and enlightened, most Newfoundland English lived with a distrust of the Catholic church, particularly its vocal and antagonistic bishop. For now, though, there was an uneasy alliance of Irish Catholics and English Protestants.[2]

Finally, in March, 1832, Newfoundlanders received news they had been granted representative government. There would be a General Assembly made up of fifteen men elected by the people, and a Council of six to be appointed by the governor. The franchise was given to all men "of sound understanding," twenty-one years of age or older, who had occupied a house for a period of at least one year, had never been convicted of a criminal offence, and a British subject by birth.

Rejoicing in the wake of this announcement was not indicative of the violence and strife that the new freedom would engender. Though the first election went off fairly smoothly, this portent was foreshadowed by a media quarrel between Henry Winton and the Irish candidate for St. John's, John Kent, Patrick Morris's nephew and Bishop Fleming's soon-to-be brother-in-law. Sometime during that opening

---

1. Gosse, who came to Newfoundland from England in 1827, worked as a clerk for the firm of Slade, Elson at Carbonear, where he became interested in local flora and fauna. He left for Lower Canada in 1835 because of his uneasiness with Newfoundland's "social state."

2. According to J.B. Darcy, Bishop Fleming did not initially favour local government, as he feared it would increase the rivalry between the various factions. (Fire Upon the Earth: The Life and Times of Bishop Michael Anthony Fleming [St. John's, NL: Creative Publishers, 2003]).

campaign, Winton's position on the idea of self-government had begun to be seen as more conservative. Initially believing that the franchise would be much narrower, and the island's affairs conducted by those he felt had made the greatest investment, namely the merchants, he now warned his readers:

> *If our House of Assembly is not to be composed of men of respectability in the community - if it is to be filled by demagogues and visionaries - by inflated schoolboys, or superannuated old men, let us in the name of God retrace our steps, and frankly tell our enemies that they have judged rightly of us - that we are not yet ripe for these institutions of which so many of the younger colonies have for so many years received the benefits.*

Winton's reference to "inflated schoolboys" and "superannuated old men" indicated a pair of candidates who were to become his greatest opponents, John Kent and William Carson. The impetuous Kent took offence, responding in a rival newspaper that he detected "an odour of prejudice" from *The Ledger*'s editor. With an egotistical flourish he added that there was a contingent in St. John's who, "if I were an imbecile, would elect me." His pompous attitude upset Winton, but this was only the start. The next day Kent circulated a pamphlet accusing Winton of "an uncompromising hatred of Irishmen and Catholics." Whether they were premeditated or accidental, Kent's choice of words was the spark that precipitated Newfoundland's fifty years of politico-sectarian hatred.

Had Winton been more easily intimidated, or less opinionated, the debate might have ended there. But he was not a man to reverse his convictions, and his response inadvertently impelled the powerful Catholic bishop to step into this war of words: "Sure we are that the Right Rev. the Bishop at the head of the Church of which Mr. K. is a member will not tolerate such conduct, nor permit it to be tolerated by any of his respectable clergy."

Bishop Fleming might have had the ability to ignore Winton's indiscretion, but not the desire. He could have doused the carelessly ignited flames of discord with some calming words. Though he might not have avoided the inevitable clash between Protestant and Catholic voters, he likely could have mellowed Winton's literary attacks, and gained an ally instead of an enemy. The bishop, however, was as incapable of restraint as either Kent or Winton. Perhaps he felt compelled to aid his future brother-in-law. Or more likely, he saw this as an opportunity to further the political interests of his underprivileged flock, a motive that was not necessarily unwarranted. Either way, it was not Fleming's smug response in *The Newfoundlander* that irked Winton, but that he had signed his letter with the insignia of the cross. Winton's counter to Fleming was unrestrained:

> *What shall be said of you when you can so far prostitute your sacred calling to secular purposes of so unworthy a character - when you can affix the emblem of the cross to your name for the purpose of furthering your views in a mere trumpery contested election squabble! You are not beyond the influence of the Press, which has only begun to deal with you. In your collision with it, take care that you do not overrate your own strength.*

Meetings in several major towns resulted in Winton being accused of all sorts of degeneracy as well as cowardice. This last affront was supposedly made by John Kent's brother, James. Winton's editorial insinuated that a public street might be a better place to determine Kent's allegation. Kent did not respond.

In the end, though, Winton lost this round, as Kent topped the polls. The ensuing condemnations from *The Public Ledger* might have sounded like sour grapes to those less aware of the politico-sectarianism which began with the first election, but they represented the opinions of many wealthy citizens. *The Ledger* would become a sounding board for powerful mercantile conservatives and their candidates.

The unaccountable defeat of Carson, one of the strongest advocates for self-government, and the first to announce his candidacy in the first election, did afford Winton some satisfaction. Even that was short lived, as a by-election was called when Governor Cochrane announced the appointment of one of the St. John's members to the Legislative Council. This move gave the ambitious doctor another opportunity for political stardom, one that he was determined not to relinquish a second time. The public would learn that the media exchanges of the first election were benign compared to the social upheaval they would face.

CHAPTER 8

HENRY WINTON: PART ONE

Christmas Eve, 1833. The angry crowd outside Henry Winton's home on Water Street was clearly not there to wish him all the best of the Yuletide season. They had been gathering since early afternoon, growing louder and more disorderly by the minute. As Winton observed the menacing mob from an upstairs window, someone stepped to the forefront and delivered a very emotional and apparently very drunken speech, complete with coarse language and name-calling, and contrived to agitate the crowd. As the gentleman's oratory grew to a fevered pitch, so too did the response from the already maddened audience. A rock hurled at the front of Winton's house was quickly followed by others that smashed several windows and pounded thunderously on the wooden floors. The situation had turned ugly; fearing for his family's safety as well as his own, Winton retrieved the loaded musket from his closet, and opened the window to take aim at the crowd below.

* * * * *

This episode resulted from Winton's political support for the ostracized Roman Catholic candidate in the St. John's by-election, Timothy

Hogan. An Irish merchant who had earlier offended Bishop Fleming, and who was not receptive to the bishop's politics, Hogan had announced his candidacy in opposition to the liberal Carson. Fleming then spitefully declared Carson to be the workingman's representative, and the clear champion of the underprivileged. Hogan soon realized the futility of his aspirations, when it became obvious that the Catholic electorate was supporting Fleming's man. Embittered and hurt by his own bishop's rejection, Hogan had published an astonishing letter in *The Public Ledger:*

To the Independent Electors
of the District of St. John's

Gentlemen - the die is cast! In the hour of victory I am constrained to retire from the contest, and abandon the hope of being useful to you as your representative.

A Rev. Gentleman has announced from the sacred Altar, that it would promote the interests of religion to elect my opponent, and has thundered forth in Prophetic anathemas that he would cause grass to grow before the doors of those who would vote the contrary.

Thus the will of the Rev. Gentleman must be considered as the text of your choice in a Representative. Single-handed I had nothing to fear, and everything to hope, but in order to preserve the peace of the community which I very much feared would be disturbed in your struggle for the Purity of Election against an influence which it is well known I was at all times unwilling to oppose, I determined to leave my opponent in possession of an inglorious field.

Adieu my friends, I sincerely thank you for your able and kind exertion, and most ardently hope our common country will not suffer by the admission into its counsels of any Gentleman who is not the subject of the people's choice.

Fleming was not amused by Hogan's bold assertions, and the would-be politician was compelled to publish a letter of apology to the "Rev. Gentleman" or suffer the consequences. Winton was incensed by the entire affair, and launched into an ongoing, full-fledged literary assault upon the Catholic clergy. Convinced, and not without probable cause, that the reform movement was being used by Bishop Fleming to wrest control of the colony from its English gentry, Winton now published one of his more offensive editorials:

> *Some months ago we ventured to affirm that His Majesty's government had committed an egregious error in conferring upon this country an elective franchise on the extremely broad principles upon which we posses it; and that conviction was founded upon the knowledge that a large majority of the population is made up of the uneducated and laboring classes of the Roman Catholic persuasion, whose superstitious veneration of the priesthood is in this country not one whit behind that which is entertained in the obscurest villages in the southwest of Ireland; and it is therefore as clear as the noonday sun that the mental slavery which pervaded their minds, might, with the utmost facility be rendered subservient to any political intrigues in which their spiritual pastors and masters may find it convenient to indulge.*

There was no turning back. Winton's true colours were revealed for all to see, and the Irish spoiled for a fight. An enraged mob descended on the office of *The Public Ledger* soon after the brazen editorial was published, and destroyed the front of the building. Never easily intimidated, Winton continued his attacks on Fleming and the Roman Catholic clergy. On the night of December 22, and again on Christmas Eve, unruly mobs attacked Winton's home. As a result, he secured his family's safety by strategically placing numerous weapons throughout the house, and appealed to the governor for military protection.

* * * * *

With his forefinger now on the trigger, Winton shouted defiantly at the crowd to leave, lest he be forced to shoot. The response from below was equally defiant, with more stones being thrown through the few remaining panes of glass and challenges to shoot if he dared. Pleas for peace and threats of judicial reprisal from several magistrates and constables who appeared on the scene brought no reprieve, however, especially since they were grossly outnumbered by an indignant mob half-drunk with rum.[1]

The crowd scorned and derided the authorities, and continued to hurl rocks through Winton's windows, as the anxious newspaperman remained with his gun lodged in readiness across the shattered sill.

Even after darkness had fallen over the troubled scene, the crowd showed no signs of disbanding. If anything, their numbers had grown, and their fury now turned on the magistrates and constables. Winton's home was in shambles, every front window shattered, and dozens of stones littered the floors upstairs and down. Winton was now convinced that deadly force was unavoidable in ridding himself of his tormentors. To Winton's great relief, however, a contingent of eighty soldiers, led by Lieutenant Rice, then marched into view. They were quickly arranged into a phalanx in front of Winton's house and, in this manner, the rioters were briefly kept at bay.[2]

After the lieutenant appealed several times to the mob to disburse, with no success, the military was then formed in lines three deep, and the Riot Act was read.[3]

Still to no avail. Frustrated, but determined to clear the streets, Rice then gave the order to fix bayonets. The taunts and challenges from the rioters grew frenzied. Rice answered by having his men parade back and forth, finally driving the mob away, or at least into hiding. An uneasy quiet then settled over the entire area, during which time Winton ventured outside to inspect the damage to his home. After conversing with the lieutenant, it was decided that sentries be placed in the immediate vicinity for the remainder of the night, in the event of further trouble. The soldiers then retired to the courthouse to await a continuance of the evening's troubles.

---

1. Probably though attempting to minimize the integrity of the demonstrators, several witnesses later claimed that the crowd was "emboldened by strong drink."

2. A phalanx was an ancient military formation where troops were arranged in the shape of a square or rectangle.

3. See Appendix 1.

They did not have long to wait. Within minutes the beating of a sentry's drum signalled Rice and his men once again to Winton's house to face a replaying of the earlier scene. This time while clearing the street the military exercised much less restraint, severely injuring a number of rioters with bayonets and gunstocks. Stones and bricks were hurled in response. The noise of crashing glass, yells of anger, curses, and screams of pain filled the air. The mob, though bold to the finish, could little resist the orderly advance of Lieutenant Rice's men, and swiftly gave way.

It was now 9:30 p.m. The crowd had been rampaging for almost six hours, causing some people in the city to wonder about the very existence of law and order, while others, who were sympathetic to the mob, would later blame the authorities for unnecessary and excessive use of force. At about this time the figure of a Roman Catholic priest, Father Edward Troy, appeared conspicuously among the rioters, exhorting them to cease the violence and to retire to their homes. What magisterial pleas, riot acts, and bayonets could not accomplish, a cleric in a black robe could. In less than half an hour Water Street was empty, and peace and quiet returned like an unsettling presence. It was an impressive example of ecclesiastic authority, albeit somewhat belated.

A meeting between Bishop Fleming and Governor Cochrane the next day should have calmed the masses, but merely created a new conflict. Following this meeting Fleming published a letter in *The Newfoundlander* stating that the governor had assured him that using the military had not been his idea, and, furthermore, he promised a "minute investigation" of the entire affair. An irate colonial secretary, James Crowdy, immediately sent a rebuttal, informing the bishop that he had "entirely misconceived" the governor's statements. In fact the governor *had* authorized use of the military on December 25. This letter, which came close to accusing Fleming of intentionally misleading the public, somehow turned up in print, outraging many of his supporters. Already believing their governor to be a bigot, many Roman Catholics now also began to see him as a liar.

In the days that followed, Winton, ever audacious, some would say ever insolent, blamed the whole business on Bishop Fleming. His "scandalous abuse from the altar," wrote Winton, was responsible for encouraging his "loyal, obedient, but ignorant flock" to resort to violence in defence of their religion. Several prominent reformers immediately stepped into this spiteful propaganda war, among them William Carson, Patrick Morris, and John Kent. They called a meeting of all interested parties to decry "with unmixed indignation, the introduction of a large military force into this hitherto peaceful town," and to announce that "to Doctor Fleming are due, and are hereby given, the grateful and heartfelt thanks of the inhabitants of St. John's."

The members of this meeting obviously did not speak for most Protestants, or for those whom Governor Cochrane termed "respectable Catholics," people infuriated with the lawlessness they had just witnessed. The newspapers were soon filled with more prejudiced editorials and biased rebuttals, fuelling the fires of religious, ethnic, and political hatred. For the next several months there would be little reprieve from the heightened rancour prompted by the violently contested St. John's by-election. Winton's *Public Ledger* was now a bitter enemy of the reformers, a position as much self-declared as publicly pronounced, with apparently one driving mission: narrow the elective franchise and keep the Roman Catholic clergy from political ascendancy.

Winton, though, would find the voice of his opposition growing substantially louder, for the reformers had found a new champion in the press. Robert J. Parsons had been foreman at *The Public Ledger* for six years, but a bitter dispute, probably over political differences, had caused him to break with Winton, and, in partnership with other leading reformers, he started a newspaper of his own. The editorial feud between *The Newfoundland Patriot* and *The Public Ledger* was prolonged and nasty. It had no rules, scorned compromise, and scared both combatants in ways they had no way of comprehending in 1833.

As things moved swiftly in the wake of the Christmas commotion in front of Henry Winton's home, the population of Newfoundland would soon have a chance to differ once again. This time, however, the cause of the fuss would not be political in nature, but, ironically, two horrendous crimes that should have helped to unite rather than divide the citizenry. The circumstances surrounding these cases incited more sectarian hostility, particularly since the victims were well-to-do Protestants and the accused Irish Catholics.

Chapter 9

The Exhibition of the Body of a Malefactor

While feelings so praiseworthy and essential to the well-being of society received every encouragement from me, it was not long before I discovered that it was but a smooth surface, covering the seeds of discord, which only required a sufficiently exciting cause to shoot into life.

Governor Cochrane to Lord Stanley
April 8, 1834

The stench of rotting caplin rose from numerous gardens in the town of Harbour Grace on the night of July 11, 1833. It blended with the sultry air, was carried eastward on the light summer breeze, and finally dissipated out over the cold waters of Conception Bay. Though nobody realized it at the time, the smell could easily have been symbolic of the foul business about to occur in their midst. Incredibly this smell would be considerably less offensive than that which would fill the air on nights to come.

As the clock neared 11:00 p.m., two dark figures skulked through the shadows, their design simple yet devious: murder their employer, Robert Crocker Bray, then rob the hundreds of pounds they suspected were concealed somewhere inside his house. But for one of the schemers preserving his own neck would soon be more important than either money or loyalty. For the other, the lesson of knowing whom to trust would come too late, and the price would be high. Observers of the whole affair would argue over justice served or justice denied, and the results would have far-reaching repercussions for the community and beyond.

Patrick Malone was not only employed by Bray, but also lived with him and his family in an apparent atmosphere of mutual trust. In a later interview, Malone recalled a day when his master's infant son, Samuel, had even been left to his care for a brief period of time. According to his testimony, Malone claimed that that day Peter Downing, a fellow Irishman in Bray's employ, had come to Bray's house to convince Malone to help him search for the money.[1]

Either out of respect for his employer, or more likely a fear of being caught, Malone refused, and asked Downing never to speak of the matter again.[2]

However, according to Malone, Downing was convinced that the money was theirs for the taking and, during the next several months, became more persistent in recruiting Malone. Malone eventually relented. Downing's cruel intentions were revealed, so Malone would claim, one night during a heated discussion, when Downing announced that he "would not scruple to kill one of their religion." That murder was now a possibility might have startled Malone, but the realization that he could be a victim if he wasn't a participant completely unnerved him. Fearing for his own safety, Malone now found himself embroiled in this sinister scheme.

As Downing and Malone neared Bray's back door, barely 200 yards away three other men stood watch over several pigs that had been confined after roaming the streets, a clear violation of the Nuisance Act by their owners. Conversation among these men was hushed, owing to the late hour, and mostly revolved around local matters, particularly the town's astounding rebirth since the devastating fire one year earlier.

The conflagration of 1832 had wreaked tremendous hardship on the businesses of Harbour Grace. Though many were unable to

---

1. Several sources use the spelling "Downey." It is difficult to determine which is correct, as both variations are still found in and around Conception Bay.

2. Patrick Malone and Peter Downing were both employed as servants for Robert Bray, their work being mostly in the line of husbandry. From the records it seems that Downing was the oldest. He also appears to have been in Bray's employ the longest, having previously lived with the man for a period of twelve months as a "shipped man." By the summer of 1833 he had a wife and family, and was living in a house of his own.

recover from their losses, for others the fire was an opportunity. All around new buildings stood in various stages of completion. The despised merchant, Thomas Ridley, was even *expanding* his holdings along Water Street. There were new entrepreneurs as well, among them, William Punton and John Munn, who had formed a partnership and purchased the premises of the bankrupt Danson and Company. In many respects, the gloom of the recent past was quickly being replaced with optimism.

Unconcerned about this resurgence in local business, Malone and Downing were about to enter Bray's back door. Malone quickly located the tools he had hidden earlier, one of which, a gruesome-looking little tomahawk, he handed off to Downing. Shouldering a cast net that had hung on the wall, Malone led the way inside the kitchen, just as Bray entered through the parlour door opposite. A single candle flickered and sputtered on the table, throwing strange shadows on the walls.

"Peter! What brought you down?" Bray asked, at first expecting nothing amiss.

Downing's response betrayed none of the anxiety he was feeling. "Sir, I was wondering whether you had any commands for the morning."

A perplexed look crossed Bray's face, for immediately after the men had taken supper in this very kitchen he had clearly informed them of their duties for the next day. With the scull just over, cartloads of caplin were needed to fertilize Bray's substantial vegetable gardens. Malone and Downing should have remembered his simple instructions; now Bray's puzzlement was evident in his voice: "No, nothing but what I told you before."

Malone tossed the net noisily on the table as Bray turned towards the large hearth, presenting his back to Downing. Seizing the opportunity, Downing swung the butt end of the tomahawk at his employer's head, knocking him to the floor. As Bray lay groaning and semi-conscious, Downing dealt the fatal blow, a vicious swing that plunged the tomahawk into the base of Bray's neck. A horrible crimson flood poured from the wound, soaking Bray's cravat and running underneath his body.

Just then a voice from upstairs startled the two villains, reminding them that, even though Bray's wife had left town earlier, there were still two others present, the infant Samuel and the maid Ellen Coombs.

Downing bounded up the stairs, holding the weapon still dripping with Bray's blood, while Malone remained behind long enough to retrieve the candle from the table. Upstairs, Malone found his partner in the servant girl's room, standing over her bed. Ellen sat upright, her hands folded as if in prayer, and begged that her life and the child's might be spared. But there was no mercy in the heart of Peter Downing as he swung the tomahawk into the side of her skull, and again, to be sure she was dead. A third blow killed the infant lying beside her. In seconds the savagery was over, and the only sound to be heard was the killer's heavy breathing.

Ignoring the horrible scene they had created, Malone and Downing then frantically searched the house. Downing's initial confidence quickly turned into a demented rage, as he scoured one room after the other, breaking open desks, cupboards, and bureaus, all to no avail. When the ransacking of the house was complete, the spoils amounted to £40 and a silver watch, not an insignificant amount, but considerably less than the cache they had expected to find.

Dejected and exhausted, Downing then suggested that Bray might have buried the money somewhere on the premises. The ironic twist of this statement was in its simple logic. In the wake of the terrible fire of '32, Bray had most likely been clever enough to bury his fortune in order to protect it from similar disasters in the future.

Now the final stage of the plan had to be put in place: the cover-up. Gathering clothes at the head and foot of the stairs, they set them alight, and fled through the back door. Hungry flames spread quickly, eating through the dry floorboards, licking at the bedsheets and curtains, climbing the walls, sparing nothing in its path.

Fortunately, the fire did not go unnoticed for long. Of the three men guarding the rogue pigs, Edward Pynn was the first to become aware of an eerie glow in the sky. Memories of one year earlier were fresh in his mind, so he wasted no time abandoning his post to race toward the scene. Upon his arrival, huge tongues of orange and red were shooting through the tarred roof and out the upstairs windows. Plumes of black smoke billowed upward, chased by hordes of glowing sparks and flankers. Believing that Bray and his family might still be alive and trapped inside, Pynn raced up to the front door, rapping and shouting loudly. Forcing his way inside, he discovered Bray's body, but not until he attempted to lift him did he notice the pool of blood underneath. Realizing that this was a murder scene, and that the murderer might still be inside, Pynn swiftly retraced his steps, and went to seek help.

A second man, Thomas Kitchen, had also seen the fire and, while rushing toward it, passed the two culprits as they escaped over the hill behind Bray's house. They were shouting "Fire! Fire!" in what Kitchen later recalled as "feigned voices."

After hurrying along the footpaths, Malone and Downing reached the relative safety of Bears Cove in the east end of town. There, they buried the watch and money, before returning to the scene of the crime in an effort to divert suspicion from themselves.

By now every household in the immediate area was awake and aware of the blaze. As fire bells rang and shouts of alarm sounded, a huge crowd gathered, staring helplessly at the disintegrating home of Robert Bray. With the second floor completely engulfed, flaming timbers collapsed onto the floor below. Rising from the smoke and embers was the nauseating smell of burning flesh. Horrified and sick-ened, many of those present turned away. By morning, all that remained was charred sticks of wood, a blackened hearth and, beneath the pile of smoking ash, the remians of three humans.

An investigation was immediately begun, and the initial sense was that the fire had been accidental. That was, until word spread that Pynn had discovered Bray's body in a pool of blood. More evidence of foul play came to light when it was learned that no money could be found anywhere on the site, despite verification from a shocked Mrs. Bray that her husband *did* have a substantial number of coins stashed throughout the house. Speculation of a dastardly crime alarmed the population, and instigated a coroner's inquest to determine the true cause of the deaths. After three days of deliberation, and close examination of the bodies by Dr. William Stirling, the jury, headed by John Stark, declared with certainty a verdict of "Wilful murder against some person or persons unknown."

Rumours and innuendo quickly became the order of the day. But the authorities already had their eyes on Patrick Malone and Peter Downing. Evidence from several individuals who reported the suspicious behavior of these two men piqued the interest of the investigators. Without an alibi to prove their whereabouts at the time of the triple homicides, and with robbery as the likely motive, both men became key suspects, and were arrested several days after committing the heinous act.

Finding himself now confined to a small, damp cell, Malone soon began to think of self-preservation. When the jailor, John Currie, informed the distressed prisoner of a proclamation by the governor guaranteeing clemency for any accomplice to a crime who informed upon his or her partner, Malone's decision was easy. On July 20 he gave a full confession before Magistrate Danson, Dr. Stirling, and at least one other witness.

Learning of his companion's betrayal, Downing offered his own version of the events of July 11. Needless to say, both stories were virtually the opposite of each other, with Malone blaming Downing, and Downing blaming Malone. To bolster his credibility, Malone made a second, more detailed confession several days later, even leading investigators to where they had buried their loot. With at least some of the authorities believing Malone's story, and key witnesses being interviewed to support the case, the Crown prosecutor quickly moved for a trial. It would not soon be forthcoming, though, owing to the sudden, unexpected resignation of Chief Justice Richard Tucker. Months of anxious incarceration lay ahead for the two Irish servants-turned-criminals.

In the meantime, more horrifying news was reported in Conception Bay. On September 11 *The Star and Conception Bay Journal* informed its readers of another murder, this time in the community of Port de Grave. The victim, John Snow, a planter of that town, was also suspected of having been killed by one of his servants and an accomplice. More shocking was the rumour that Mrs. Snow had been carrying on an affair with one of the suspects, and had been the key conspirator in her husband's death. Mrs. Snow, originally from Harbour Grace, was still at large and reportedly seen in her hometown by people who knew her.[3]

More important news for the entire colony, however, was the arrival of the new chief justice, Henry John Boulton, on November 20. Judge Boulton's tenure would not be lengthy, but it would be controversial. During his appointment he would instigate sweeping changes to established customs and modus operandi, and preside over some of the more infamous cases the colony would ever witness. His stern demeanour and harsh sentences would cause him to become known as "the hanging judge," a most unfortunate bit of luck for Downing and Malone, who had both earlier been transferred to the jail at St. John's.

The Supreme Court was a busy place in the fall of 1833, with a long list of capital cases to be heard. It was not until January 3, 1834, that Downing and Malone finally stood trial before three Supreme Court justices. It was a relatively swift proceeding, lasting approximately eight hours following jury selection. Though the prisoners were reported by the press to have shown little emotion, the same could not be said for many observers in the courtroom, particularly when the widowed Mrs. Bray entered to give evidence. The pitiful woman appeared quite distraught, and even required physical assistance in order to take the stand. A total of twelve witnesses were called by the Crown, including Downing's twelve-year-old son, Michael. With no witnesses called by the Defence to refute the strongly condemning evidence, and with Malone's confession disallowed because of a technicality, a guilty verdict was assured for both of the accused.

Judge Boulton felt it necessary at that point to admonish the two prisoners for their crimes, prior to passing sentence upon them. Downing, however, was uncooperative, and repeatedly interrupted the judge, complaining loudly of his perceived injustice. It was a senti-

---

3. This report would later be proven to be incorrect.

ment shared by many who believed that Malone had been the main instigator, and who felt that Downing should have received a lighter sentence. But Judge Boulton had the final word. He ordered them executed on the following Monday, and their bodies dissected and anatomized.[4]

But the saga of these two Irishmen did not end quickly, and it now took a rather unexpected turn. Their incarceration and trial had attracted much attention in and around St. John's, where the largest portion of the population was also Irish. Great sympathy was expressed by many who felt their plight to be just another example of Irish persecution at the hands of the English autocracy. One individual who took a keen interest in the case was John Valentine Nugent, an educator from Waterford, who was destined to become one of the more radical voices in Newfoundland politics. Immediately after the death sentence was passed, he petitioned the king against the illegalities of the entire trial, conviction, and sentencing. His argument was based on three complex points: first, one of the three judges had been unilaterally appointed by Governor Cochrane during the absence of Honourable Judge Des Barres; second, the constitution of the Grand Jury was illegal; and third, the "character" of the Grand Jury differed from the usual, in that they were all inexperienced, unintelligent, and not from the district where the crime had been committed. Judge Boulton, who initially received the petition on the day after the trial, completely ignored it, however, and proceeded to carry out the sentence he had pronounced.

Between the hours of 11:00am and 12:00 noon on Monday, January 6, the two condemned men prepared for their fate. A gallows had been erected for the occasion, just off the northwest window of the courthouse. Attended by two Roman Catholic priests and guarded by several constables, Downing emerged from his cell first. By all eyewitness accounts he displayed no emotion, apparently having accepted his end with stoic finality. Down the hall he walked, through

---

4. It was common at this time for qualified surgeons to be allowed to dissect the bodies of executed criminals for the purpose of anatomical study.

the Sessions Room, and out onto the platform where he would make his last stand. The anxious crowd, numbering in the thousands, watched intently from below, as the anonymous hangman, garbed in the traditional disguise, first placed the hood over Downing's head, then the rope around his neck.

Contemporary records disagree as to the last minutes of Downing's life. At least one newspaper reported that he took the opportunity to say some last words to the crowd, while others said he remained silent. Either way, he did not linger long before the trap door was sprung. After several involuntary convulsions, the last spark of life was extinguished, and Peter Downing's body swayed silently, suspended about ten feet above the ground.

Those in the crowd with an insatiable appetite for gruesome sights were to be somewhat disappointed on this day, though. Just minutes before his partner's execution, Malone had been informed of the mercy of the Court, which had rescinded his death sentence based on the proclamation for clemency that had been read to him prior to his confession before the Harbour Grace magistrate. Malone was to remain confined "until His Majesty's pleasure be known." Eventually, he was banished from the colony.[5]

In many respects the conviction of these two men fuelled a smouldering fire. Convinced of the Court's ulterior motive, many Irish living in and around Harbour Grace greatly resented the decision to have Downing's body remain hanging in chains on or near the site of the crime, as a letter to the editor of the *Star and Conception Bay Journal* reveals:

It has been satisfactorily proved that a species of exhibition serves only to outrage humanity, and is not at all calculated to effect the object for which it was intended. The unfortunate man's corpse is still lying in the Courtyard (of course in a high state of decomposition).

---

5. The following summer he was still in the St. John's jail. A letter from Deputy Sheriff Aaron Hogsett, dated June 23, refers to his "dangerous state of health," and forwards a request that the prisoner be moved to Prowse's Lodging House to recover.

We are now to be disgraced and insulted with a Gibbet being stuck up amongst us. I would therefore suggest the propriety of committing the body of this miscreant to the earth, and not insult us with its exhibition.

As well, the editor of *The Star*, a known liberal, felt moved to offer his opinion on the gibbet:

If the inhabitants of Harbour Grace, or the majority of them, feel aggrieved at the appearance of so disgusting an object as the body of Downing must present, they should petition the governor on its removal. We cannot, for the life of us, discover the good to arise out of the exhibition of a malefactor.

Dr. Stirling, certainly one of the Crown's key witnesses at the trial of Downing and Malone, soon realized the extent of the public's displeasure. In the early hours of the morning, months after the trial, a tremendous rapping on his door stirred him from his sleep. Shaken by the apparent urgency, Stirling stumbled down the darkened stairway, candle in hand. After struggling with the latch for a few seconds, in exasperation he finally swung the heavy door open. Immediately, a large, black form collapsed in on the startled doctor, and crashed to the floor with a sickening thud. Before he could collect himself, he was nearly overcome by the putrid smell of the strange object. Gathering up the candle, which had fallen from his hands, Stirling's usual composure deserted him, and a terrified scream escaped his lips. Lying at his feet were the rotten remains of Peter Downing. A small piece of parchment pinned to the corpse fluttered slightly in the breeze blowing in through the open door. After his initial revulsion had passed, Stirling managed to approach the ghastly form, and snatched up the paper. Scribbled in poor handwriting was the message:

Dr. S. This is your man you were the cause of bringing him here take and bury him or Lookout should you be the cause of allowing him to be put up again we will mark you for it so Do your duty and put him out of sight. Truly A friend from Carbonear.

The triple murder of Robert Crocker Bray, his son, and house-maid, followed by the execution of Peter Downing, horrified and disgusted many citizens in and around the community of Harbour Grace. Sadly, the family of the executed man also suffered tremendous hardship and humiliation in the aftermath. Undoubtedly shunned by local society, and unable to provide for themselves, Mrs. Downing and her children quickly became anathema. A brief letter to James Crowdy, the colonial secretary, from three Harbour Grace magistrates is most plaintive:

> *receiving His Excellency's permission to send the widow and children of the late Peter Downing to Ireland by the brig Kingarlock, that vessel's accommodations were so taken up that it was quite impossible for them to proceed in her, and no opportunity having since offered, they still remain a charge of the District, being entirely destitute of any means of support.*

Several weeks later the Downing family, no longer welcome in Harbour Grace, was sent to St. John's, where it was hoped that passage could be found for them to New York. They disappear entirely from the records after this, leaving us to wonder about their fate.

CHAPTER 10

A WRETCHED, SINFUL WOMAN

*I am sure a dozen Catherine Snows of the Protestant faith might have
been executed under similar circumstances and no Protestant clergy or
layman would have presumed to call in question the decisions of the Judge
or Jury and pray for pardon on no other ground than their own impression
of the innocence of the party nor have attempted to vilify the public authorities because their increasing interference had not been adhered to.*

Governor Cochrane to Lord Stanley
August 2, 1834

The crowd of spectators outside the courthouse was surprisingly quiet
on this dreaded Monday morning, the faces of many bearing despair
instead of anticipation. In the dim light of early morning, numerous
individuals clasped prayer beads and whispered appeals to a higher
justice, in hope that the Almighty would spread His supreme mercy
upon the one they felt was innocent of the horrible crime for which
she now stood convicted. That Catherine Snow's execution had been
moved forward by two hours was confirmation for many that the hard
hand of man's justice was determined to have its way, despite the
intervention of several clergy on behalf of the condemned.

Several days earlier Fathers Troy, Waldron, and Ward had called
on Chief Justice Boulton at his home with a petition signed by
hundreds, declaring that Mrs. Snow had been unjustly convicted of
the murder of her husband, John Snow, a successful planter in the
fishery. Boulton had responded to this impressive display of support
with a letter that declared his willingness to hear any new evidence
which might vindicate the "unhappy woman." Boulton, though soon
to be deplored by the Roman Catholic clergy and the entire reform
movement, did not sound unreasonable in his letter:

As I told you personally so do I now repeat, that it is not the number of signatures which can have any weight in relieving this prisoner from the melancholy fate impending over her, but the legal reasons which can be urged to the Court to influence them in this matter. It is not too late to hear reasons against her conviction; and if it can be shown that she was illegally convicted, God forbid that I should be necessary for her condemnation!

However, Boulton also admonished the priests for their ill-timed defence of the condemned woman:

It is further to be observed that every circumstance put forth in your memorial was equally well known the day after her trial in January last, when the law, out of tenderness to her offspring interposed, and she was respited until this term, and therefore if an honest conviction were felt that she had been illegally convicted, why were not measures taken by you to bring her case under consideration of the King's government, when by this time an answer might have been received.

One of the circumstances Boulton referred to was the fact that Mrs. Snow had been tried along with her lover, Tobias Mandeville, and her late husband's servant, Arthur Spring, co-conspirators in the murder. Mrs. Snow's supporters felt that trying all three at the same time unfairly prejudiced the jury against her and argued that, had she been tried alone, the jury would have returned a different verdict. This argument, predictably, went nowhere with Judge Boulton.

Most troubling of all, however, had been Mrs. Snow's revelation at the time of her sentencing that she was pregnant. A jury of Court-appointed matrons privately examined her the next day, and found that she told the truth. Consequently, the Court agreed to delay her execution until the following term, by which time the child would have been born. This case scandalized and further divided an already estranged population.

The entire affair had begun several years earlier on a trip to Harbour Grace from Catherine Snow's home in Salmon Cove, near Port de Grave. According to Mandeville, a cooper for the firm of

Jacob and Martin in Bareneed, their first intimate encounter had been in the woods near an area known locally as "the ponds." Their feelings for each other had grown during the ensuing years, and their "encounters" more frequent. Living with a husband whom she claimed was abusive apparently made the decision to murder him an easy one. Recruiting Arthur Spring, who later testified that his master had treated him cruelly, had also been relatively easy.

On the last day of his life, August 31, 1833, John Snow had gone to Bareneed with a boatload of fish, accompanied by his wife. As Snow went about his business, completely unaware of either his wife's long-term infidelity or her treachery, Catherine met with Mandeville and confirmed their plans to carry out the murder that night. The Snows stayed until nearly sunset before heading back across the harbour.

Later that evening John Snow returned to Bareneed alone, as was usual on a Saturday night, to pick up Mandeville and bring him back to Salmon Cove. Since Snow was unable to read or write, over the years Mandeville had received a modest remuneration for doing up Snow's books at the end of every week.

Unsuspecting of any sinister design, when they reached his wharf John momentarily remained behind to tie on the boat. Mandeville hurried ahead to the stage and, as planned, Spring waited with a loaded gun. Though Spring had learned to despise his master over the past several months because of the alleged cruel treatment, when the time came to commit the foul deed, his nerves failed him. Watching Snow approach the doorway, Spring's hands trembled uncontrollably and he dropped the butt of the gun.

"What are you about?" growled a disgusted Mandeville.

"I haven't the courage to fire," replied Spring.

Mandeville then snatched the weapon from his partner and ordered him to stand aside. Just as Snow was coming through the door, Mandeville squeezed the trigger. The full blast took Snow in the chest and blew him onto the broad of his back without even a groan, dead instantly. Months of planning, watching, and waiting for the right moment were over with the flash from the gun. Tobias

Mandeville, Arthur Spring, and Catherine Snow, now murderers, had sealed their fates.

Quickly, in case somebody had heard the shot, Mandeville and Spring lugged the dead man down to his boat, trailing a stream of blood. With the body hidden below the gunwales, they rowed far out into the mouth of the harbour, where they sunk it with a grapnel, naively secure in the belief that they would never be discovered. Once back ashore, the two felons proceeded to Snow's house, and informed the widow that the deed had been done. Having had the foresight to send her two eldest daughters and a servant girl named Catherine White to a wake at Cupids, a mile or so away, Catherine warned her co-conspirators to say nothing to anyone. Then, with the younger children already asleep, she went to her brother-in-law's house farther up the road.

News of John Snow's disappearance went around the harbour quickly enough, however, so that by Monday, when he still had not shown up, Magistrate Pinsent of Port de Grave ordered Constable John Bows to investigate. To Bows's surprise, he found Tobias Mandeville still at John Snow's house and, instead of a distressed wife pleading for help in locating her lost husband, he was met by an irate woman who wanted to know why "Mr. Pinsent was meddling himself about the business."

The constable's report raised some eyebrows within the tiny police force at Port de Grave. Pinsent, Bows, and several others immediately returned to Salmon Cove, where they obtained statements from Spring, Mandeville, and Mrs. Snow. At this point the authorities were not even sure they were looking at a murder case. As far as they knew, John Snow was simply missing. But as a result of their inquiries, on September 5 Spring and Mandeville were both arrested on suspicion of foul play. To his astonishment, Pinsent was approached by Mrs. Snow as he and a constable were taking Mandeville to the lockup at Port de Grave. At the time, she appeared very anxious and determined to have Spring released on bail, claiming that her hay and potatoes would spoil if he were not there to do his work. Catherine Snow's pleas for the liberation of a man believed to be involved in her husband's disappearance seemed extremely odd.

As a result of their suspicions, the authorities decided on a clever ruse to be played out during the remanding of Spring and Mandeville in the tight quarters of the jail. Prior to placing the two suspects in adjoining cells, a third man was ordered to remain hidden beneath a nearby table to overhear any conversation between the two prisoners that would implicate either them or Mrs. Snow.

The craftiness of the investigators was rewarded when Spring and Mandeville realized they had been duped. There was hardly any need to hear a statement from the concealed constable, for almost immediately Spring sent word to the magistrate that he had something important to communicate. Probably aware of the same deal that had been offered to Patrick Malone, Spring no doubt felt assured that a full confession would get him off easy. His words on entering Pinsent's quarters said it all: "We killed him. Mandeville, myself, and Mrs. Snow."

With his partner likely to shift the blame, Mandeville soon volunteered a partial confession of his own. Though each man accused the other of the actual shooting, one fact was common in both their stories: Catherine Snow had been a full participant in the plot to murder her husband and dispose of his body. His suspicions now confirmed, Pinsent ordered Bows and others to head for Salmon Cove to arrest the deceitful Mrs. Snow.

But they were too late. Having realized that Spring and Mandeville were behind bars and likely to confess, Catherine did not wait around for the constables to come knocking. With help from some of her closest friends she spent the next several days and nights moving from one safe house to the next.

On September 7 three search parties combed the nearby communities, but all three returned near dusk, empty-handed. Similar search parties on September 8 had the same result. But a rumour that the fugitive was in Cupids brought the constables to Dennis Hartrey's house on September 9. After first being denied entry, the police finally discovered Catherine resting in bed. Her life on the run brought to an end, Catherine was taken to the jail at Harbour Grace, where she gave her own statement before Magistrate Thomas Danson.

A great deal of public anxiety quickly arose around this case and the concurrent saga of Downing and Malone. With sectarian tensions still high only months after the violent by-election of Dr. Carson, the citizenry split along religious lines as to whether they supported the Crown or the Defence. Since the defendants in both cases were Irish Catholic, the Irish population was quick to rally to their side. Local Englishmen, however, still smarting over their recent loss at the polls, became incensed with the sympathy offered to the accused, and were further offended because the second case involved a romantic affair between two of the defendants.

As with Downing and Malone, it was not until early in the new year that Mandeville, Spring, and Snow finally went to trial at the Supreme Court in St. John's. On the day of the trial, Friday, January 10, the courtroom was filled. The intricacies of the law in 1834 determined that Mandeville was charged with murder, but, owing to their different relationships to the victim, Spring and Snow were both charged with a specific type of murder referred to as "petit treason."

The proceedings commenced at 11:00 a.m. and continued through the afternoon and into the evening. Numerous witnesses were called, and the statements of the three accused were read. A particularly moving part of the trial occurred when Mandeville was given the opportunity to speak in his own defence. Realizing the harm he had brought upon his lover, he likely now wished to clear her of any involvement in the murder of her husband. As for his earlier testimony that Catherine had been fully aware of the scheme, Mandeville asserted that any statement he had made to that effect was incorrect and unintentional.

By 10:30 p.m. the Court had heard both arguments for the Crown and the Defence, and Chief Justice Boulton addressed the jury. He ordered them to pay particular attention to the evidence against the widow Snow, urging that, if they "did not consider the evidence sufficiently conclusive," they were "bound to give her the benefit of the doubt." These instructions might cause us to speculate that Boulton was either unconvinced of Catherine's guilt, or wished to demonstrate to the public a leniency toward the "softer sex."

The twelve-man jury deliberated for a mere half-hour before

returning with a guilty verdict for all three accused. One newspaper reported that Boulton made an "impressive display" of immediately pronouncing death upon the prisoners. As with their predecessor Downing, the bodies of both Mandeville and Spring were to be hung in chains. Although the final outcome may have been a forgone conclusion, the astonishment of those in attendance to Catherine's revelation of her condition at this time could afford no pretence. As expected, the court-appointed jury of matrons confirmed the next day that Catherine Snow was pregnant. Boulton subsequently respited her sentence until the following session of the Supreme Court.

In the meantime, Bishop Fleming, who had already begun his meditations with Mandeville and Spring, earnestly offered prayers and celebrated Mass in their cells in an effort to prepare them for the hereafter.

At the allotted time on a cold Monday, January 13, the condemned men walked through the upper window of the courthouse and out onto the platform where they would make their last stand, accompanied by Fathers Troy and Ward. The editor of one Catholic newspaper thought the two, dressed in blue jackets with white gloves and trousers, "really fine young men"—not a description typically assigned to convicted murderers, but certainly indicative of Catholic sentiment. Henry Winton of *The Ledger* remarked that the two had resigned themselves to their awful fate, but not with "the same firmness which marked the conduct of their predecessor, Downey."[1]

After a few moments of prayer, they were "consigned to another realm."

Having been suspended for the required thirty minutes, the bodies were removed from the gallows for the last order of sentencing. However, according to Governor Cochrane's account of the trial, upon "the interference of Roman Catholic priests" the hanging in chains was remitted. Dr. Edward Kielley, a Roman Catholic but self-professed Tory at odds with his clergy, was to have performed the usual dissection of the bodies; however, the jail was soon surrounded

---

1. Winton used the alternate spelling.

by a noisy, threatening mob. Fearing for his own safety, Kielley merely scratched the neck of the dead convicts with a penknife so as to have formally carried out his duty, then gave the bodies up for burial.

In a lengthy letter to Lord Stanley, the governor expressed his extreme displeasure, stating that "the subsequent funeral was more that of Majesties than Felons." The furor over this double hanging, following immediately after Downing's execution, had the Irish population in an uproar. With Catherine Snow awaiting her death, it was beginning to look as if the new chief justice had his own plan for exterminating Irish Catholics in Newfoundland.

The public's attention was soon diverted by other news, however, particularly a scandal involving another Supreme Court judge, and the condemned murderess, Catherine Snow, was briefly forgotten.

Several months passed, until one day the cries of a newborn infant sounded throughout the halls of the jail. The arrival of this child was hardly a joyous occasion though, for it signalled the mother's impending demise. Having displayed only a reckless disregard for her situation up until her delivery, Catherine Snow was brought before the Supreme Court once again in mid-July, loudly protesting her innocence. Her behaviour on the day of her last arraignment was tantamount to the rantings and ravings of a madwoman. Her contempt for the court that had convicted her was manifested in a violent episode that shocked many onlookers, but further convinced supporters of her innocence.

It was shortly after this appearance that Father Troy became actively interested in the case. Reviewing the transcripts of the original trial, he was convinced that the evidence against Catherine Snow was circumstantial. This, along with the belief that she should have been tried separately from Mandeville and Spring, solidified his determination to get her death sentence remitted. Troy's main argument was, in fact, a convincing display of his legal knowledge. He pointed out that, aside from the confessions of the co-accused, there was no evidence to substantiate that a death had even occurred—after all, there was no body. Troy maintained that if Mrs. Snow had been tried on her own, the confessions of Mandeville and Spring would not have been permitted as evidence against her, and therefore the jury would have had no choice but to acquit.

The point was not even debatable, replied Boulton, who used a simplified example to demonstrate his position:

> *If A hired B to drown C, and B upon his apprehension for the murder confessed his crime and that he had sunk the body in the sea - it would be a monstrous proposition that although B confessed his guilt, A could not be convicted as an accessory, the hiring being clearly proved.*

Not willing to concede defeat that easily, Troy went about collecting signatures to petition Boulton to reconsider:

> *That Your Lordship's Memorialists are impressed with the conviction that Catherine Snow owes her condemnation not the fact of any proof of guilt being addressed against her, but entirely to the circumstances of her trial having occurred concurrently with the trial of the unfortunate men who suffered for the murder of John Snow.*

It was to this position that Boulton replied with a willingness to hear any new evidence favourable to the condemned woman, but stressed that the number of her supporters was not enough to overturn her conviction.

After responding to the judge's admonition, and getting nowhere, Troy took his argument to Governor Cochrane in the form of a letter. The only answer to this appeal was a notification that the execution was being moved forward by two hours. It is not certain who ordered the move, but Cochrane's letter to Lord Stanley two weeks later apparently recognized the distress that it caused among the condemned woman's friends:

> *It must be wholly unnecessary for me to point out the mischief that may be created among such an ignorant class of people as compose the majority of this population by impressing upon them the idea that a fellow creature and one of their own station in life has been*

*unjustly executed and that the only answer to petitions on her behalf
was the hurrying forward her sufferings.*

Whoever ordered the move, and for whatever reason, the fact
was that Catherine Snow's mortal existence was to be cut shorter than
expected on the morning of July 21, 1834, ten months and twenty
days after she had conspired to murder her husband.

Just before dawn on the last day of her life, Catherine prayed
earnestly with Fathers Troy, Ward, and Waldron. Having accepted her
fate, she feared now for her soul. For days the priests had been her only
companions, and thoughts of spiritual salvation her only concern. She
cared not at all for her physical well-being, having hardly eaten or drunk
since her last arraignment. Even her own family was dismissed, and the
newborn, who had given her extended life, only a vague memory.

With the sun rising in the east, and a grey light slowly flooding
the dingy cell, Catherine gazed on her reflection in the crude mirror
she had been permitted on this, her final day. What she saw was a
frail, dishevelled creature, with hollow cheeks and sunken eyes. But
most startling was the long, black "gown of the dead," hanging loosely
about her emaciated body, that had been provided for her execution.
Sight of the grotesque vision provoked a shocking reaction from
Catherine. As she stared at this frightful image, a lengthy, bone-chilling
scream escaped her lungs, unnerving all within earshot. Prisoners in
nearby cells, startled from their restless dreams, shouted in horror
and fear. Jailors immediately came running. The distraught woman
wailed and thrashed about with her arms and legs, until finally, after
several minutes, her disturbing outburst subsided into pitiful whimpers.
With the aid of the priests, Catherine slowly regained her composure
and rejoined them in solemn prayer.

At about 8:45 a.m. Monday morning, July 21, 1834, Catherine
Snow was led from her cell and escorted out onto the gallows, followed
closely by the priests, who murmured the last rites in unison. Below
the gallows the crowd awaited. Not all were here to assist the
condemned woman with prayers. Many needed to watch the final
moments of a condemned murderess, and to witness the discharge of

justice they felt was deserved. When asked if she had any last words, Catherine declared that she was "a wretched and sinful woman," but as innocent of any participation in the crime for which she was about to suffer "as the child unborn." Then, with stoical reserve, she waited as the hood was pulled over her head, and the noose placed about her neck. A momentary eerie silence preceded the collapse of the trap door through which passed the body of the "unhappy woman." It was over quickly, remarkably quickly, considering the months of remand, trial, and pregnancy. After several involuntary leg thrusts, the spark of life was extinguished, and the lifeless form twisted ever so slightly in the warm summer breeze. Following a collective moan from the crowd the moment after her neck snapped, there was silence.

After the body was cut down, Dr. Kielley took possession of it for the customary anatomical dissection. Knowing the mood of the crowd that once again surrounded the jail, Kielley made a small incision upon the neck as he had done with Mandeville and Spring.

A day or so later, one of Catherine's daughters applied to have the body returned to the family, whereupon it was laid to rest in the Roman Catholic cemetery. As the church did not bury murderers within hallowed ground, the significance of the interment of the three convicted parties in this case was not lost on Governor Cochrane and others. The Catholic Irish had long felt deprived of equality and justice in Newfoundland, in many instances with good reason. This case, along with that of Downing and Malone, thus signalled another step in their ever-increasing distrust of the authorities. To the English Protestants, however, the guilty had received their just reward, and their Catholic support was confirmation of Irish criminality.[2]

---

2. The ultimate fate of Catherine Snow's children, of which she had eight, cannot be determined with any certainty. However, there appears in the records of the Colonial Office at PANL (GN2/2, f368) a letter from A. Hogsett, Deputy Sheriff, requesting support for Catherine Snow's "child." It can only be assumed from this letter that the child survived its birth, and probably lived to an old age. No doubt some of Catherine's direct descendants still live in the Salmon Cove - Port de Grave area.

CHAPTER 11

THE FLAMES OF DISCORD

Two or three months ago we appeared to be subsiding into Peace, and even our Island papers announced the pacifying fact. It is with infinite regret that I see the flames of discord again breaking out in various directions, and defeating all my hopes.

Governor Prescott to Lord Glenelg
January 17, 1836

The authorities would refer to the events of January, 1835, as a "state of rebellion," perpetrated by an uncontrollable Irish priest. The residents of St. Mary's Bay probably thought more of a *war of independence*. Most likely neither side anticipated the magnitude of the relatively minor affair, yet both were prepared to defend their position to the bitter end. As Chief Justice Boulton declared, "Duffy and the whole rabble will be brought to heel, and with them the Irish faction in the House of Assembly, and Bishop Fleming as well." Diplomacy was certainly not one of Boulton's better attributes, and his brash prediction would later return to haunt him.

It had begun innocently enough the previous fall, with Father James Duffy seeking a good location to rebuild the Roman Catholic chapel at St. Mary's, destroyed earlier in a wind storm. The site he had chosen was on the sheltered part of the beach, close enough to the houses to be more convenient for parishioners travelling to and from Mass. John Martin, agent for the local mercantile establishment of Slade, Elson and Company, was totally opposed to the reverend gentleman's site selection, however, and made his opposition well known. As a rule, the merchant's word, or that of his representative, carried much weight in rural Newfoundland, but Martin was also the local magistrate *and* the district's representative in the House of

Assembly. Even though Duffy faced an influential opponent, he was in no way intimidated, and a verbal jousting match between the two continued for several months.

Ignoring the threats of legal admonishment from his adversary, Duffy had the church constructed on his chosen site while Martin attended the latest session of the House at St. John's. Suffice it to say, there was plenty of magisterial and personal rancour from Martin on his return, to find the church standing defiantly on the beach. Not willing to concede defeat, Martin ordered the construction of a large fish flake directly in front of Duffy's church, close enough to block the entrance. Admission was only possible through one of the side windows. So much for the convenience of the parishioners.[1]

Duffy, used to having his own way, was irate, and not at all impressed by Martin's social and judicial status. In fact, Duffy had had some legal training prior to his spiritual calling. Thus, preferring to proceed along legitimate avenues, he communicated his objections to Martin in a formal letter, asking that the flake be removed. Duffy pointed out that the beach was public property, and Martin had no right to make it the private domain of Slade, Elson. He concluded his letter with a momentary lapse from legal propriety by warning Martin that failure to accede to his wishes would result in the forced removal of the flake by his congregation.

Martin immediately warned Duffy to keep his hands off the flake or suffer the consequences. Incidentally, the matter of Duffy having constructed the church without permission in the first place had yet to be dealt with. As he departed again for St. John's, Martin spitefully left orders that the mischievous priest was to be sold no household supplies or any other goods by Slade, Elson.

By mid-January Duffy was sufficiently incensed that, legal propriety

---

1. One version of this story, as related by Bishop Fleming, said that Martin had the flake erected on the beach *prior* to Duffy's constructing the church. Numerous requests by the priest to have the flake removed went unheeded. Once the church was completed, Duffy *then* ordered the destruction of the flake. While much of this version is entirely plausible, most sources claim the church came first, then the flake.

aside, at Mass on January 13, he ordered the men of his congregation to get their axes and chop down and burn the offending flake, warning that the devil would go with them to their grave if they did not obey.

Word of the priest's misconduct reached Martin in St. John's; however, he was at a loss as to his next move. The situation was a delicate one, for Father Duffy and his flock had clearly defied Martin's wishes, but any sudden reaction on the part of an English Protestant in an Irish Catholic community might re-ignite the already flaming emotions in the capital. Finally, after a lengthy delay, Attorney General James Simms drew up a warrant for Duffy's arrest. But the forces of justice were either slow moving or indecisive, for it was well into November before a constable sheepishly appeared at the priest's door to take him into custody.

An event then occurred that played out almost as a tragicomedy. Just before Christmas, two constables masquerading as shipwrecked sailors showed up at St. Mary's to arrest the men who had destroyed Martin's flake. Local suspicions were immediately aroused, since neither of the men appeared to have gone through such a terrible ordeal as a shipwreck, plus they immediately asked to be directed to the magistrate's house. That night the two policemen revealed their true identities to the local constable, and announced warrants for the arrest of eight men suspected to have been involved. Clearly understanding his difficult position and quite possibly facing years of personal harassment from his neighbours, the town constable refused to aid in apprehending the eight men. This left the two strangers to their own devices and, as predicted, they were met with great resistance when many of the townspeople turned out to protect their own. Both police were severely beaten before they managed to escape and make their way back to the colonial brig *Maria*, which had been waiting offshore to transport the prisoners back to St. John's. Probably fearing for his own life following this incident, Martin now wrote a letter to Governor Prescott, informing him of the "outrageous conduct" of the men of the community, and earnestly requesting more assistance.

It was on hearing of this latest fiasco that Boulton expressed his desire to bring the whole rabble to heel, and advised the governor to request a Royal Navy warship to be sent to St. Mary's. The governor received a favourable hearing at the Colonial Office, and Lord Glenelg immediately sent notice that the Admiralty would dispatch a vessel.

For all outward appearances, up until this time the leader of Newfoundland's Roman Catholic church had been mostly silent, while playing the part of moral and spiritual adviser to his troubled people in St. Mary's. In truth, Bishop Fleming had never been one to sit idly whenever a fight was brewing. Just how active he was behind the scenes is difficult to say, but on learning that the eight individuals sought by the authorities had been declared outlaws by "Royal Proclamation," Fleming calmed the waters by ordering the men to turn themselves in. His pastoral letter, though, was far from a condemnation of their actions:

> *You are considered in a state of rebellion against the king, and warships are to be sent to blockade your harbour and a regiment of soldiers to be quartered upon your households. Let us contemplate with fear and horror the establishment of soldiers upon your houses, at a time when you men will be absent at the fishery, abandoning your wives and children, without protection, to these licentious soldiers.*

The strength of Fleming's word was clearly demonstrated when all eight fugitives, accompanied by Father Duffy, showed up at St. John's shortly afterwards.[2]

Not feeling very conciliatory, Boulton delayed bringing the case to court, obviously hoping to inflict as much inconvenience as possible. Winter turned to spring. With no signs of a trial, the eight men returned home to go fishing, while Duffy continued to hike the woods and barrens between St. Mary's and St. John's in an effort to have his day in court.[3]

---

2. While most sources claim that there were eight men arrested with Father Duffy, nine names appear: John Bowen, Michael Yetman, Thomas Whealan, Geoffrey Quilty, Patrick Tobin, John Bishop, Stephen Conners, James Fagan, and Thomas Murray.

3. It was during these numerous trips back and forth to the capital that Father Duffy discovered his now famous spring near Salmonier.

Once again Fleming utilized his persuasive prowess and convinced the governor to order Boulton to either proceed with the matter or throw the whole thing out.

If diplomacy was not one of Boulton's better attributes, neither was it one of Duffy's. Now, finally in the dock, he antagonistically declared that an Irish Catholic could find no justice in Boulton's court. This statement was not one calculated to win any sympathy among Protestant observers. Duffy then had the temerity to demand that he and his co-defendants be represented in court by one of their own faith. Word soon spread, and Duffy's support grew considerably as several petitions reached the governor from Roman Catholics all over the colony. Finding a qualified Roman Catholic barrister in Newfoundland in 1836, though, was easier said than done. Thus, Duffy chose to act in his own defence.

Once the proceedings finally got under way it didn't take long before some legal *improprieties* surfaced. For unexplained reasons, two of the Crown's main witnesses, John Martin himself, and William Lush, chief clerk for the firm of Slade, Elson, could not make their court appearances. Instead, written depositions from both men, sworn before the local magistrate, were forwarded to the Supreme Court. Of course, it will be remembered that the local magistrate was John Martin. Boulton ignored the obvious conflict of interest, and permitted the questionable depositions to be admitted as evidence.

Some facts of the case were indisputable. Duffy had certainly instructed his congregation to destroy Martin's flake, even admitting this himself. But it was the motive that Duffy tried to justify. He claimed that the flake caused undue hardship to the residents of the community because it not only blocked admission to the church but also the path across the beach to neighbouring communities. To support his position he argued that several years earlier a local man named Fewer had erected a flake on the same spot. Martin had ordered Fewer's flake dismantled at that time, stating that the beach was public property - basically the same point that Duffy was arguing now.

Martin and Lush, in their depositions, both claimed that Duffy had been agitating civil disobedience ever since his arrival in St. Mary's, and finally succeeded in coercing his flock by threatening severe ecclesiastical punishment if his instructions were not obeyed.

Tension between the defendant and the judge was apparent throughout the trial and, at the end of the proceedings, Boulton angrily charged the jury that it could bring in no other decision but guilty. The return, however, was not at all what he had called for. Amid much cheering from the spectators, a Not Guilty verdict was read, to Boulton's complete disgust. It was a bitter defeat, one of several that would eventually bring about his downfall.

But Duffy's star did not shine for long. It came as no surprise to many of Duffy's enemies that his stubborn disposition later landed him in more trouble, this time with his own superior, Bishop Fleming. Apparently not willing to forgive his trespassers, Duffy carried a grudge against William Lush and the man Fewer, whose issue with Martin he had argued as support for his own case. Fewer had afterwards sold some of the land in question to Martin, an insult that the clergyman did not forget. Having gained the abhorrence of his foes and the admiration of his friends, Duffy quickly elevated himself to the level of supreme ruler of St. Mary's. Sitting on the local Roads Board along with Lush and Fewer, a committee to which he had been appointed chairman, Duffy refused to call any meetings until both men resigned. This stalemate resulted in absolutely no roadwork being done for several years, and caused unnecessary hardship to his own people. By 1841 the new magistrate, Mr. Blackburn, wrote to Fleming demanding that something be done with the obstinate priest. What transpired between the two clerics may never be known, but the result was evident in Duffy's silence over the next ten years. He finally departed Newfoundland in 1851, for an appointment to Guysborough, Nova Scotia, where he immediately became embroiled in a bitter dispute with the priest of a neighbouring village.

Stubborn, unforgiving, and controversial are words that describe the personality of Father James Duffy, yet his legacy to the people of St. Mary's is that of a devoted man of the cloth who challenged the authorities and prevailed.

CHAPTER 12

HENRY WINTON: PART TWO

Now Orangemen gentry wherever you be,
Whether in Newfoundland or home over the sea,
Don't treat the poor Papist with scorn or with jeers,
Just remember what happened to Winton's two ears.

"Croppy Winton"
Anonymous

Against the advice of his friends, Henry Winton travelled to Conception Bay on business in May, 1835. For much of the trip he was alone, a brave but foolhardy exhibition of his contempt for the unremitting threat of personal harm, all the more real in recent weeks since posters had appeared in St. John's and some of the larger towns calling for the assassination of the controversial newspaperman. Satisfied that the pistol beneath his coat was all the protection he needed, Winton walked the streets of Harbour Grace and Carbonear, arrogantly defying the cold stares and whispers he knew were being directed his way.

His presence in this hotbed of radical liberalism produced a feeling of incredulity in his enemies. On the one hand, they could not believe his audacity to show up in their midst, without an escort – a man who embodied the very essence of all they detested, hated for his admonishment of the lower orders, the reform movement, but more particularly, the Roman Catholic priesthood. At the same time, the opportunity which now presented itself was nothing short of answered prayers for many. Here was the perfect chance to repay Winton for his insolence. Once Winton showed his face in public, it did not take long for devious voices to whisper foul plans. But for several days conspirators distanced themselves from the malefactor, to watch his every move and to await an opportune moment.

By late afternoon of May 19, the belligerent newspaperman was seen leaving Carbonear for Harbour Grace on a borrowed horse, his intention being to take the *Express* back to St. John's at 9:00 the following morning.[1]

His departure was viewed by cunning eyes, with eager anticipation. Winton would have something worthwhile to print in his heretical rag, and he would be taught a lesson he would not soon forget.

Unaware of the plot being set in motion, Winton passed over the bridge at the southern end of town, and was joined by a familiar gentleman, Captain William Churchward of the brig *Hazard*, who was also heading to Harbour Grace. After initial courtesies had been exchanged, the conversation likely switched to the troubled state of Newfoundland politics, and the heavy-handed influence of the Catholic priesthood over its "submissive flock." Churchward was undoubtedly subjected to quite a diatribe of anti-clerical rhetoric during this journey. Whether or not he agreed with his companion, we cannot be certain.

The ascent of Saddle Hill, the infamous prominence that had to be traversed on the road out of Carbonear, was slow and arduous, as the dusty road wound through thick woods and over little brooks. A gradual incline at the bottom turned into a significant climb before its summit was reached. The Saddle had a reputation of its own. It had lately been the scene of rowdy gatherings by local sealers determined to convince, or bully if necessary, prominent merchants into paying fairer wages, demonstrations which Winton had criticized in his paper, even referring to the sealers as "Conception Bay rabble."

Eventually the two travellers left the town of Carbonear far behind, and began the slow descent into the thickly wooded Mosquito Valley, halfway to Harbour Grace. It was now mid-afternoon and the sun was low in the western sky, casting its final rays on the deceptively tranquil scene below. Tall, handsome evergreens grew close to the narrow

---

1. The *Express* was a small cutter which left Harbour Grace for Portugal Cove at 9:00 a.m. every Monday, Wednesday, and Friday. Winton appears to have missed the *St. Patrick*, another vessel which made the trip to Portugal Cove from Carbonear every Tuesday, Thursday, and Saturday.

roadway, their shadows slowly spreading eastward. Aside from the rhythmical clip-clop of the horse's hooves, all was quiet and peaceful.

Suddenly, from out of the shadows on the right, two figures appeared, and walked towards Winton and Churchward. It wasn't until these figures were almost upon him that Winton saw that their faces were hideously painted with red and yellow ochre. He was briefly bewildered by the sight, but then realized that these men meant to harm him. Underneath him the mare also sensed danger and became restless. In haste and confusion, Winton attempted to draw the pistol from his pocket, while at the same time struggled to control his mount. The taller of the two painted figures seized this opportunity and hurled a large rock, striking Winton on the skull and knocking him to the ground. More figures appeared and attacked Captain Churchward, dragging him into the trees before he could lend any assistance. Dazed from the blow, Winton was instantly set upon by the first two men, who slammed more rocks down on his head. Mud and gravel were stuffed into his ears, as still more blows rained down. Amazingly, Winton remained conscious, and heard one of his attackers order the other to hold his hands. This individual then produced a clasp knife, the sight of which terrified Winton into the realization that his time may have finally come.

"Do you mean to murder me?" he stammered.

"Hold your tongue, you bastard!" was the reply.

In an instant the knife slashed two pieces from Winton's right ear, and took the left ear off completely. Finally, with a scream of agony and fear, the battered man fell mercifully into darkness.

Minutes later, to his own astonishment, Winton regained consciousness. The pain in his head was almost unbearable but, with a valiant effort, he struggled to his feet. Blood streamed over his face and soaked his jacket. Through a blur he could perceive two figures, and instinctively reached for his gun once again. But the friendly, consoling voice of Captain Churchward broke through the drumming inside his head, assuring him that the danger had passed. As Winton teetered on his feet, his shocked companion examined the dreadful wounds. To Churchward's surprise, the beaten man even made the absurd suggestion that they attempt to follow and apprehend his attackers. A wiser head prevailed, however, and upon the captain's insistence they proceeded as swiftly as Winton's condition would allow towards Harbour Grace, a mile and a half away. Once there, Dr. William Stirling provided shelter and medical attention for the injured and humiliated newspaperman, and sent word of his condition to the authorities:

> *I have seen Mr. Winton within the last half hour and am happy to say that though dreadfully mutilated he does not appear to be in any danger. He bears his misfortune with great fortitude and meets with much sympathy from all the upper classes, though I really believe that many of the lower ones are chuckling at his situation.*
>
> Judge Edward Benton to Colonial Sec. James Crowdy
> May 20, 1835

In the spirit of the times, when Benton spoke of the "lower" classes he was primarily referring to Roman Catholics. Indeed, it was generally assumed that Catholics were responsible for the assault on Henry Winton. Even Governor Prescott observed "a matter of open triumph and rejoicing to the Catholics of low degree, even female servants and children expressing the greatest satisfaction." In a letter to the Earl of Aberdeen two days later, the governor sounded more reproachful:

> *There can be no doubt that Mr. Winton has been thus barbarously mutilated in consequence of the unhappy dissentions existing here and has been repetitively denounced from the altar of the Roman Catholic chapel as an enemy to Bishop Fleming and priests. It is much to be feared that the wretches by whom this diabolical act was perpetrated may have believed themselves to be performing a meritorious deed. It is superfluous to say that the public mind is in a state of great ferment on this melancholy occasion.*[2]

---

2. See Appendix 2 for the order to clear trees from the side of Carbonear Road, in consequence of this act.

There was some truth in the assumption that Roman Catholics garnered much amusement from Winton's misery, for pretty soon a jaunty little ballad entitled "Croppy Winton" was being whistled and sung throughout the island, to the delight of young and old alike. Some members of the liberal press also commented, with some sense of vindication, on their antagonist's just deserts. The editor of *The Newfoundland Patriot*, Robert J. Parsons, had this to say: "If ever mercy was deservedly extended to crime - this case above all others demands it."[3]

The sober business of apprehending and punishing the perpetrators began in earnest, with the government offering a £500 reward, and dozens of St. John's merchants who favoured Winton's politics chipping in another £800, an astronomical figure for the time. Posters announcing this substantial reward were nailed up everywhere, only to be ripped down by unknown hands. A shroud of secrecy descended over Conception Bay. Allegations of a Catholic conspiracy throughout the land appeared in the newspapers and were the subject of debates within the House of Assembly. A determined team of special constables and magistrates headed by the attorney general himself was convened, and began a vigorous investigation, which ultimately dragged on for months. The final result, however, was an unsolved mystery. No one was ever arrested for the bloody assault on Henry Winton, though within certain circles the identities of the culprits were said to be common knowledge.[4]

It has remained astounding that, despite the small fortune offered as a reward, no one with any connection to the crime or the people involved ever volunteered any information. This may have been due to fear of a brutal retaliation, or because those involved were truly and totally committed to their ultimate cause.

---

3. Parsons, a former employee of Henry Winton, had worked as foreman of *The Public Ledger* for six years. A dispute in 1833 forced him to leave Winton's employ, and to form his own paper, *The Newfoundland Patriot*, in association with John Valentine Nugent.

4. See O'Flaherty, *Old Newfoundland*, 248.

Chapter 13

The Strange Case of Mr. Parsons

Boulton had undoubted ability, but he was the worst possible selection for both the Council and the Bench. His views, both of law and legislation, were most illiberal; as a technical lawyer he was mostly right and sublimely independent, but his harsh sentences, his indecent party spirit, and his personal meanness caused him to be hated as no one else was ever hated in this Colony.

D.W. Prowse
A History of Newfoundland

Another bizarre and unfortunate series of events occurred in May, 1835, one seeming to verify all the bad press Chief Justice Boulton had received in the wake of Catherine Snow's execution the previous January. The audacious editor of *The Patriot*, Robert J. Parsons, had been unrelenting in his diatribe against Newfoundland's conservatives, and further agitated Boulton by printing a letter that satirized his remarks at the opening of the central circuit court. The anonymous author of this letter was quite obviously offended with Boulton's lecture to the jurors on the benefits of hanging criminals. Considering the times, however, one might think that the judge's words were not that inappropriate, unlike his actions that followed the publication.

Charging Parsons with contempt for having printed the letter, Boulton took it upon himself to act as prosecutor, judge, and jury in the subsequent trial. This was an appallingly unorthodox and improper mode of proceeding, one that immediately raised a few eyebrows as well as quite a few objections. Ignoring the public outcry, Boulton sentenced the erring editor to three months in jail, and fined him £50. The outcry became an uproar.

Several of Mr. Parsons's influential supporters reacted by forming a "constitutional society," with two purposes: to free the imprisoned newspaperman and eliminate Boulton. Rumours of mob violence by the rank and file had spread in the days after the sentencing, and petitions were circulated and forwarded to the Colonial Office in London.

For his part, Parsons seemed to revel in the attention, knowing well that the judge's gross miscalculation could only end with his ultimate censure. In a lengthy letter, smuggled from his jail cell, Parsons affected the role of the persecuted hero:

> *When these lines shall have met the public eye, four dreary weeks of my allotted time shall have been numbered, and I shall have wiped off nearly one third of the score.*

Though possibly full of a greater sense of his own worth than was warranted, Parsons did have a strong argument for appeal. He was rewarded when Governor Prescott received instructions from the Colonial Office to free him and to repay his fine.[1]

The celebrating was loud and prolonged, to the utter dismay of conservative hard-liners.

Boulton attempted to defend his actions but, as Parsons had predicted, wound up being chastised for his oppressive methods. Humiliated, and fearing for his personal safety (not without good reason), Boulton travelled to London to plead for a transfer from the colony. His request was denied, and the unhappy man had to return to St. John's to face more criticism and ridicule.

After this case, Boulton should have re-evaluated his position on some of Newfoundland's social issues, for it was clear that his action against Parsons had nothing to do with criminal behaviour. Journalists on both sides had a flair for nastiness, and during the 1830s this colony was no place for a politician or official easily offended by the press.[2]

---

1. The anti-mercantile party had succeeded in having Thomas Cochrane replaced as governor in 1834. There were high hopes for Prescott, whose first action, in an attempt to appease the Catholic masses, was to drop a libel suit against Father Troy that had been levied by Cochrane.

2. It was widely suspected that Father Troy wrote the offensive letter.

But if Boulton was battered, he was not yet beaten. He had wealthy, powerful allies within the mercantile community, people who saw him as a champion of conservatism. He also had an insider who kept him abreast of developments within the Catholic church, someone who reported faithfully to him on clerical indiscretion. Eliza Boulton, wife of the ultra-conservative chief justice, was a Roman Catholic.

Boulton survived this latest round of attacks, having learned a valuable lesson about his antagonists; they too had friends in high places, liberals within the British House of Commons who were not to be trifled with. Among them was Daniel O'Connell, the charismatic Irish M.P., who could name Bishop Fleming as one of his greatest supporters. Indeed "The Great Dan" was soon to be Fleming's ace in the hole.

If Boulton was feeling a bit more intimidated by the now infamous Parsons affair, having to watch his back a little more as he walked the streets of St. John's, it was not apparent in the way he continued to handle his courtroom. Nor was it evident in his other role as head of the Executive Council, a position that allowed him to influence the drafting of certain legislation.[3]

Rigid and tough though he might be, Boulton faced a relentless opposition. The ongoing saga of Father Duffy would drag into the new year, and continue to antagonize Roman Catholics, adding mounting evidence for their case against the judge. Even Governor Prescott was becoming annoyed with Boulton's antics, going so far as to recommend his removal in order to preserve peace within the troubled colony.

By 1836, Boulton's days in Newfoundland were numbered. But he had one more vital part to play in the turbulent history of Newfoundland politics.

---

3. This dual role was a gross conflict of interest, and a great source of debate within the Lower House.

CHAPTER 14

BLUDGEONS, BAYONETS, AND ARTILLERY:
THE GENERAL ELECTION OF 1836

Carson, Morris, and Kent forever!
The sacred cause they will promote!
The chains of slavery they'll sever!
Spite the vile apostate's brazen throat!
Spite of his four years venal, venal, venal vote!
The Newfoundland Patriot
October 26, 1836

With serious concerns about the ideological makeup of the new Assembly, but in keeping with the agreed four-year legislative mandate, Governor Prescott announced a general election for the fall of 1836. In the four years since the initial contest, Prescott's reservations had not been proven unfounded. Since 1832 the electorate had grown stauncher in its political loyalties, and increasingly more displeased with the opposing side. This was particularly true of the Roman Catholic Irish, whose leaders were labelled "radicals" rather than "reformers" by the conservative press. The changes they promoted were interpreted by conservatives as "political ascendancy." In plain language, this meant an Assembly dominated by Catholics, or members supported by the Catholic clergy. This possibility was especially alarming to the merchants, who were quick to realize its repercussions: higher taxes and increased wages. Naturally, the lower orders, in particular the Catholic Irish, would select politicians who had their interests in mind and not those of the people responsible for their sustained dependency in the first place. There was already plenty of evidence that the lower orders were becoming more politically ambitious.

Aside from politics, the local Irish had a notion that they were continually being persecuted by their English "betters." In many instances this was true, but the perception may not always have been correct. For example, in the recent highly politicized trials any impartial observer would have difficulty saying that the execution of Peter Downing, or, for that matter, even Catherine Snow, was an intentional mistreatment of Irish Catholic citizens. On the other hand, the Father Duffy affair was indeed a systematic prolonging of abuse by the chief justice. The result was aggressive petitioning by the reformers and, eventually, open violence that bordered on insurgency. While some of the violence may have seemed justified at the time, the revolting behaviour of some extremists only hardened the opinions held by many Protestants. The most flagrant example of this was the attack on Henry Winton on Saddle Hill. Even though this incident had certainly made Winton the brunt of many jokes among the Irish, it did not silence his criticism of the reformers or the Roman Catholic priesthood, and, in fact, merely raised his status within conservative circles. Contrary to that, Bolton's blatant exploitation of authority in the case of Robert Parsons, confirmed, for the Irish and the reformers, that there was no justice in an English conservative courtroom.

So now, both sides had their martyrs, and were prepared to argue on the pages of opposing journals. But if the conservatives thought for one moment that election hostilities would be confined to the press, they had either forgotten about Dr. Carson's by-election or had grossly misunderstood the strategies for political success in Newfoundland.

Campaigning began in October, several weeks before the actual election. Signs of trouble appeared almost immediately. On October 23, a huge reform rally gathered in front of Patrick Mullowney's house in St. John's, and proceeded from there to a large field in Waterford Valley, where they were entertained by stirring speeches from popular candidates William Carson, Patrick Morris, and John Kent.[1]

---

1. At this time in Newfoundland there were no clearly established political parties, just common doctrines that individuals either followed or rejected. Those who desired a change to the status quo were considered reformers, the majority of which were Irish. Conservatives were often known as the "mercantile party" as their greatest support came from within that group.

At 5:30 p.m. the crowd returned to the city with music playing and banners flying. Prominent among the leaders of the parade were Father Edward Troy and three other Roman Catholic priests, whose presence clearly indicated a goal to unseat the English Protestant merchants, and to replace them with candidates more favourable to the Irish Catholics. The excited crowd shouted slogans and cheered as they marched through the streets. Almost on cue, some members began insulting known conservatives that they passed along their way. It was after dark before the crowd dispersed, with many following the priests to church.

Winton's predictable disapproval appeared in the next issue of his newspaper under the heading "Scandalous Outrage and Violation of the Peace!" There were, of course, the usual accusations of harassment and assault, at least some of which were true, but what most upset Winton's readers was that this rally occurred on a Sunday. For most puritanical Protestants this was a gross violation of the Sabbath, and they loudly voiced their indignation.

Parsons's version of the event clearly conflicted with Winton's, but was equally biased, and read like the report of a Sunday School garden party:

> *From Mr. Mullowney's the immense multitude proceeded towards Waterford Bridge along the picturesque and fertile vale that leads to that romantic spot - the day was remarkably fine - it was one of those Indian summer days, so well known in the October month in Newfoundland.*

Parsons made no reference to a disturbance on their return to the city, and chose instead to exaggerate the positive aspects. The same could not be said for all his editorials, however, many of which were just as offensive as anything Winton could write. On October 29 he railed about a long list of conservative supporters that had recently been printed in *The Public Ledger*: "We are very glad that these lists have been published; because we shall have, when any reference may require it, the whole band of dirty Orangemen before us in one long, filthy row."

The appearance of the "O" word in this editorial was grossly irresponsible, but also certainly deliberate, for Parsons had a penchant for unnecessary innuendos, which were meant to incite his readers. This allusion to Orangeism would not be his only one, and it was bound to have the desired effect, even though there was no established Orange Lodge in Newfoundland at the time, nor would there be for another twenty years or more. Not surprisingly, the events at Harbour Grace during the next few days would prove that some electors were only too willing to follow the examples of reproachful leaders and reckless newspapermen.

Seven candidates were nominated to fill the four existing seats in Conception Bay. Peter Brown, Robert Pack, Anthony Godfrey, and James Power were running under the reform ticket, challenged by three conservatives: Thomas Newell, the former right-wing editor of *The Conception Bay Star*; Robert Prowse, a merchant from Port de Grave; and the wealthy, and unpopular, Thomas Ridley of Harbour Grace.

An ominous harbinger of what was to come occurred the day before polling started. A large crowd of reform supporters gathered in Carbonear, parading the streets with banners and music, much like the St. John's rally one week earlier. Things got out of hand, though, when the crowd began smashing property belonging to known conservatives. The local police, being too few in number, were unable to control the mob and, when the rampaging had ended, the town, according to one eyewitness, presented "the appearance of a town just delivered from the tremendous bombarding of a powerful enemy." Having completed their work in Carbonear, the mob then proceeded to nearby Harbour Grace for a similar show of force.

So it was that two of the most troublesome districts were already up in arms, even before the opening of the polls.

On November 1 the Conception Bay election began in Harbour Grace amid plenty of fanfare and no small amount of anxiety. A crowd of between 150 and 300 people, carrying an ensign and a blue Ridley flag, gathered at 10:00 a.m. to show their support for the conservative candidates. From their location near the hustings they could hear the drums and flutes of the approaching parade of reformers, mostly Irish and nearly 700 strong, who had been gathering in Carbonear since the early morning hours.[2]

Though several witnesses would later claim that this procession had only peaceful intentions, the truth was borne out in the menacing message emblazoned in Gaelic upon one of its banners: translated, "Clear the road. Keep away from the wind of my cudgel." Many in the crowd were armed with pickets and bludgeons fashioned out of heavy wood, and some were dressed in flamboyant outfits. Particularly noticeable was Roger Thomey, who wore red and green ribbons around his hat, and a green sash over one shoulder decorated with a flower. He carried a hefty, knotted stick that he twirled and swung overhead in a threatening manner. Upon reaching the hustings the crowd immediately began to boisterously chant, "Down with the Tories! Down with the merchants!"

Not wanting to be driven from the field, Ridley's supporters, evidently overawed by their opposition, offered a pathetic little cheer of their own.

Minutes later, as the first of conservative voters to be tallied came forward, the processionists suddenly charged. Swinging their sticks in a brutal assault that smashed limbs and cracked skulls, they quickly overwhelmed Ridley's unarmed men. Screams of agony, shouts, and curses filled the air, as the attackers drove their quarry away, many of whom had to be carried because of the severity of their injuries. Thomey, arrested soon afterwards, was seen attacking Thomas Goss with his stick, while others hit and kicked the stricken man.[3]

At the same time, Pack and Power, clearly horrified by the

---

2. Witnesses at the subsequent trials gave differing estimates of the size of both groups, but the numbers here appear to be the most accurate.

3. James Currie, the jailor at Harbour Grace, claimed that he saw Roger Thomey strike Thomas Goss on the head with a stick, while twenty or thirty others also beat him. Goss himself, an elderly planter from Spaniard's Bay, claimed that Thomey first hit him with a stick as he was leaving the polling room. He was then attacked by "a great many other men." The numbers given by Currie appear to be exaggerations.

conduct of their people, had mounted the hustings, imploring them to cease the violence.[4]

The attack, though swift and shocking, was over in ten minutes. The vanquished, driven from the field in the end, huddled inside their houses, too hurt and too scared to return to the hustings, while the mob triumphantly paraded the streets, chanting and hurrahing.

With a repeat of the same proceedings imminent the next day, and fearing for the lives and property of their supporters, Ridley and Prowse both announced their resignations, but under protest. Newell, in the words of Robert J. Parsons, didn't even "come to the scratch."

News of the riot shocked and angered conservatives around the island, some of whom, rather prematurely, demanded the abandonment of the charter that had granted elected representation to the people of Newfoundland. This was something Winton had been preaching since Carson's dubious by-election victory three years earlier. The editor of *The Patriot*, however, felt like gloating, and lavishly declared, "Triumph for Reform! Toryism Defunct in Conception Bay!" Any mention of the terrible violence used to gain the desired result was purposely omitted, Parsons again choosing to ignore reports of hooliganism.

Meanwhile, on the same day as the Harbour Grace riot, another rally was held in St. John's by hundreds of reformers. Though there was no sign of trouble, the ever-critical Winton coloured his report of the event with some scathing journalism:

> *In the van were some three or four little dears, from eight to twelve years of age, out at knees and elbows, but innocently recreating themselves with the most amusing gambols. Then came an ancient little lady of the name of Cahill, and one Mistress Eleanor Tappin (the same that was up before the Magistrates a few days ago, and held for bail for a breach of the peace). After that the Rev. Father Troy, Dr.*

---

4. It was pointed out at the trials that both Pack and Power must have known that dozens of their supporters were armed, for they had all walked from Carbonear together. For that reason, some charged that the two candidates were also guilty of the violence on November 1.

*Carson, John Kent, Pat Morris, and about 400 men, women, and
children - such a motley group as we have rarely seen.*

If Winton's editorial sounded nasty, that of Parsons in the
November 2 issue of *The Patriot* was downright obnoxious:

*Electors! Beat the Tories from the hustings by your votes - knock out
their political brains by dashing plumpers against them - Drive them
(not to hell or Connaught but) to private life by whacking the ambition
out of them by defeat.*

This shocking passage was probably *not* what it first appeared to
be, a thinly disguised play on words meant as a call for more violence.
It was likely an ill-conceived metaphor, yet, in consideration of the
rioting in Harbour Grace, it was certainly in poor taste. Plus, when
news of the deaths of two riot victims was released several days later,
it could also be said to be poorly timed.

And the fireworks were far from over.

On November 9 a discovery was made by those investigating the
Harbour Grace troubles that no election writs in any district bore the
mandatory Great Seal. While this development clearly required a higher
ruling than local officials could provide, Boulton's opinion that the
Conception Bay election results should be nullified seems to have been
an attempt to over-exaggerate the problem. Unwilling to call off the
entire general election until he had heard from the Colonial Office in
London, however, Prescott ordered that the discovery be kept secret.

Another disturbance in St. John's, this time at a rally held by
conservatives, added more volatility to the already dangerous situation
there. On the night of November 10, supporters of conservative candidates Nicholas Gill, James Grieve, and Patrick Kough,[5] who had

---

5. Patrick Kough, a talented stonecutter from Ireland, would go on to construct
many prominent buildings in Newfoundland. During the 1830s Kough was
considered by many Irish to be an "Orange Catholic" because of his close
relationship with the St. John's mercantile class; he was therefore ostracized by
his clergy.

assembled at their committee room, were dismayed to learn that several hecklers had hidden among them. Having disrupted the proceedings, the hecklers were quickly ejected from the building, only to be joined outside by dozens of their friends, who stoned the committee room, smashing windows and splintering doors. Several members of the rally sustained injuries when they attempted to drive away their tormentors, but the remainder clustered inside, hoping that assistance would soon arrive. When it finally came, about half an hour later, it was in the form of a Roman Catholic priest, who urged the rioters to desist and return to their homes. In the days following this attack, the authorities were able to apprehend only three of those involved: Thomas Shortall, Patrick Lynch, and Geoffrey Power. Many people attending the rally claimed they were unable to positively identify others because it was dark. In a letter to Governor Prescott written much later, though, Boulton presented his own theory for the small number of detainees.

As polling day drew near, many St. John's conservatives feared a spectacle similar to that which had occurred in Conception Bay. Their concerns grew when John Walsh, a Roman Catholic at odds with his clergy, was assaulted after leaving a meeting on Friday, November 10. He had five broken ribs and numerous bloody gashes after being pushed into an open cellar and jumped on by two men. Except that several passers-by heard his groans, Walsh would likely have died.

Fully aware of the heightened state of alarm throughout the city, Winton made one last attempt to convince the Roman Catholic electorate of the "correct" vote. The tone of this latest editorial sounded much more conciliatory than anything heard from him in recent months:

Protestants! Lend your energies to the sacred cause of Civil and Religious Freedom - and Catholics! You and those like you, who but a few short years since, at a numerous assemblage in your own chapel, gave us a hearty, a cordial, and a kind and liberal vote of thanks for the interest which we had uniformly taken in your cause,

*when you had no other Press to represent your interests, will you
disregard our admonitions now! Rely upon it we will not mislead
you. We concurred in your emancipation from your national
disabilities; but we are equally desirous that you should be relieved
from all other disabilities that would render you anything else than
free and honest citizens.*

The effort was probably futile, as most Catholics no longer
subscribed to Winton's paper anyway, since Bishop Fleming had
banned it the previous year. Besides, Winton's continuous denun-
ciation of the priesthood had burned too many bridges. Even those
inclined to accept Winton's politics, like John Shea, the moderate
editor of *The Newfoundlander,* who was running as an independent
in the district of Burin, could hardly forgive his impudence. The
dividing lines had been drawn much earlier and, at this stage,
Winton's appeasements were almost pointless. With some notable
exceptions, the Roman Catholics of St. John's were voting reform.

But, if Winton was a bigot, there were some incidents which lent
credence to his literary attacks on the clergy. The most notorious of
these occurred on Sunday, November 13, the day before the St.
John's election was to begin.

During a celebration of Mass at the Roman Catholic chapel,
Father Edward Troy launched into a vicious verbal assault on the
"mad dogs," the term given to Roman Catholic electors like John
Walsh, men despised by their co-religionists for their conservative
politics and for their brazen defiance of clerical authority on such
matters. Two men in the congregation known to fraternize with the
enemy, Michael Scanlan and Thomas Grace, were singled out by
Troy and ordered to leave the chapel at once. When Scanlan questioned the priest as to what he had done wrong, Troy threw off his
vestments and advanced towards the offender. At this point, a burly
labourer named Patrick Brawders grabbed Scanlan and pushed
him down, then turned roughly on the man's wife and daughter.
Pandemonium broke out, with the Scanlan family being jostled and
pushed outside into the churchyard, where they were surrounded

and further threatened. Except for the levelheadedness of men like John Shea, the situation could very well have been much worse.[6]

News of this shocking display soon reached Winton, who was only too happy to relate the entire affair to his conservative readers and to use the opportunity to further castigate the politically motivated Roman Catholic clergy:

There is no mystery about it; they openly and shamelessly desecrate their altars to the service of a most unholy cause . . . They deny the rites of the church to those whose political creed does not square with their own, and they oppress and persecute by all manner of means those who offer the slightest resistance to their political domination.

Losing his ears had certainly not stilled Winton's tongue nor mellowed his opinions. Knowing that Troy had clearly crossed the line, the anti-reformers now had proof that some Roman Catholic clergy were indeed trying to influence the vote. This was provocative material, but the authorities had to tread lightly when it came to clerical chastisement, matters that were clearly the bishop's responsibility, and Winton's hobby. But they had no problem arresting Pat Brawders, once the Scanlans came forward with their depositions.

It was an acrimonious prelude to the St. John's election. Regrettably, the actions of Father Troy, a priest of high renown among his followers, appeared to justify, or at least condone, the use of physical intimidation. On the same night as the affair in the chapel, a rambunctious crowd proceeded along Water Street and halted in front of a store owned by another of the so-called mad dogs, Michael McLean Little.[7]

---

6. A young Ambrose Shea, a witness to the incident, made a statement before a local magistrate, but only after being assured that his statement would not be made public.

7. Troy had earlier ordered a Catholic boycott of Little's store, declaring that, until Little was "made a beggar, he could not be a good Catholic." This action stemmed from what Troy and Fleming considered political insubordination. But both would soon discover that Little was not someone to be pushed around. His subsequent petition against the clergy would reach the Colonial Office in London, and even the Vatican.

After shouting insults and threats, the crowd took out their rage upon the front of Little's premises by smashing the windows and doors, a course of action that was turning out to be standard behaviour for the reformers. Having made their intentions clear, the crowd moved on to other targets, leaving Little standing amid the rubble.

Cloaked in this atmosphere of violence, the six St. John's candidates proceeded to the hustings at 10:00 a.m. on November 14 for compulsory nomination: Kough, Grieve, and Gill for the conservatives; Carson, Morris, and Kent for the reformers. The predominantly Catholic crowd was in a nasty mood, stirred up by the previous day's events and encouraged by the presence of Troy and four other priests.

As Kough ascended the hustings to deliver his campaign speech, a tumultuous, disapproving roar erupted from the crowd, almost completely drowning out his words. Insults and threats were exchanged by members of the opposing sides, but were quickly replaced with sticks and stones. The entire scene swiftly descended into a riot, fulfilling the expectations and fears held by St. John's authorities. Many special constables sworn in in anticipation of such a turn of events were assaulted and beaten. William Townsend was particularly mistreated by the mob, who kicked and nearly strangled him to death, then dragged him by the hair along Water Street. Another constable, John Eakes, was knocked to the ground and kicked repeatedly. He somehow managed to reach his horse, and was about to escape, only to be again hauled to the ground where the beating continued. Amid the chaotic scene, the Riot Act was read in a pitiful attempt to subdue the lawlessness.

Property of known conservatives was attacked next, once the constables were overwhelmed, one of the main targets again being the home of the unfortunate Little. Fearing for the lives of his family, Little had refused to accept a position as a special constable, and remained at home during the nomination proceedings. But his discretion did not win him any accolades on this day. The mob, preferring to reinforce its earlier message, again descended on Little's property and hurled more stones through the already battered storefront. When his wife was struck and injured by one of the rocks, Little lost all sense of restraint and furiously charged out to confront his tormentors. As he was being pelted by mud and rocks, an indifferent Patrick Morris drove by in his carriage, deliberately ignoring the wanton acts of his supporters.

Because of the almost-continuous rampaging, no actual polling was conducted that first day. By 4:00 p.m., when the polls were officially closed, the mob stood dangerously close to having complete control of the town. The civil authorities then called on the military, which formed up in front of the courthouse and attempted to clear the streets. During the course of the evening many individuals were roughly treated by the soldiers, Parsons of *The Patriot* even claiming that numerous citizens had been bayonetted.

But if the military thought they had regained law and order, they were sadly mistaken. Later that night, a large number of men surrounded the home of Constable Eakes in the west end of town and warned him that, if he returned to the hustings the next day, they would destroy everything he owned. They emphasized their point by firing several shots into the air. It was surely no idle threat, but one that was probably unnecessary, as Eakes was too injured to even get out of bed.

Tuesday dawned over a city that trembled with uneasiness. Another immense crowd had again gathered about the hustings, fully prepared to batter their political opponents into submission. As they noisily chanted "Down with the Tories," someone noticed the guns of Fort Townshend aimed at them from above. A meeker bunch would have been overawed with this shocking display of force. This crowd was not so easily deterred, however, and continued their hurrahs, all the more encouraged by the new threat. Whether the military would have actually fired on the people with their artillery cannot be determined, since the order to do so was never required. As the reformers gave every indication that they had no intention of backing down, the three conservative candidates officially resigned, and the returning officer declared Carson, Morris, and Kent elected.

The vanquished conservatives now had to endure the humiliation of watching their foe triumphantly parade the streets of St. John's. Filled with anger and disgust, many still did not realize they had just been taught a hard lesson in dirty politics. The voice of the reform movement, Robert Parsons, could not help but flaunt their win:

Mr. Morris and Mr. Carson rode each in his carriage. Mr. Kent, dressed in a green velvet foraging cap and green silk waistcoat, and carrying an elegant little green banner in his hand, rode on horseback, accompanied by so many equestrians that they appeared like a regiment of cavalry led on by a victorious general.

This commentary was followed with some ominous insinuations:

And we are the more thankful when we reflect that had one life been closed by the bayonet the probability is that a fearful retribution would have followed. Had the life-blood of one man been unjustly spilled, we tremble at the retrospect - the innocent would have fallen with the guilty, and there is no knowing where the red hand of massacre would be stayed! The great and good God be praised that the imaginary event has not been realized! And that at the present moment there is so little to interrupt the joy of victory, calmly and peacefully obtained over Tories, bludgeons, bayonets, and artillery!!!

One has to wonder at Parsons's state of mind and his credibility after this article, for his claim that the victory had been "calmly and peacefully obtained" was nothing short of a blatant lie.

Although the voting was over, there was still unfinished business to be taken care of in Conception Bay. Ongoing investigations by the authorities had resulted in charges being laid against numerous men suspected of being involved in the November 1 riot, including Robert Pack and James Power. Two particularly nasty incidents now came to light.

In the tiny community of Mosquito, near Harbour Grace, at about 10:00 p.m. on November 15, a large number of men with blackened faces surrounded the home of Joseph Pippy, shouting insults and threats. Pippy had been injured during the election violence two weeks earlier and had filed statements against Roger Thomey for assault and battery. The mob had come with the purpose of convincing

Pippy that he had erred. As he cowered in a hiding place under the stairs, the crowd smashed out all his windows before charging through the door. Ransacking everything as they went, they discovered Pippy's frightened wife, trembling in her bed. She was dragged downstairs, where she was subjected to more indecencies, and made to beg for mercy.[8] Joseph's brother, William, who was also in the house, had a musket placed to his head and ordered to reveal his brother's where-abouts, or be shot. With no apparent recourse, the terrified man was compelled to give up his brother. Joseph was then seized from his hiding place and, after being bludgeoned about the shoulders and back, told to recant his earlier statement against Thomey and provide proof of such on the following night, when the mob would return. They left then, warning Pippy of the dire consequences should he fail to heed their instructions.

On the same night, the home of Simon Levi, a Jewish merchant living in Carbonear, was also invaded by a crowd of men. Like Pippy, Levi had been injured during the polling at Harbour Grace and had made a statement before a magistrate. Having smashed out all the windows, the mob then entered the house, but unknown to them, neither Levi nor his wife were at home. A servant girl who had been left in charge of Levi's children was knocked unconscious by one of the invaders, just about the time that a clergyman showed up, pushing his way through the mob, and implored them to leave. Having realized that their search would not be rewarded on this night, the men spirited away in the dark.

In spite of this significant resistance, and already smarting from their embarrassing defeat at the polls, the conservatives sought revenge through the courts. Several upcoming trials, involving defendants from St. John's as well as Conception Bay, lasted well into the new year. But even in court the conservatives were stymied. Either through some clever wrangling by defence lawyers, or simply sheer luck, most of the juries were composed of sympathetic reformers. Though many

---

8. Mrs. Pippy had her nightgown torn off by one of the mob, but another man covered her with a rug and carried her back to bed.

of the cases seemed cut and dried, the majority of the defendants successfully avoided any punishment, their trials ending in a variety of sheepish convictions or absolute acquittals. Judge Boulton still presided over the Supreme Court, however, and he now spitefully countered the leniency of the petit juries, with heavy-handed sentencing. Three Carbonear men, including Thomey, were jailed for twelve months. Thomas Shortall was put away for six months, and ordered to pay two £50 sureties. A man named Ryan was fined and sent to jail for one month for having struck a magistrate on November 14. Also, Patrick Brawders was fined £25 for his actions.

But these men were just a fraction of those involved in the election violence, and the failure to secure more convictions impelled Boulton to write to Prescott. He was convinced that witnesses were being threatened, and that the police were simply not doing their job by making more arrests: "I am of the opinion that a great deal of turbulence and insubordination visible in this island is to be attributed to the feeble and inactive character of the police." For this he blamed the flawed system that hired and paid members of the constabulary based on funding approved by the elected Assembly. The result, he said, was that the police were reluctant to arrest candidates, or their supporters, who might soon be paying their salaries. Though his notion of police complacency was difficult to substantiate, there was certainly evidence of witness coercion.

The defeated conservatives still had one more ace up their sleeves, however. Having received a cautious reply from the Colonial Office regarding the missing writs, in early January Prescott announced the decision to nullify the results of the late election and hold a new one in the spring.

Reformers loudly voiced their belief that this was just a conservative ploy to rob the victory. They were likely correct, for even the officials in London felt that Boulton and his clique were just being petty over the whole deal. Needless to say, R.J. Parsons was not stuck for words. Nor were 1,800 residents of St. John's who sent a petition to the Colonial Office claiming there had been no indication of disorder in the late November election but that which had been practiced by the mercantile conservatives against the supporters of "liberal principles." This was no mere misinterpretation of the facts, but a bold fabrication.

For his part, Winton renewed his criticisms of the Newfoundland franchise and continued to lobby for its abolishment. Many of his mercantile associates were undoubtedly of the same mind, and by now believed that it was blatant hypocrisy to be involved in a system which favoured their opponents.

The political rematch held in May, 1837, was hardly worth the effort. Except for several seats in the Protestant districts of Trinity and Bonavista, where they were guaranteed a victory, the conservatives nominated no candidates, and returned two poorly qualified representatives to the Catholic-dominated Assembly. The times were changing.[9]

The humbled conservatives had one more defeat to concede. Having examined the petitions of the incarcerated Catholic men and their supporters, Lord Glenelg of the Colonial Office determined that Judge Boulton had been unnecessarily harsh in his sentencing. With less than half of their time served, the three "Glorious Martyrs" from Carbonear, as Parsons called them in a March issue of his paper, were to be released and their fines repaid. With this overruling Boulton's days as chief justice of Newfoundland were clearly numbered. Having gained almost total control of the House, and with the power they now held, the reformers showed him no mercy. They were relentless in their objective to have the despised Boulton removed from office.

The 1836 general election was one of the most violent in the island's history. It was also a turning point in the relationship between the colony's Protestant English and Catholic Irish, since the Catholics

---

9. It is interesting to note that Robert Pack, an English Protestant merchant, did not run in the 1837 election, despite being almost guaranteed another victory. According to the *Dictionary of Newfoundland Biography*, he quit because the liberal reform party had become "too closely identified with the Roman Catholic church and Irish radicalism" (s.v. "Pack, Robert [1786–1860]").

were now in total control of the lower House. Over the next four years, though, developments showed that the reformers could be just as intolerant as the men they had displaced.

The magnitude of the violence surrounding the 1836 election may have horrified many people in Newfoundland, but the fact that the election *was* marred by violence should have come as no surprise to anybody. There had been numerous warnings during the campaigns of several candidates in the two most volatile districts. The press on both sides had long been aggressively critical of their opponents, to the point that undignified personal attacks had become the norm. The aftermath of Carson's by-election four years earlier had also demonstrated that violent behaviour could be used for political advantage. Most notable, however, was the increased activism of some Roman Catholic clergy, and their successful attempts to wed Catholicism to the reform movement. This union had taken place long before 1836, but the election proved the lengths to which some clergy were willing to go in order for reform to triumph. While it is unfair to place all the blame on the priests, for it should not be said that they actually *promoted* violence, they clearly had the power to either calm their people or arouse them accordingly. Independent Catholics who may have been inclined to vote conservative, though few in number, to be sure, were overawed by their clergy's forceful presence on the hustings. To face the wrath of their spiritual leaders, some of whom were known to withdraw their services for political transgressors, was terrifying for most Roman Catholics.[10]

---

10. CO 194/97, f421 contains a list of Roman Catholics who were denied the sacraments by certain clergymen because they were known to be "mad dogs." One of the most flagrant examples was that of Lawrence Barron, a prominent St. John's cooper and past president of the Mechanic's Society, who, having died as a result of injuries he sustained during the election violence in the capital city, was refused a Christian burial. See Appendix 5 for Mary Barron's deposition against Father Troy's refusal to give her husband the last rites (GN 1/1, Governor Prescott's Despatches 1836-7, Miscellaneous #37). The respect and/or fear that parishioners held for their clergy is exemplified by the statement given by Mrs. Michael Scanlan before Magistrate Carter on November 23, 1836: she "refused to utter a syllable" of what was said by Father Troy during the scene at the chapel.

Whether there was a need for such tactics is very doubtful, since it seems quite clear that the vast majority of Catholics were already solidly in the reform camp.

In the end, the Irish Catholic electorate, along with their small but not insignificant number of Protestant allies, pulled off the victory. It was arguably long overdue. On the other hand, the predominantly Protestant conservative population had been clearly unprepared, or unwilling, to participate in the physical campaign offered by the Irish Catholics. Following 1836, Newfoundland had indeed become a reflection of troubled Ireland.

CHAPTER 15

THE STRANGE CASE OF DOCTOR KIELLEY

Oh did you see Dr. Kielley, oh!
With his boots and spurs, and styly, oh.
Anonymous

With newly acquired power, the reformers went on the offensive, immediately launching an investigation into the affairs of the justice system, as they had promised. On July 3 the Assembly ordered Chief Justice Boulton to relinquish all information on the major criminal cases of the previous two years, as well as depositions sworn against the Roman Catholic clergy for their involvement in the most recent election. These aggressive demands particularly annoyed Boulton, as the acquittal of Father Duffy had occurred only a few months earlier. The reformers were relentless and, by the fall of 1837, felt they had enough evidence to draw up a petition asking for Boulton's removal. They delegated Carson, Morris, and a relatively new voice of contention, John Valentine Nugent,[1] to bring the petition before the colonial secretary in London. Not surprisingly, another unofficial representative, Bishop Fleming, also headed overseas to aid in the ousting of the chief justice.

Boulton's supporters, and he had many within the conservative population, quickly rallied to his side. Armed with a petition of his own, compiled of at least 1,000 signatures and endorsed by the St. John's Chamber of Commerce, the beleaguered chief justice followed his antagonists overseas.

---

1. Nugent moved to Newfoundland from Waterford, Ireland, in 1833 and began teaching in a private school in St. John's. He was elected to the House of Assembly in 1836, quickly becoming one of its more radical reformers.

However, the affairs of the world's greatest empire were many, so it was not until January, 1838, that the Assembly's delegation got to address the colonial secretary, Lord Glenelg. In addition to their case against Boulton they also took the opportunity to speak of other concerns, one of which was the ongoing French Shore debate. On this issue the delegates received some small conciliation when the British government agreed that, contrary to French assertion, they did not, in fact, own "exclusive rights" to the fishery anywhere along Newfoundland's coast. While this news was inspiring, the main aim of the visit was to hasten the removal of Boulton, a man who, according to Carson, "ought never to have been permitted to contaminate our shores."

Boulton's rebuttal was extensive and impassioned. Though he addressed all the major complaints made by the reform delegates, his efforts may have been in vain. At this time there was a strong desire within the home government to have the colonies handle their own affairs, and the reform representatives had made it abundantly clear that this could never occur while Boulton remained in his current position.

Following the presentation of both arguments, the final decision regarding Boulton's future was left to the appropriate Privy Council committee. The accused and accusers then returned home, forced to carry on with business as usual, and to endure a lengthy wait.

Upon their arrival in Newfoundland, Boulton and the delegates quickly ascertained that the political atmosphere had not changed since the time of their departure. Ironically, the reform party was entangled in a mess that would prove its members just as despotic as the conservatives had ever been. Already charges of political patronage were being levelled against them, a claim that was somewhat legitimized when the Assembly's Supply Bill proposed to increase the salaries of Roman Catholic constables, while decreasing those of some Protestants. More significantly, an attempt to have Dr. Edward Kielley's duties and salary reduced now sparked a bitter episode.

Kielley, a native Newfoundlander of Irish descent, had long been designated a "mad dog" by the Catholic clergy for his non-compliant political views. Being a friend and confidant of the most notorious conservatives, Kielley was as much admired by high-ranking Protestants as detested by Roman Catholics. The scandalous events which unfolded, no doubt, partially resulted from Kielley's political affiliations, but may have been exacerbated by a vengeful Dr. Carson, who had lost his position as District Surgeon to the upstart Kielley in 1834.

The affair began in the House of Assembly with John Kent questioning Kielley's ability to perform all the duties previously bestowed upon him, and recommending a reduction in Kielley's salary. Slighted, Kielley later confronted Kent when the two men had the misfortune to meet on Water Street. Insults were exchanged before Kielley threatened to "pull Kent's nose." No doubt feeling intimidated as well as humiliated, the sensitive Kent scurried back to the House, claiming that his privileges as an MHA had been violated. Foolishly, Carson, as speaker of the House, issued a warrant for Kielley's immediate arrest.

The following day, having spent the evening in the custody of Thomas Beck, the sergeant-at-arms, Kielley was hustled before the Assembly and ordered to apologize, as the House had determined there had indeed been a breach of privilege. Kielley refused to apologize, claiming that his dispute with Kent was a private not a public matter. He also asked to be permitted to call witnesses on his behalf, but was denied. He was then ordered to be kept in Beck's custody until the Assembly decided what to do with him; the impetuous Kent even proposed a lengthy jail term for his brazen antagonist. Though the partisan crowd that filled the gallery cheered this motion, cooler heads prevailed, for the moment at least.

During the following day's session, Peter Brown, a representative for Conception Bay, suggested that Kielley be ordered to apologize to the Assembly and Kent with these precise words, "I exceedingly regret that I have been guilty of any act or expression which has been considered by your honourable House to be a gross breach of its principles." Following this apology Kielley would be reprimanded and ordered to pay all unspecified expenses.

Kielley was again brought before the House, had the drafted

apology placed in his hands, and was asked to read it aloud. Not surprisingly, the exasperated Kielley displayed the same determination as before, and again questioned for what alleged offence he was being asked to apologize. The members of the House, clearly unwilling to tolerate any insubordination, ordered him to respond with a simple yes or no. Kielley then asked for, and was given, permission to retire from the House for a few minutes to consider his options. However, his position on return did not change. Now aware that Kent and his friends intended to humiliate as well as penalize him, Kielley refused to make the apology. The belligerent Dr. Carson immediately issued another warrant, ordering the sheriff to escort Kielley to the jail. These highly irregular proceedings, comedic though they were, were about to get entirely out of hand.

On August 10, Assistant Judge Lilly declared that the actions of the House were void, and ordered the sheriff, Benjamin Garrett, to have Kielley released. The ensuing response from the Assembly was both despicable and arrogant. After deliberating, the members decided to have Kielley rearrested and, for good measure, also ordered the arrest of Sheriff Garrett and Judge Lilly. Anticipating such an action from the House, Kielley had already hurried off to his friend Winton, who lent his assistance by hiding the doctor in his attic.

An outrageous scene occurred when the sergeant-at-arms, accompanied by numerous others, showed up at the Supreme Court, and practically dragged the judge from his chambers. Along with Garrett, Lilly was then paraded through the streets of St. John's, followed by a throng of delighted citizens who jeered the degraded officials.

Governor Prescott did not share the sentiments of his subjects, however. In his judgment this was a House completely out of order, and one satisfied to ignore the rules of proper procedure. On August 13 he prorogued the Assembly, and had Lilly and Garrett released, to the great consternation of the public spectators. Immediately, the newly liberated judge delivered his decision on Kielley's arrest, stating that this Assembly had no right to imprison for a perceived breach of privilege.

The conservative press was quick to print the decision, along with some choice words for the so-called "liberal reformers." Winton, as usual, made his position quite clear: "no man's liberty is safe," he said. "How can it be, when even our Judges may be dragged from the judicial bench and subjected to every indignity!" The disgruntled editor again called for the abolition of representative government, a requisition that by now had developed into an obsession.

Kielley had already demonstrated that he was not easily pushed around, so it should not have come as a surprise that he now initiated a vengeful counterattack against the members of the House of Assembly. Upon the reopening of the House on August 20, Kielley had his lawyer, Bryan Robinson, serve writs of illegal imprisonment against Carson, Kent, Brown, and Beck, among others. Astonishingly, the reform members responded by giving serious consideration to having Robinson also arrested, along with the proprietor of *The Newfoundlander,* for having earlier published Judge Lilly's decision. After much discussion, however, the House managed to pull back from the brink of total absurdity, and agreed that it was not prudent to "resort to the exercise of extreme power."

Though the conservatives seemed to have taken the upper hand in this latest round, news from the Colonial Office soon deflated their optimism. The committee of the Privy Council investigating the allegations against Chief Justice Boulton had decided that, despite a lack of evidence to suggest corruption or dereliction of duty on the judge's part, he had permitted himself to become involved in the colony's partisan politics. The committee therefore recommended that Boulton be removed as chief justice.

This was a devastating blow to the conservatives, and a tremendous triumph for the reformers. Public displays of celebration went on throughout the capital city and all major towns. Bishop Fleming even ordered the singing of the "Te Deum." Predictably, a string of vicious editorials flowed from the conservative press, matched by gloating editorials from Parsons and his colleagues.

Instead of alleviating the problems of governing such a divided population as now existed in the colony, the removal of the conservative champion only widened the gap between Catholic reformers and Protestant merchants. The latter group was now totally convinced, if they had not been before, that Winton was right, that the system of government with its liberal franchise only encouraged corruption. A series of petitions was sent to London over the next few months demanding that the home government re-evaluate Newfoundland's charter. The most potent of these came from the St. John's Chamber of Commerce, quite possibly the most prominent body of citizens on the island. Similar correspondence was sent from the merchants of some of England's larger cities, many of whom still had a financial interest in Newfoundland's fishery.

More distressing news reached the conservatives in late December, 1838. The Supreme Court, under Newfoundland's new Chief Justice, John Bourne, brought down its judgment in the Kielley v. Carson case, deciding against the plaintiff. The one dissenting voice was that of Judge Lilly.

Armed with this latest advantage, the newly energized Dr. Carson strode about town letting it be known that the Assembly would soon set its sights on the president of the Chamber of Commerce, John Sinclair. The reformers seemed quite willing to tread all over the rights of citizens they viewed as enemies.

Kielley, however, was not about to quit just yet and, with the financial and moral support of local merchants, he appealed to Her Majesty in Council. As always, the wheels of justice turned slowly, and it was not until January, 1843, five years after the initial infraction with John Kent on Water Street, that Kielley finally received the answer he had been waiting for. The Lords of the Privy Council had determined that Newfoundland's House of Assembly *did not* have "the same exclusive privileges as the ancient law of England has annexed to the House of Parliament." In essence, the Assembly did not have the power to imprison for any perceived breach of privilege.

Although this was a final victory for Newfoundland's conservatives, in what was clearly a case of vengeful persecution, it was one of their few successes during those five years. As one historian has stated, "What politics was chiefly about was religion."[2]

---

2. O'Flaherty, *Old Newfoundland*, 191.

And, with Catholic reformers controlling the House, the Protestant conservatives were on the run. Political campaigning had become a tool of Roman Catholic priests for furthering their agenda, something which, to the Protestants, often appeared suspiciously similar to Irish insurrection. The persistent clashes between these groups was "the bane of our peace," said Governor Prescott in 1838, and it would continue to be so for a long time.

St. John's harbour, circa 1750.

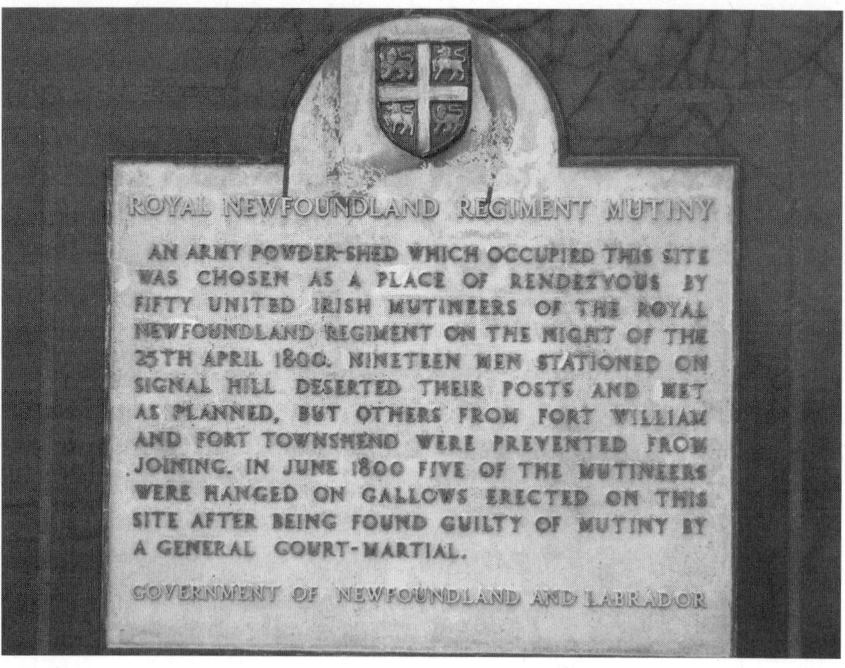

This plaque is situated on the corner of Bellevedere Street and Barnes
Road in St. John's. It marks the location where five United Irishmen were
executed in 1800.

Water Street, Harbour Grace, looking east. Circa late 1800s.

Left - Victoria Street, Harbour Grace, looking south. Hundreds of Liberal and Conservative supporters clashed here during the especially violent election of 1861.

Right - Bishop Michael Anthony Fleming

The ejection of Hogsett and Furey from the Assembly Room of the Colonial Building on May 13, 1861 precipitated one of the worst riots in Newfoundland's history.

St. John's, 1857. Two years after the granting of responsible government the old capital was poised for a prosperous future.

The Anglican Cathedral of St. John the Baptist was constructed amid much controversy over the allocation of relief funds following the devastating fire of 1846.

This stone building, recently restored, once housed the offices of Ridley and Sons in Harbour Grace.

Harbour Grace Courthouse dates from 1830 and is still in use today. Peter Downing, Patrick Malone, and Catherine Snow are among those who have spent time within its walls.

This empty shell on Water Street, Harbour Grace is all that remains of the once opulent home of Thomas Ridley.

Constructed by Governor Thomas Cochrane in 1831, the cost of Government House far exceeded its original estimate. Government House replaced the old, drafty residence at Fort Townshend where Francis Pickmore had succumbed to the extremely harsh winter of 1817.

Opened in 1850, the Colonial Building was the home of Newfoundland's House of Assembly until 1959. Its exterior was much damaged during the riots of 1861.

The Cathedral of St. John the Baptist (left). Courtesy of the Archives, Archdiocese of St. John's)

St. John's from Government House. Drawing by W.R. Best. Lithographed by W. Spreat's Litho Establishment, England, 1851. The building with the tower in front of the cathedral is the first Mercy Convent in the New World (1842).

Thirty-six voters from the little community of Salmon Cove, today called Avondale, played a pivotal role in the 1861 general election.

Today called Conception Harbour, in 1861 the tiny outport of Cat's Cove was the scene of a deadly riot that gravely affected the outcome of that year's general election.

Looking over Carbonear from Saddle Hill. "The Saddle" holds its own prominence within local lore.

CHAPTER 16

LONG LOOKED FOR IS COME AT LAST

*The repetition of so barbarous an outrage must inspire the colonial commu-
nity with a great sense of indignation against the authors of it, at the same
time that their sympathy is excited on behalf of the unfortunate person
who has suffered so severely and undeservedly.*
Despatch from Lord John Russell to Governor Prescott
June 25, 1840

Over the years, Herman Lott had grown accustomed to the endless
stream of threats against his employer, Henry Winton. Everything
from assault to assassination, he had heard it all. The hideous scars
borne by Winton constantly reminded everyone at *The Public Ledger*
of the price sometimes paid by outspoken, unpopular newspapermen.
But it was his employer's resilience in the wake of the Saddle Hill
assault, although a continuing source of irritation to Winton's enemies,
that Lott viewed as admirable. Winton's bold opinions had not
wavered, despite threats. It was as if the now infamous assault had
caused merely a stumble in Winton's parade of brazen editorials. If
possible, his criticism of those "incorrigible tyrants" grew even more
determined, the assault convincing him more than ever of the correct-
ness of his opinions.

During six years of employment at *The Ledger,* Lott probably
understood his controversial employer more than most. Contrary to
the accusations of Bishop Fleming and the clergy, Lott did not believe
Winton was "anti-Catholic." Winton had, after all, strongly supported
Catholic emancipation in the late '20s, and had been truly surprised
and offended at the delay that Newfoundland's Catholics had to
tolerate before their liberty was officially recognized. During that
campaign for liberty Winton had exposed the grave injustices faced

by Newfoundland's Roman Catholic citizens, a task for which he had been publicly commended by Bishop Fleming himself. In the succeeding years, however, the direct involvement of Fleming and his clergy in Newfoundland's politics had soured Winton's opinion of the Catholic leadership, and had turned him into something that Lott knew him to be—not anti-Catholic, but stubbornly principled to the point of being obstinate. His disapproval of the radical priesthood became widely misinterpreted by most of the Roman Catholic citizenry, since Winton had begun referring to many of them in the wake of recent troubles as an "ignorant, gullible, and misled rabble."

With much dismay, Lott observed the erosion of law and order in Newfoundland brought on by the widening rift between Catholics and Protestants. As an employee of *The Public Ledger,* the possibility of an attack upon *him* personally had entered Lott's mind on more than one occasion, but never to the extent that he felt afraid to walk the streets of St. John's. It was, after all, Henry Winton, whom the dangerous radicals hated and wanted to see punished. In the arena of Newfoundland politics, Lott considered himself an insignificant observer, a position that he believed sheltered him from harm. But this mistaken sense of security was soon shattered.

Thursday nights, publication night, were normally busy at *The Public Ledger.* However, February 13, 1840, was a little slower than usual. At around 11:00 p.m., young Lott saw an opportunity to leave the office to meet Lucy Westcott and escort her home from a visit to a friend's house. Lucy had been the object of Lott's attention for a short period of time, and for both of them the seriousness of the relationship was yet uncertain, though her parents seemed to favour the courtship.

As the young couple walked along Water Street, they encountered several people coming from the theatre and stopped briefly to speak with William Morrison. Being a conscientious worker, and not wishing to upset his employer by taking a lengthy break from the office, Lott allowed himself only a short conversation before he and Lucy continued on, arm in arm towards her parents' house. After leaving Lucy at her front doorstep, Herman hastened back to the office for the final printing of Friday's paper. Not suspecting that her gentleman friend was in any danger, Lucy watched as he disappeared around a corner, both of them completely unaware they had been followed.

Less than ten minutes later, and only a few hundred feet from the office, a voice called to Lott from the shadows of an alleyway. Lott stopped and peered into the darkness, trying to discern who had hailed him. For several seconds he could barely make out the dark figure standing featureless and unmoving. Caution permitted Lott to betray no emotion when he responded: "Yes, who is it?"

Silently, the apparition moved closer, becoming more defined, but its face was partially hidden behind a scarf. When the figure spoke from about eight feet away, the voice, though unfamiliar, was not necessarily threatening: "Come back with me as far as the Orphan Asylum School. Young Winton is up there, very tipsy, and will not come home."

Though it was widely known that both Wintons, father and son, enjoyed their share of strong drink, there was something unlikely about the stranger's statement. Despite young Winton's inclination to overindulge, Lott could not imagine him intoxicated and staggering about the town on publication night. The request made Lott uncomfortable, so he tried to explain that he was expected back at the office, and that it might be better if he spoke with his employer or somebody else at the house first.

A slight impatience became evident in the stranger's voice as he insisted that harm might come to young Winton if Lott did not bring him home straightaway. Lott again hesitated, but against his better judgment finally agreed to go.

They had only gone a short distance when they were joined by another man, whose face was also concealed behind a high collar and scarf.

"Are you going up again?"asked this new stranger of the first.

"Yes."

In an area near "the crossroads," Lott's two companions suddenly turned upon him.[1]

---

1. This may have been what is today known as Rawlins Cross.

In a swift, skillful manoeuvre, Lott was grabbed and his arms pinioned to his sides by a length of rope. At the same time, the second man snatched Lott's handkerchief from his pocket and tied it tightly around his eyes. Struggling to break away, Lott shouted, "Why are you serving me in this manner? I am sure I did nothing to you!"

"Hold your tongue!" was the firm reply. "Follow us, and no harm shall come to you."

Lott was roughly spun around several times before being led away. For fifteen minutes they walked without speaking, the frozen snow crunching beneath their feet and their breathing laboured. The slight tremble that had developed in Lott's knees was not entirely due to the cold winter wind that stirred up little puffs of snow. Along the way, he tried his best to determine the direction these men were headed, all the while hoping this was not a journey from which there was no return. Finally, they came to some steps, and Lott was led up to a door. One of his abductors knocked out a distinctive rhythm, indicating to Lott that they were expected. Once inside, Lott was led into a room and ordered to sit in a chair. A third stranger entered and removed Lott's blindfold.

The scene before him was surreal. In an obvious effort to disguise the premises, the entire room, including the ceiling, had been covered with white sheets. An open fireplace in which several logs burned remained visible, as well as the door through which Lott had been escorted. Near the fireplace was a small table, behind which sat two men, both dressed in long black gowns, their heads covered with black hoods. One of the men held a pen, with some paper and an ink bottle on the table in front of him. The dancing firelight was all that illuminated the room.

As Lott sat in fear and confusion, through slits in the hoods the black figures stared towards him, until the apparent leader, the one without the pen, finally spoke.

"What is your name?" It was another unfamiliar voice.

"Herman Lott."

"What is your persuasion?"

"Protestant."

Lott observed the second hooded man scratching his responses onto the paper.

"Was not your father a Catholic who turned Protestant?"

"No."

At another time and place these questions would have been merely peculiar, but not in the city of St. John's in 1840, particularly in the situation in which Lott now found himself. However, being a peaceable man, and not at all used to personal insult or outrage, he now attempted a small show of indignation. "I should like to know what reason . . ." But before he could complete his demand, he was abruptly cut off.

"You are to ask no questions!"

The interrogation continued, with the hooded man querying Lott about operations at *The Public Ledger*, its patrons, and, most significantly, its owner, Henry Winton. Not long into the process it became apparent to Lott that these men did not intend to harm him, unless he failed to co-operate. Several questions regarding the episode when Dr. Kielley had taken refuge with Winton were clear indications that Winton's house was being watched. Other questions regarding the possibility that Winton had loaded firearms around his house and on his person may have unintentionally disclosed a more dreadful intention. An assassination attempt on Winton had always been a likelihood, especially since the Saddle Hill attack.

Finally, after almost two gruelling hours, the questioning ended. A few minutes of uncomfortable silence passed before the interrogator stood up and glared at Lott menacingly. "Winton has stated that the Irish immigrants are refugee Ribbonmen. Well, he and others like him may soon find out that there is indeed a Ribbon Society in Newfoundland, equally as terrible as ever it was in Ireland! He may soon find his house a little too hot for him."

The threat was clear. These men were to be taken seriously. They were not just local ruffians with a score to settle. There had long been rumours of covert societies within Newfoundland's Irish population, ever since the UIS uprising forty years earlier, though no clear evidence of such had ever been uncovered.

The hooded man's final words to Lott were emphasized with a pointed finger: "Remember that you dare not divulge one word of what has transpired here tonight! What has been done cannot injure you. Keep silence, or perhaps an *unseen and an unknown hand* will be in your way. We are done with you."

Lott was once again blindfolded and, at the sound of a small bell, was led out of the house. In an attempt to further confuse him, Lott was escorted back along a different route than before and, after being spun about several times, was released. Physically and emotionally shaken, he attempted to pull the blindfold off, but staggered against a nearby fence and fell into a snowbank. For several seconds he could hear the sound of retreating footsteps, but toward what direction he was unsure. Trembling from the experience he had just endured, as well as from the cold, Lott tried to collect his thoughts and energy to find the quickest way back to Winton's house. With the hooded man's warning still ringing in his ears, he wondered how he might convincingly explain his absence to his employer.[2]

Meanwhile, Henry Winton had grown increasingly concerned for the welfare of his missing apprentice. Lott had always been a dependable worker, and it was most unlike the young gentleman to leave the office for such a long period. Fearing that some harm had befallen Lott, around 2:30 a.m. Winton ordered two of his other assistants to search for him.

They had not been gone long when there was a frantic ringing of the hall bell. On answering the door Winton was taken aback to find young Lott standing dishevelled and visibly upset. Winton quickly ushered him into the parlour where he could clearly observe that his wayward employee was pale and shaking. Winton's first impression was that Lott had been drinking, but the young man's adamant denial and frightened appearance persuaded him otherwise.

Several glasses of wine and a warm blanket helped to sufficiently relax Lott to the point where Winton was able to coax the entire

---

2. The events and conversation related here are taken directly from Lott's testimony (GN 2/2, beginning on page 119).

story from him. The tale, though very disturbing, did not entirely surprise Winton. Considering the countless threats he himself had received, along with his own assault by still unknown hands, Winton was convinced that his employee was telling the truth. A little later, after Lott had retired to his quarters for some much needed rest, Winton noticed Lott's hat lying on a table. Inside was the young man's handkerchief. Close observation of this item revealed a pattern of wrinkles consistent with those of a blindfold.

News of Lott's tribulations spread quickly, to the astonishment of his abductors, no doubt. Their warnings had gone unheeded, so they could now expect a determined investigation, something which probably did not alarm them tremendously since they had gone to such lengths to hide their true identities. Besides, any meddling by authorities could easily be handled by well-placed "friends."

Things became a little uneasy for the self-proclaimed "Ribbonmen" several days later, though, after Lott had taken his deposition to local magistrates Peter Carter and Charles Simms. The chief constable, James Finlay, was immediately ordered to go with Lott to try and identify the house to which he had been taken. After several hours, the two men arrived at a home on Circular Road commonly known as Hally's Cottage. The owner was John Delaney, who, as it turned out, was a doorkeeper for the House of Assembly. Probably taken completely off guard by the appearance of these men, Delaney denied them permission to enter, an action somewhat inconsistent with that of an innocent man. Undeterred, the constable and Lott returned later with Carter and Simms. This time Delaney met them in front of his house, apologized for his earlier behaviour, and declared they were welcome to search his entire premises. Despite a firm belief that he had found the correct house, Lott was unable to make a positive identification.

This story was incredible enough without any further developments, but the actions of the House of Assembly, once the particulars of the case became known to the general public, caused an even greater uproar. Rather than offering a reward to aid the authorities in their investigation, many members of the House became incensed that the eye of suspicion had been cast on one of their minor officers. Heated discussion in the House on February 18 displayed an inexplicable "sympathy for the unknown offenders."[3]

Two of the reformers were exceptionally prejudicial with their comments, even to the point of publicly slandering Lott as a "drunken young scoundrel."[4]

But, while Lott received his share of abuse, the House was particularly enraged with the magistrates. Lott, after all, was a private citizen who had made a complaint, whereas the magistrates were public officials who could be held accountable for their deeds.

A committee was immediately organized and headed up by John Nugent, one of the most vocal critics of Magistrates Carter and Simms. Nugent was subsequently responsible for a House vote that would reduce the magistrates' salaries, an astonishingly vindictive display of partisan politics.[5]

In an obvious attempt to smear the names of Carter and Simms and to belittle their investigation, the House Committee examined all witnesses related to the case and the magistrates themselves. Finding no discrepancies in the evidence, Nugent then petitioned the governor to hand over all depositions that had been made in order "to arrive at a correct conclusion as to the grounds whereon suspicions have arisen that a secret and illegal association was entertained at the house of an officer of the Assembly." Prescott apparently suspected this request was an attempt to tamper with evidence and flatly refused the petition, a decision for which he later received the support of Britain's colonial secretary. Without any just cause to further slander the magisterial investigation, Nugent's committee eventually adjourned after several weeks, returning no report.

---

3. Governor Prescott's own opinion, as expressed in a letter to Lord John Russell, dated May 23, 1840.

4. The words of John Valentine Nugent.

5. Initially the attempt to cut the magistrates' salaries was unsuccessful: however, the persistence of reform members finally resulted in a vote that approved the salary reduction. Governor Prescott overturned the bill, however, and the magistrates' pay was restored in full.

The proceedings of the House during this affair were quite extraordinary, and more than a little suspect. An application from Carter and Simms for Governor Prescott's intervention stated that the actions of some members were "of a nature to deter judicial, and other public officers, from the impartial and proper exercise of their duty, and calculated to obstruct the due course of justice." This was no lame accusation on the part of offended officials; this was bold finger pointing. Even the governor had commented on the MHAs' unacceptable behaviour. The nature of the reformers' actions left many opponents wondering what, or whom, the members were protecting. While there may have been no definitive answer to this question, the perpetration of another shocking act would soon appear to many Protestants as irrefutable evidence of the presence of a secret society within Newfoundland's Irish population.

In more ways than one, Herman Lott might easily have experienced déjà vu on the afternoon of May 15, three months after his abduction. He had been in Conception Bay for a week on newspaper business and now sauntered along the dusty road atop Saddle Hill, heading towards Harbour Grace. It could have been a pleasurable afternoon, with the fresh smell of spring in the air, a warming sun on his face, and a cool but gentle breeze stirring the evergreens. Lott probably took no notice, knowing well the significance of this place. It was nearly five years to the day since his employer had suffered his humiliating attack along this same stretch of road. Wisely, Lott was no longer willing to take his own safety for granted and, since February, carried a sword stick for protection.[6]

Near a small house at the top of the hill, Lott met two women headed toward Carbonear. Despite the exchange of polite greetings, Lott sensed something odd about their demeanour. It may have been the way they looked at him, or something in their voices; he could not be sure. An overactive imagination on his part, maybe? Frayed nerves? Or did these women know something?

---

6. A sword stick was a popular gentleman's weapon of the 1800s. It was a short sword hidden inside a walking cane.

Hardly ten minutes later, as Lott drew close to the big farmhouse in the valley owned by David Connors, two figures suddenly appeared from behind some trees, closely followed by two others. All four had their faces disguised with black crepe and, as they rushed forward, one of them exclaimed, "Long looked for is come at last!"

Clearly realizing their intent and unwilling to allow himself to be abused as before, Lott drew his sword and pointed it threateningly from one man to the other. One of them ignored Lott's warning, in all probability believing that this puny little newspaperboy did not have the nerve to use his weapon. To his surprise, Lott reacted with a flick of the blade that opened a gash along the man's cheek.

Injured and enraged, the man wiped his face with his sleeve and swore, "Blood for blood, you bugger!"

Quickly, one of the others jumped and landed a solid blow with his fist that knocked Lott to the ground. In an instant all four men were pummelling him with their fists as he screamed for help. Lott was then lugged, kicking and flailing, into the woods, where they continued to beat him. In a replay of an earlier performance, clay was stuffed into his mouth and ears, and his head repeatedly pounded with a rock. Finally, a merciful darkness closed over him. Somewhere within this strange dark world Lott could vaguely sense the presence of his enemies, but what they were doing to him he did not know. He felt no pain, only a numbness that paralyzed his entire body.

Sometime later, Lott's return to consciousness was greeted with a tremendous thundering in his brain. His attackers had fled, but the trees and clouds spun wildly above him, making any attempt to regain his footing nearly impossible. Blood ran into his eyes, down his neck, and onto the lapels of his jacket. After lying on the ground for several minutes, waiting for the spinning to stop, Lott examined himself to determine the extent of his injuries. Tenderly moving his fingers over his face and along the sides of his head, to his horror he discovered a huge lump above his right eye, and that both of his ears were missing. Along with the terrible physical pain, a great despair swept over him, for he knew all too well the ridicule and discomfort he would now endure.

After several minutes, Lott realized that if he did not get medical attention soon he could perish right there in the woods of Saddle Hill. Mustering his remaining strength, he struggled to his feet and stumbled out onto the roadway, only to collapse again. He remained there for an unknown period of time before noticing a man approaching from the north. The stranger, seeing Lott's mutilated condition, was initially reluctant to offer assistance, possibly fearing for his own safety. Lott's repeated pleas, however, convinced the man to help him to his feet, and the two proceeded slowly toward Harbour Grace. A few hundred feet along the way, though, the stranger left his charge leaning against a fence, and disappeared down a side path, evidently unwilling to let himself be seen aiding the injured newspaperboy. Almost immediately, a second man passed Lott, headed toward Carbonear, but offered no assistance at all. Lott had to walk the mile or so to Harbour Grace alone.

By the time he got there, he was barely conscious. The pounding and dizziness inside his head, combined with the loss of blood, had weakened him tremendously. Stares and whispers followed him as he stumbled along the street, and finally collapsed at the door of Robert Lee Whiting, a personal friend of Winton's.

During the next few days Lott remained at the Whiting house, closely attended by Dr. Stirling. A written report to the Harbour Grace magistrates by the doctor indicated Lott's painful, but swift recovery:

His person was much disfigured by coagulated blood and clay, the countenance being exceedingly pale from loss of blood; portions of both ears had been removed, evidently by a sharp cutting instrument, the wounds being all the character of incised ones, that of the left being the most extensive one, and the most dangerous. The hemorrhage (owing to the clay, which completely filled the cavities of both ears) was not as extensive as it otherwise would have been . . . a severe contusion appeared in the frontal region above the right superciliary ridge. Friday night complains of severe lancinating pains in his head with other distressing symptoms. Fifteen ounces of blood were taken and cold applied. Saturday, says he feels much better, contusion much less; changed dressing of wounds. On the whole, up to the present time (3 p.m.) improves.

Not surprisingly, the population reacted differently once the news got out. The majority of Protestants demanded an intensive investigation, with harsh punishment for the culprits, whom they felt were undoubtedly Irish Catholic. A reward of £300 was offered by local merchants, and matched by Governor Prescott. The talk going around was that this latest act of violence was Lott's punishment for not keeping quiet about the incident of February 13, irrefutable proof for many Protestants that secret societies were indeed operating in Newfoundland. Henry Winton's editorial on February 19 was direct:

We shall devote our next (issue) to the exposure of a system of villainy which has been secretly working its way in this colony for some time past. We shall show that there is an organized Ribbon Society in this country - we think we shall succeed in showing that the House of Assembly is connected with it - above all shall we show that the young man who has been subject to the outrage . . . has been the victim of it.

Obviously the loss of both ears had not mellowed Winton's opinions much, but accusing MHAs of being tied to covert rebel organizations, especially without solid evidence, was inviting a libel suit. By not naming specific individuals he likely avoided such an action.

A code of silence once again settled over Conception Bay. Numerous individuals living in the area of the assault were questioned extensively, especially after it was learned that some had been working in their gardens at the time and may have witnessed the entire event. These people, however, were either unable, or unwilling, to divulge any helpful information. Authorities became so enraged with the lack of co-operation that several potential witnesses were briefly held in custody, under somewhat dubious grounds.

Contrary to common belief, not all Irish Catholics were pleased with the reputation for violence they had been reaping, and at least one editor of an influential Catholic newspaper was as shocked by recent events as any Protestant. Edward Shea of *The Newfoundlander* said in his May 21 editorial:

> *We regret sincerely to be called upon to place so revolting an outrage upon record. This information was received here on Sunday last, and has naturally awakened feelings of indignation in this community. The perpetration of so foul a deed in open day, and upon an unoffending individual! Can it be believed that in a civilized community men can be found so to outrage the common feelings of humanity. It is high time that the people of that district are called upon to aid in bringing the offenders to justice.[7]*

This expression of anger was not necessarily a split within the Irish ranks but more a call for law-abiding Catholics to take their rightful place in Newfoundland society, and to renounce violence as the only means of gaining real equality.

Local authorities tried to deliver on the intensive investigation they had promised, but in the end they got nowhere. The wall of secrecy again proved impenetrable or, as Winton had alleged, the perpetrators of the deed were being protected by a network of associates with influential friends. Whatever the truth, the public soon faced other troubles. Governor Prescott, desiring to calm the sectarian waters, had earlier appointed Patrick Morris to the position of colonial treasurer, the first Catholic to hold such a title, thus creating the need for a by-election in St. John's. Polling was set to begin on May 20, and the unfolding events distracted the public's attention from Saddle Hill. Besides, all indications were that this investigation was pointless. On the day the polls opened, Judge Lilly sent a letter to Secretary James Crowdy, one that probably reflected the sentiments of most Protestants:

> *I beg to inform you that every means has been used by the magistrates to discover the perpetrators of so foul an act, but I am afraid that, as in Winton's case, it will never be discovered who (they) are.*

---

7. Edward had taken over as editor after his brother, John, had left Newfoundland three years earlier.

Chapter 17

A Pure Love of Dissension

To the polls then, men of all Creeds! To the polls, Merchants, Mechanics, Fishermen and Farmers! To the polls and secure for yourselves and for your children liberty, Civil and Religious! To the polls, and break down a Tyranny more galling than Egyptian bondage.

The Newfoundland Patriot
Friday, May 22, 1840

Early indications were that this was going to be a quiet election. Initially, following the governor's mandatory proclamation calling prospective candidates to announce themselves, no one came forward. For the conservatives this was deliberate. Still sulking over their last defeat, they had no intention of involving themselves in any further contests with people they considered unworthy of holding public office. There seemed little chance that a conservative was going to get himself elected in St. John's, as long as the priests continued to influence the vote.

For the past few years, however, the normally opinionated Bishop Fleming had maintained an uncharacteristic political silence. Through certain channels Fleming had learned of an ongoing campaign by powerful individuals on both sides of the Atlantic to have him ousted from Newfoundland, the most conspicuous being Governor Prescott. Fleming was incensed by the governor's treachery, but not tremendously surprised, or overly intimidated. In truth, Fleming's political hiatus had more to do with recent correspondence from the Vatican that urged him to control his priests.

The slow response of the reform party to Prescott's proclamation was less understandable than the conservatives' and, in fact, may have had little to do with Fleming's deceptive indifference. However, with both parties showing little interest, this election was shaping up to be a rather boring exercise. Thus, when a Scottish Presbyterian named James Douglas stepped forward, there was probably a collective sigh of relief throughout the liberal media. Douglas had been in the reform ranks for some years, and was now supported by many influential colleagues, notably Carson, Kent, Nugent, and the Irish merchant Laurence O'Brien.

But the ink had hardly dried on the election proclamation when Fleming broke his silence. He was now in a bind. With no conservative challenging the seat it would obviously remain in the hands of the reformers, and Douglas would be declared victorious by acclamation. But Fleming, whose numerous Protestant allies shared his political ideology, had never been completely comfortable with their representation of Roman Catholic constituents. There were only a few whom he trusted to explicate the grievances of his flock, and Douglas, apparently, wasn't one of them.

As Fleming pondered his quandry, the governor, in another attempt to prove his impartiality, appointed Thomas Beck as returning officer, the same Beck who had arrested Kielley and Lilly during the ridiculous affair of '38. While this move certainly pleased many Catholics, including the bishop, some Protestants felt betrayed.[1]

Before the election ended, the governor himself would question the sanity of his lame attempts at conciliation.

Throughout it all, the voice of conservatism, Henry Winton, spent most of his time leading up to the election advising his readers to boycott the whole deal: "Since the knaves have it," he said, "let them keep it; the *trumps* will come out by and by." If "respectable" citizens showed no interest in playing the electioneering game, then

---

1. In correspondence with Lord Stanley after the election, Prescott would write: "My anxiety to act with strict impartiality between Catholics and Protestants, and to remove even plausible grounds for complaint respecting the non-employment of the former in official situations, has exposed me to great obloquy."

Winton figured the authorities in London could be easily convinced to cancel the game altogether. In several editorials he stated his belief that the representative system in Newfoundland was nothing but a cruel experiment exploited by devious, undeserving individuals. His rhetoric was persistent, and increasingly effective.

As May 20, the first day of polling, drew near, Fleming decided that he could hold his tongue no longer. He met privately with O'Brien and convinced (some say ordered) him to run against Douglas. The bishop's logic was clarified in church the following Sunday when he lectured his congregation on the "correct" way to vote, claiming that the interests of Catholicism were best handled by a Roman Catholic. Immediately, Kent and Nugent abandoned the Douglas camp and sided with O'Brien, taking many supporters with them.

This sudden split in the ranks stunned many reformers, and initiated a furious response from the editor of *The Patriot*:

> *we cannot lose sight of the hollow-heartedness and political treachery of the chief supporters of Mr. O'Brien, who, having appended their names to the requisition to Mr. Douglas, have, after having insidiously induced him into the situation of a Candidate, turned their backs upon him without cause, and given their support to his opponent.*

Parsons was at this point unaware of Fleming's involvement, and blamed the defection squarely on Kent:

> *were we to seek for a destroyer, for one calculated in all respects to ruin the party with whom he works, were we to seek all Newfoundland for such a one, we could unhesitatingly point to Mr. Kent and claim "Thou art the man!"*

Astonishingly, there had been signs of conflict within the reform party much earlier. Kent and Parsons had been at odds since at least March, publishing nasty letters back and forth. As well, Carson and Morris were going through a messy divorce, of sorts. No doubt secretly knowing of his impending promotion, Morris showed a new inclination to defend Governor Prescott on certain issues in the House of

Assembly. This was a clear breach of the reform agenda, and Carson, among others, was not amused. In a particularly offensive letter published by *The Newfoundlander* on April 23, Carson spitefully attacked Morris's personal abilities: "I cannot call to my memory having suffered greater inflictions than being obligated to listen to Mr. Morris's speeches, and to read Mr. Morris's pamphlets." It was painfully obvious that Carson and Morris no longer shared a bottle of brandy, and planned strategy together.

Thus, as the citizens of St. John's prepared to head again to the hustings, the question in many minds was not just *who* would win, but *what* was the future of the "reform" party? It was clear that this contest was turning into one of the most important elections the city, or the colony, was ever to have. With much of the populace already excited over Herman Lott's misadventure, the heightened emotions leading up to May 20 had newspapers buzzing. This time, however, the tables had turned, and the editor who would be most critical of Fleming's political re-emergence was R.J. Parsons of *The Patriot*.

Sunny skies and hot temperatures greeted voters on Wednesday, May 20, a continuation of the conditions that St. John's had been abiding for a while. No rain had fallen in weeks and, as a result, vegetable gardens were dry and barren. In a time and place when most people depended on their own sustenance, a poor crop could literally mean starvation. To add to the misery, hordes of fish flies had invaded the city, creating a potential health problem.

At 10:00 a.m. on May 20, however, most citizens of St. John's were unconcerned about either dry weather or natural pests. The crowd surrounding the hustings waited in anxious anticipation for the speeches to begin, quite possibly hoping for a peaceful contest but knowing well the likelihood of violence. These were veteran election-eers, overwhelmingly Irish Catholic, since most Protestants had taken Winton's advice and remained at home. They knew the rules: play dirty and play to win. The motivation behind the opposing sides was different, however; thus, the presence of three Roman Catholic priests was all the more significant. Easily discernable, and intimidating in their black robes and birettas, Fathers Waldron, Walsh, and Forrestal were there to ensure "the sanctity of their religion." What that meant, and how it was to be maintained, were questions, it seemed, that only Bishop Fleming understood.

The Patriot reported that at precisely 10:00 a.m. James Douglas stepped upon the hustings, surrounded by many friends, who, aside from a few banners, "had nothing to distinguish themselves beyond their respectable appearance." On the other hand, O'Brien and his supporters were adorned with green flags and badges, literally wearing their heritage on their sleeves in a clear attempt to influence the Irish vote.

The nastiness began almost immediately when the first speaker, a Douglas supporter, asked the crowd who among them could vote for Larry O'Brien, since he had once taken out a £25 writ against his own priest, Reverend Father Ivers. The applause from Douglas's men was matched by shouts of scorn and derision from the O'Brien camp, the latter already displaying a particularly ugly mood and a willingness to riot. (Parsons would later make the bold allegation that they had been "bribed to be disorderly," but by whom he would not say.)

The next speaker, Patrick Mullowney, ignited the smouldering fire when he declared that Kent, Nugent, and O'Brien were all "traitors" for having deserted Douglas in the first place. The boisterous uproar that followed made it nearly impossible for anyone upon the hustings to be heard, so both candidates agreed to proceed to the polling station without further ado.

According to the rules, each candidate was permitted four individuals inside the polling station to examine voter qualifications and to ensure that the tallies were counted honestly. Not surprisingly, two of O'Brien's appointees were Roman Catholic priests. This may not have been a violation, but the fact that religious leaders were present in this capacity certainly aroused more concerns about their undue influence over the voting public. In fact, their actions inside the polling station justified these concerns. As Parsons later reported:

> *The proceedings here were exceedingly unpleasant - the interference of the Clergy was very generally considered improper and highly*

objectionable, and they were repeatedly told so. Indeed we are decid-
edly of the opinion, for whatever pretext there may have been for
such influence in by-gone times, there was not a shadow of necessity
for it on the present occasion - it was out of place and entirely illegit-
imate.

"[H]ighly objectionable?" "[E]ntirely illegitimate?" Could this have been the same man who had bragged about the victorious election of '36, and who had publicly praised the actions of Father Troy and other priests during that contest? If so, it seemed as if there had been an about-face. One can only imagine Winton's condescending smile as he sat in his parlour reading *The Patriot*'s account of these early developments.

Another anomaly was the sight of several conservatives within the crowd of Douglas supporters, most notably Walter Grieve, John Ryan, and Robert Carter.[2]

Amid the pending collapse of the reform party, their presence likely lifted Parsons's spirits, because he interpreted it as a sign that the reform movement was no longer exclusive to the anti-mercantile class. In this he was at least partially correct, though at this time he may have been overly optimistic.

At the end of day one plenty of accusations had been spread around, mostly by the Douglas camp, but the count showed him in front of O'Brien by eleven votes.

Thursday began with an expectation that the ugly mood would quickly turn violent. Bishop Fleming returned to the city on this day, having been on Kellys Island supervising the stone-cutting for his new cathedral. Jumping immediately into the fray, from his residence he preached to a crowd of the need to vote according to the honour of their religion. It was probably not his intention, but his speech further inflamed the already agitated masses, many of whom understood that the end now justified the means.

Immediately after the polling station reopened there was trouble.

---

2. Robert Carter was a lieutenant in the Royal Navy, and Magistrate Carter's brother.

The clerk, Robert Hildey, feeling that it was impossible to proceed with the voting, agreed to do so only if the magistrates were present. One of these, C.F. Bennett, witnessed a terrible assault on a cooper named James Tubrid. Having cast his vote for Douglas, Tubrid, a Catholic, was walking toward Water Street when two men ran up and struck him several times, knocking him down. Other men joined in, lugging the poor man as far as Beck's Cove, repeatedly hitting him, and finally trampling on him. A futile attempt by Bennett to rescue Tubrid was easily warded off.[3]

Moments before this, two of Douglas's committee men, Patrick Brennock and Kenneth McLea, had been severely beaten, with McLea being lucky to escape alive. In his deposition before Magistrate Simms, McLea later declared his belief that voters were being "deterred from exercising their franchise with freedom" as a result of the terrible threat of violence, a belief echoed by many constables who were trying to maintain some form of order.

Scenes such as these continued throughout the afternoon despite the presence of magistrates and police constables, who were so outnumbered that they wielded little or no authority. At one point High Constable James Finlay even refused to arrest one of the men suspected of having assaulted Tubrid, knowing well that he himself would have "suffered similar treatment from the mob."

Reports of the rioting were continually received by Governor Prescott, who finally instructed Secretary James Crowdy to authorize the swearing in of "as many constables as may be necessary to keep the peace." For insurance, he also ordered Colonel Sall to have his troops prepared for the next morning should the police be unable to contain the rioting.

The tally at the end of day two showed Douglas still leading, but only by a mere six votes.

The Patriot and *The Public Ledger* of Friday, May 22, reported on the terrible conditions under which this latest election was being

---

3. Tubrid suffered several broken ribs, and bruises and lacerations. He had a lengthy recovery.

conducted. Their severe criticisms of the clergy's involvement would probably be the first and only time that these two editors would be in agreement. It seems unlikely, though, that either man was prepared to exalt the other. It would take more than one riotous election to make them allies.[4]

Yet, when Parsons stated "it degrades any man's religion to see their priests, without necessity, the leaders in the local politics of the country, and becoming well-practiced politicians instead of well-practiced priests of the living God," he sounded suspiciously similar to his old rival. Again, Winton's reaction can only be imagined.

Polling continued the following week, as did the fighting, despite the best efforts of the newly sworn constabulary. Dozens of Protestants now appeared at the hustings to vote for Douglas, adding more volatility to the crowd. They were probably responding to *The Patriot*'s call to "break down a Tyranny more galling than Egyptian bondage." It seemed clear that the "Tyranny" Parsons referred to was the same as that Winton had been railing against for years.

Originally, May 26 was to have been the last day for voting within the city before the hustings was moved to the outports of Torbay and Petty Harbour, both of which were within the electoral district being contested. For clearly partisan reasons, however, the returning officer extended the voting in St. John's to the end of the week. This caused more anxiety among the authorities, who feared a lengthier period of unrest. Despite the fact that the police were unable to control the mob, Governor Prescott hesitated in calling out the troops, possibly mindful of the backlash that had followed the 1836 election when even the threat of cannon fire could not deter the masses.

Wednesday dawned with an air of dreadful expectancy, especially since a full-scale riot had barely been averted the previous evening. Rumours had spread that numerous strangers from out of town had shown up to aid the O'Brien campaign.[5]

---

4. In fact a journalistic jousting match between the two papers over Herman Lott's credibility regarding his February misadventure continued into June.

5. *The Public Ledger* twice reported on the appearance of "a gang of ruffians from Carbonear," but the legitimacy of these reports is uncertain.

Throughout the day the weary constables tried to separate the opposing sides, and took more than their share of physical abuse and mistreatment. Allegations of wrongdoing by the returning officer and O'Brien's committee surfaced. Beck was either grossly inept and incapable of doing his job, or was in cahoots with O'Brien. Whatever the case, it was true that Beck frequently deferred to J.V. Nugent, one of O'Brien's men, for a final opinion on the qualifications of voters, a clear and blatant conflict of interest. Amid the chaos, polling finally ceased at the usual time of 4:00 p.m., with Douglas still holding onto a narrow lead.

Instead of the crowd dispersing at this time, however, many people remained near the Douglas committee room, either waiting to hear some encouraging words, or waiting to jeer and heckle, depending upon their affiliation. As Lieutenant Robert Carter listened to his candidate's address, he noticed a scuffle between several men, followed by a general rush forward. Carter immediately grabbed a fellow named Denis McCarthy, and dragged him inside the committee room, where he was detained until several constables showed up to make the arrest. But it was during the walk back to jail that the real trouble started.

As the police escorted their prisoner past Bishop Fleming's residence, they were suddenly attacked by a gang of men. A melee ensued as the mob attempted to free McCarthy, with the constables getting the brunt. High Constable James Finlay grappled with several men who were trying to take his pistols. Fearing their intent, Finlay fought savagely and eventually escaped his attackers, still in possession of his weapons. Nearby, Edward Cahill, one of the special constables who had been recently sworn in, battled for control of his police staff with a man who turned out to be the messenger for the House of Assembly. When Cahill shouted that he recognized his combatant, the man hurried off in shame. Meanwhile, Special Constables John Halliday and Walter McPherson did not fare so well. Both were punched, kicked, and, in McPherson's case, beaten over the head with a stick. As the mob swiftly gained the upper hand, the outnumbered police had no choice but to give up their prisoners in order to save their own lives.

Disgusted with the lack of support they had received, following this incident thirty-seven special constables threatened to resign unless they were provided with the promised military assistance. Their petition was backed with a letter from Magistrates Simms and Carter begging the governor to act. Finally realizing the seriousness of the situation, Prescott ordered Colonel Sall to put 100 soldiers on the streets the next morning.

Though the military presence eventually quelled the street brawling, the shenanigans were not over. With Beck a mere puppet of the O'Brien camp, the credibility of the entire process was more than just doubtful. For unspecified reasons, but most likely to give O'Brien an opportunity to take the lead, the returning officer again extended the polling in St. John's. It would be extended twice more. The leading journals gave several reasons for complaining about the lengthy duration, not just that the entire city had been turned into a battleground. Winton correctly pointed out that as long as the citizens were being distracted by the election the main business of the fisheries was put on hold, costing the city and the entire colony thousands of pounds.

In the latter stages of the contest, as O'Brien's party attempted to rally as much support as possible for their final surge at the hustings, a regrettable choice of words sparked a new fire. While speaking to a gathering of followers, Nugent, in a moment of overzealous misjudgment, was alleged to have exhorted his audience to "Drive the copper-colored natives to their native woods!" To many of those present the meaning was not lost. Nugent, an immigrant from Ireland, clearly felt that the native Newfoundlander was inferior. Whether or not this was his true sentiment it is difficult to say, and to be fair, the man adamantly denied having said those exact words, even trying to cozy up to the "natives" in a later speech. Indeed, it would seem ridiculous for a political campaigner to risk offending a large number of his followers by making such outlandish statements, especially in the middle of a close contest. Still, the damage was done, and many of O'Brien's supporters felt a deep sense of betrayal. The incident refused to disappear, and turned out to be much more significant than many reformers realized.

The polling finally closed on June 6, after eighteen days of riotous electioneering. Many people on both sides felt disillusioned with the whole exercise, and these emotions were substantiated with the announcement that O'Brien had won with a slim margin of eight votes. Douglas's followers, convinced they had been cheated, demanded a recount. It was set for Tuesday, June 9, but, in truth, hardly anyone in the city had confidence in the appeals process, as Beck was also responsible for the so-called Court of Revision.

Their cynicism would soon be justified, as Beck continued to deny the right of franchise to several Douglas supporters whose votes clearly should have counted. At one point during the recount, Beck's legal adviser, an independent barrister named Stewart, who was obviously shocked by the unethical procedure he was witnessing, asked Beck if he intended to follow the law in scrutinizing the votes. When Beck answered in the negative, Stewart responded, "Mr. Returning Officer, I have a character to sustain, and I cannot think of compromising it by remaining here any longer to sanction by my presence such illegal and unjustifiable proceedings." Douglas and his solicitor, George Emerson, also withdrew, knowing well their chances of receiving fair treatment was practically nonexistent. By the end of the recount, Beck had disallowed a further twenty-four of Douglas's votes, thus handing the victory to O'Brien with a more comfortable majority of thirty-two.

Parsons, in an obvious attempt to prove the real winner, then published a list of dozens of discrepancies in voter qualifications. Included were men like John O'Neil, a convicted felon who had been permitted to vote for O'Brien, while at the same time men like Charles F. Bennett, a wealthy merchant, magistrate, and supporter of James Douglas, had his vote disallowed without any apparent reason for the omission.[6]

No doubt with some sense of vindication, Winton took the oppor-

---

6. Bennett would soon begin his own day in the political spotlight. He would be appointed to the new Amalgamated Assembly from 1842 to 1848, and would even make prime minister in 1870.

tunity to expound once more on his opposition to Newfoundland's liberal franchise. He offered a convincing argument that immigrants who had resided only a short time in Newfoundland en route to either the Canadas or the United States, were being given the "right of exercising a control in the return of members to serve in the colonial House of Assembly." Since most of the transient population consisted of Irishmen with lasting memories of the harsh conditions back home, their political ideologies would naturally be at odds with the conservative mercantile party.

In a letter to the colonial secretary, Governor Prescott did not mince words when he articulated his thoughts on the source of this latest trouble: "Dr. Fleming, without the slightest reasonable pretext, or any rational motive, but apparently from a pure love of dissension, has again blown up the flames of religious strife, and produced new discord in a community which appeared to be subsiding into peace and tranquility." It was a sentiment being repeated by reformers and conservatives alike.

Bishop Fleming's re-emergence on the political scene was, at the very least, a serious misjudgment on his part. By all accounts James Douglas would have been a worthy reform representative, a leading citizen of liberal ideologies and one who had already shown his support for Irish Catholic grievances. The betrayal of so many former friends and allies, especially Nugent, Kent, and O'Brien himself, could only have dampened some of Douglas's enthusiasm for politics. It was a most unfortunate loss, all around. Ironically, some unsuspected developments were unfolding that temporarily bridged the turbulent waters. Winton took note: "A great moral change has been wrought in the minds of the people, who have begun to perceive that their votes at elections, either on one side or the other, do not necessarily involve the condition of their souls." While there was a new willingness on the part of many Roman Catholics to separate religion and politics, this was not necessarily a realignment Nf ideologies. Winton and others may have mistaken the change as an embracing of conservatism.

If there is truth in the saying that politics makes for strange bedfellows, then the St. John's by-election of 1840 is a case in point. Hardly anyone would have expected Parsons and Winton to agree on any issue, but their editorials during this contest read as if they had been written by the same person. Though they would never become allies, these two combatants, for the moment, found themselves endorsing a brand new political idea.

CHAPTER 18
THE FORMATION OF THE NEWFOUNDLAND NATIVES' SOCIETY

About this time in Newfoundland's history there was an increasing desire for identification as "Newfoundlanders" with some sense of patriotism, a race of people—unique. There had been earlier glimpses of this, but prior to 1840 many residents still considered themselves British subjects, or Irish émigrés, who planned to eventually return to the land of their birth or move on.

For this reason, at least in one of his assessments, Henry Winton was correct: there *was* a transient character within much of the population, and it had existed for literally hundreds of years, ever since the beginning of the migratory fishery. But in the nineteenth century the industrialization of the eastern United States, along with the limitless prospects of its westward expansion, was tremendously alluring to footloose immigrants, most of whom were Irish seeking a better life. Newfoundland often became just a stepping stone in the journey to a promised land, a place to earn enough savings to make the rest of the trip. It was of these people that Winton complained when he stated:

[Newfoundland's] resident population consists of about an equal number of Protestants and Roman Catholics, but superseded to the latter are the fleeting emigrants from Ireland, who are yearly brought to this colony, and having resided in it for some time, move off to the Canadas or the United States; but upon all men who have occupied for one year any tenement of the smallest value, and who have not been convicted of any infamous crime, is bestowed the right of exercising a control in the return of members to serve in the Colonial House of Assembly.

However, Winton was mistaken in thinking that the poor Irish were the only transients. Many leading merchants and bureaucrats (not to mention clergy) were also in Newfoundland on a semi-permanent basis. Once their wealth was made or their tenure complete, they retired quite comfortably back to England. Their residency in Newfoundland was often little more than a temporary, albeit lucrative, assignment.

The native-born were increasingly offended by these temporary citizens, who took no vested interest in the improvement of life in the colony. A growing number of the population were second-, third-, and fourth-generation Newfoundlanders.[1]

They had fished here long enough to know every shoal and sunker, and had laid claim to the land for many years. Many had ancestors who fought the Americans and the French. Yet, despite the constitution of 1832 and the granting of representative government, Newfoundland's affairs were still run by outsiders, or by newly arrived political saviours. There were close ties to the Old World, but there was a culture, an identity, and a new sense of pride here. John Nugent's inopportune words awakened this awareness.

Having played a role that was more observer than active participant in the latest election, Henry Winton quickly interpreted the rift within the reform ranks and offered praise for the "intelligent Roman Catholics" who had broken from "the thraldom in which they had been held by their clergy in matters relating to more temporal concerns." Winton was in his glee, but if he was to have any hope of convincing more Catholics to think independently of their clergy, he would have to stop delineating them as either "intelligent," meaning conservative, or "ignorant," meaning reform. It was a nasty habit that he had developed over the years.

There was likely plenty of confusion as to who was on whose side in the wake of O'Brien's election, with *The Patriot* and *The Ledger* both attacking the priests for their interference. But when R.J. Parsons started talking about "a new era," many native Newfoundlanders, Catholic and Protestant, merchant and fisherman, took notice, and

---

1 Some families, notably the Pikes, the Garlands, the Badcocks, and the Dawes, can trace their lineage back to the early 1600s.

recognized the need to organize as one body. Within a month a meeting was called, and attended by several hundred native citizens of St. John's.

It is difficult to imagine this gathering of old-enemies-turned-allies. Was it possible for these men to bury the hatchet and forget, or at least forgive, all past transgressions? Throughout the years, after all, some belligerent words had been exchanged over vastly different political ideologies. Everyone agreed, however, that this new movement needed collaboration if it was to succeed, and they quickly got down to business. An executive was chosen, with none other than Edward Kielley being elected president, and The Newfoundland Natives' Society was given its name. A list of regulations was drawn up, making it clear that the association's main aim was the advancement of the colony through the political will of native-born Newfoundlanders.

After publishing these regulations on June 30, Winton expressed his complete support: "We heartily wish the Society the most perfect success in the carrying out of its praiseworthy design." In fact, a week earlier he had articulated the need for a union of Catholics and Protestants which would "from its innate moral force and energy, overcome every factious opposition which might be brought to bear against it." Winton's calculated choice of words indicated that he believed the Society had to separate itself from clerical influence, but his endorsement had repercussions.

Naturally suspicious of any association that found favour with Henry Winton, Bishop Fleming soon had his priests criticizing the Natives' Society, proving that he was not about to step aside and relinquish his political authority without a fight. An upcoming by-election in Conception Bay, necessitated by the death of Anthony Godfrey, was about to test the allegiances of many Roman Catholics in that district. In a contest nearly identical to that which had just promoted Laurence O'Brien, rioting would be a factor. But there was now a new political entity in the colony, and for many residents its presence was a positive sign that Catholics and Protestants could find common ground in the management of Newfoundland's affairs.

CHAPTER 19
SET A FIRE, THEN SMOTHER THE FLAMES

If there were use in talking in the language of reason to men who show
how little either reason or justice are permitted to influence their conduct,
we should ask what it is that they promise themselves by such a course?
Are their interests to be promoted, or is the end they seek to attain to be
affected by such turbulence, violence and bloodshed?

The Newfoundlander
December 10, 1840

Anthony Godfrey could hardly have picked a worse time to die.
The year 1840 had already been one of the most tempestuous in
the island's early political history, and the required by-election to
replace this deceased member further aggravated the masses.
Having called for a late fall by-election when everyone had returned
from the fishery, Governor Prescott informed his superiors in
London of his reservations and warned them of the inevitability of
more trouble. In keeping with his conviction that Bishop Fleming
was largely responsible for past disturbances, Prescott, somewhat
underhandedly, renewed his efforts to have the Roman Catholic
prelate dismissed from his position, and expelled from Newfoundland.

Throughout the summer the governor sent letters to Lord
John Russell, Secretary of State for the Colonies, and to anyone
else who would listen, complaining of the bishop's active involvement in local politics. Attached to these letters were numerous
testimonials from ostracized Catholics, who sought everything from
solace to restitution from the home government. Among the most
disturbing was a statement by Lawrence Barron's widow, one from
a widower named Michael Kavanaugh, and another from the
scrappy shopkeeper Michael McLean Little.[1]

Father Timothy Browne of Ferryland, a priest who had often quarrelled with Fleming over politics and the bishop's unyielding stance on certain clerical matters, also contributed to the assault.

Word of the conspiracy soon got back to Fleming, who immediately launched his own letter-writing campaign, demanding to know the nature of the charges against him so that he could offer a complete account of his actions to his superiors in Rome:

> *I write the present letter, finding myself tormented by the most grievous anguish. This morning the news was communicated to me of another secret plot organized by my implacable enemy, Captain Prescott, Governor of Newfoundland, to disgrace me and to impede the completion of the splendid edifice undertaken by me for the glory of God and our Holy Religion.*[2]

In one letter to Lord Russell, Fleming even sounded somewhat hurt by the governor's latest attack:

> *(Upon) the arrival of Captain Prescott, I had been upon the strictest terms of intimacy with him and in the habits of the most friendly intercourse with his family. In fact, I had reason to think Captain Prescott a bosom friend at the time! I freely confided to him all my acts and intentions, I consulted with him in my difficulties, and used my every effort to support his administration.*

While there may have been friendly discourse between the two men early on, Fleming's letter exaggerated the closeness of their initial relationship in order to gain sympathy from Lord Russell, and to depict Prescott as a betrayer and unworthy of his trust.

The war of words continued into the fall, with the English gradu-

---

1. This was the same Lawrence Barron who died as a result of injuries sustained during the 1836 election in St. John's. Michael Kavanaugh's wife had died a few days after giving birth in 1837, but, because her father was politically opposed to the priests, no clergy attended her funeral.

2. The edifice to which Fleming refers is the Cathedral of St. John the Baptist, later elevated to Basilica.

ally tiring of this ongoing colonial mockery. By now they were well aware of the campaign by Winton and others to dismantle the franchise in Newfoundland, having read the editorials and petitions for years. They had also read the correspondence from Prescott and his predecessor, Cochrane, complaining of the dire political predicament faced by Newfoundland, largely because of the "illiterate and vulgar Roman Catholic bishop."[3]

Finally, the English offered Vatican authorities an ultimatum: either get rid of Fleming, or financial support for Roman Catholic priests throughout English colonies would be stopped. Furthermore, the British government would decline the admission of a Vicar Apostolic for the island of Corfu, a small British protectorate off the coast of Greece.

This new British resolve even got the pope's attention, who ordered Fleming to repair to Rome immediately to answer to these charges. The strongly worded directive was written by Cardinal Fransoni of the Propaganda Fide:[4]

> *Now, from this you will easily grasp how much is to be feared from Your Grace's behavior, not listening to the repeated admonitions of this Sacred Congregation, nor indeed of the Holy Father himself, when indeed you may see from this that both the dignity of the Holy See and the good of the Catholic religion are brought into disrepute.*

But, if Prescott and Russell thought they would be rid of Fleming simply by complaining to his boss, then they had either overestimated the Vatican's authority or underestimated Fleming's determination. The unruly bishop did not respond to Cardinal Fransoni's summons, later claiming he had not received the letter.[5]

There was plenty of disbelief and displeasure in St. John's, London, and Rome. But Fleming was on a mission, with plenty of

---

3. Governor Prescott's words.

4. A department within the Roman Catholic church responsible for missionary work. During this period Newfoundland fell under its jurisdiction.

5. See Appendix 3 for Fleming's response to the pope's censure.

work to be done, and he was not about to be sacked by treacherous politicians or misinformed cardinals.

As Fleming battled to stay in Pope Gregory's good graces, the opening day of the Conception Bay election drew near. Around the middle of October Prescott was notified that two Roman Catholics had answered the call for nominations: James Prendergast from Harbour Grace and Edward Hanrahan from Carbonear. Although both were of the same faith, Hanrahan was being supported by his clergy and Prendergast was considered independent. As they had done in previous elections, the mercantile conservatives abstained from even offering a candidate to oppose the reformers, preferring to abandon the field to their foe in a political scorched-earth policy. Their scheme was simple: allow the reformers to elect members of doubtful means and abilities, thus filling the House with characters totally incapable of governing the colony. Once the House had proven itself incompetent, the home government would have little choice but to rescind the 1832 constitution. It was a cowardly, even traitorous, plan, but the wealthy conservatives saw it as their only chance to be rid of this baleful entity: government by the clergy.

An unexpected peace manifested during the early stages of the Conception Bay election derided the fears expressed by Prescott. Opening day at Harbour Grace, November 9, was perfectly calm; it was followed by several days of similar conduct among the voters. Robert J. Parsons, unwilling to discard his liberal ideologies despite his differences with the Catholic priests during the June election in St. John's, was moved to print some scathing criticisms of his old nemesis in support of the people of Conception Bay:

> *The northern election is proceeding with vigor, and with a peacefulness highly creditable to the character of the people of the Bay. The district is that portion of the colony which, over and over again, has been described by* The Ledger *and his falsifying party, as in a state of reck-lessness and lawlessness, where outrage and crime were matters of diurnal occurrence, and where the civil power had no supremacy to check the crimes of the populace . . . we observe this election*

conducted without a single blow being struck on either side of the popular contest!

By the end of the first week, Prendergast, garnering open support from some of Harbour Grace's aristocracy, was ahead by eight votes. Though peace had been maintained throughout the first five days of electioneering, signs of discontent were evident within the Hanrahan ranks. A subscriber to *The Patriot,* who claimed to be an impartial witness, informed the editor that while "the utmost quiet and harmony" existed at present, it was "notwithstanding the inflammatory addresses which marked each succeeding evening at the close of the Poll - so inflammatory as to make the blood freeze, and uttered by the conspicuous leader of Hanrahan's party." This discontent did not ease, for the election next moved to Port de Grave, a notoriously anti-Catholic area, where Prendergast was expected to widen his lead substantially.

When the polls closed the following week Hanrahan had dropped behind by 200 votes. The harangues of numerous priests were startling, but one clergyman, Father Walsh of Carbonear, unexpectedly advised his congregation to keep the peace. Fleming swiftly transferred him to an isolated parish in Trinity Bay, and replaced him with the politically outspoken Father Cummings.[6]

Voting at Harbour Main, a Catholic district, brought Prendergast's lead back to sixty, but with the north shore of Conception Bay, a mostly Protestant area, yet to be polled, there was considerable unrest in the Hanrahan camp. The peace that Parsons had bragged of was about to be disturbed.

On the morning of November 30, approximately sixty Prendergast supporters, Protestants as well as Catholics, left Harbour Grace to walk to Western Bay, where the next round of polling was to take place. The atmosphere was joyous, for Prendergast and

---

6. The story of Father Walsh's difficult journey to his new parish, through snowstorms, and across deep, freezing rivers, is a sorrowful but inspirational tale. See John Greene, *Between Damnation and Starvation: Priests and Merchants in Newfoundland Politics, 1745–1855* (Montreal: McGill-Queen's University Press, 1999).

his people sensed the inevitable victory. Even knowing that Carbonear was Hanrahan territory, they were confident that the north shore would bring a good enough return to maintain the numbers necessary to win. Flags fluttered in the breeze, accompanied by cheering and the pounding of drums. As they entered Carbonear, however, their jubilation quickly turned to despair, for approximately 300 Hanrahan supporters had gathered on the beach. Threatening words and gestures were initially hurled at the little parade, and before long a full-scale riot had broken out. In the words of one witness, "sticks, stones, and feet" were used to batter and trample the men from Harbour Grace. A man named Mitchell was particularly ill-treated when another of his associates attempted to come to his aid, only to be assaulted by "a very stout woman" who ran from a nearby house and attacked him with a poker. As he lay on the ground, the would-be rescuer was jumped upon by a tall, foxy-haired man known as "The Soldier." Dozens of Prendergast men were quickly bloodied, including Prendergast himself, and John Munn, the wealthy Harbour Grace merchant who had sided with Prendergast on the first day of polling. The air was filled with curses and screams, and pandemonium reigned.

Having trounced the intruders, Hanrahan's party withdrew, shouting threats of more to come should the Harbour Grace men return. Among the most severely injured were John West, Michael Hartry, Patrick Barry, Michael Fitzgerald, Edward Pynn, and John Mitchell, some of whom would be bedridden for days.[7]

Magistrates Danson and Stark sent details of this latest, and not entirely unforeseen, ruckus to Governor Prescott, requesting the immediate dispatch of a company of military to aid the civil authorities in keeping peace throughout the remainder of the election. Despite shocking statements from some of the victims, such as Edward Pynn, who said that "before this election ends in Carbonear there will be blood to the knees," Prescott baulked at sending troops. Perturbed

---

7. For testimonials regarding this disturbance, see CO 194/109, ff284-290.

by the governor's uncertainty, Danson and Stark soon had adequate cause to forward a second request.

In the middle of this civil unrest the citizens of eastern Newfoundland now faced an uncontrollable fury. On November 26 a savage winter storm hammered the south coast, as well as the Avalon and Bonavista Peninsulas, sinking two schooners that were bringing provisions from Prince Edward Island. Seemingly by divine choice, the town of Carbonear was hardest hit by Nature's fury, as four of its schooners—the *Wanderer*, the *Active*, the *Shannon*, and the *Triol*—were lost. Most lamentable, however, was the wreck of the packet *St. Patrick*, which was blown off course and foundered on the Maiden Rocks, three miles north of Carbonear. Five passengers and the crew were drowned. This disaster should have awakened feelings of humanity within the citizens, yet families of the deceased barely had time to mourn their loss before news of more election disturbances reached them from down the shore. It was as if the tragedy had been but a momentary distraction.

On November 28 *The Star and Newfoundland Advocate* printed a bold editorial applauding Roman Catholics in Conception Bay who now voted in opposition to their priests:

> *We now see the people are getting their eyes opened to their true interests, and determined to judge for themselves in future, while those who would make mere tools of them (if allowed) have found that they have taken the wrong method by treating them with such severity that they will no longer bear it - horsewhipping electors we expect is getting out of fashion - and the priests in the future, will find their clerical duties more becoming them than electioneering.*[8]

Even though the editor of *The Star* lauded the newfound independence of some Conception Bay Catholics, the news from the

---

8. The reference to horsewhipping was a sarcastic remark towards Roman Catholic priests accused of whipping some of their parishioners during the June election in St. John's. The validity of these reports is difficult to determine.

north shore was not comforting. Polling there had closed on December 3, after an outrage similar to that which had occurred in Carbonear. About twenty men were reported to have attacked a larger number of men from Lower Island Cove who had been proceeding to the hustings to support Prendergast. Several Island Cove men were severely beaten, and the rest forced to return home without voting. Nevertheless, at the close of the polls in Western Bay, Prendergast still held the lead, but by a mere forty-eight votes. According to the returning officer, Robert Pinsent, if the Lower Island Cove men had voted, Prendergast's lead would have stood at 100 at least.

Everything now hinged on Carbonear. Local authorities, however, did not expect peaceful proceedings. With much trepidation, Pinsent wrote to Colonial Secretary James Crowdy on December 4: "I imagine we shall muster on Monday morning to the number of 2000 men, and many of them fighting men. I fear that we shall stand on a volcano, but we shall endure the result."·

In the meantime, Prescott had received more requests for military protection from magistrates Danson and Stark, who were now joined by their colleagues James Power and Robert Pack.[9]

Feeling the pressure, but still unwilling to unilaterally commit any troops for fear of public resentment, Prescott met with the Executive Council on December 5 to determine what should be done. It was unanimously decided that, owing to the lateness of the season and the short time remaining in the election, the request for military assistance would be denied.[10]

Lord Russell later viewed Prescott's indecisiveness as simply reneging on his duties.

The early polling at Carbonear was carried out, as predicted,

---

9. Robert Pack had won the election of 1836. He was a successful merchant, with premises in Bay Roberts and Carbonear, and by 1840 he also held a position as magistrate. Paradoxically, Pack was the first to nominate Edward Hanrahan for the Conception Bay by-election.

10. As others would later insinuate, Prescott might have been waiting for the situation to deteriorate further, in a vain exemplification of his previous warnings to Russell.

amid daily assaults, with special constables complaining that they were unable to guarantee anyone's safety. Tensions grew to a fevered pitch. On the final day, with two and a half hours of polling left, Pinsent's volcano finally erupted. Throughout the morning the magistrates knew they could not control the mob which had gathered in frenzied expectation. At 1:30 p.m. serious fighting again broke out in an area known as Powell's Brook between the Harbour Grace supporters of Prendergast and the Carbonear supporters of Hanrahan. Witnesses claimed to have seen stones thrown at a boat-load of Harbour Grace men as they attempted to land on the beach. A Carbonear man, Thomas Murphy, was shot and wounded by one of Prendergast's supporters. Mr. Punton, a partner in the Harbour Grace firm of Punton and Munn, was severely injured, as was Thomas Ridley, who was in Carbonear as a magistrate to witness the closing of the polls. Ridley was immediately conveyed to the home of John Kiely, where it was determined that he had suffered a fractured skull. The attending doctors quickly assessed the man's condition as life-threatening.

In the absence of law and order, the remaining four magistrates immediately proceeded to the hustings and informed the returning officer that "the civil power under their control was altogether insufficient to preserve the peace." Knowing that any hope for a legitimate return was futile, Pinsent closed the poll, a decision which invalidated the entire election. News of this action infuriated the mob even more, and a full-scale assault was made on Prendergast and his supporters as they attempted to leave Carbonear. The hike back to Harbour Grace resembled what military officers call a "fighting retreat," as sticks and stones were used to fend off the attackers. Battered and bloodied, the Prendergast men eventually stumbled back to their homes.

Termination of the election did not end the violence and, throughout the night, citizens of Carbonear who had supported Prendergast became the next victims. Nicholas Ash, a cousin of Edward Hanrahan's wife, paid dearly for not supporting his relative, when part of the mob set fire to his house. In defence of his family and property, Ash shot and wounded four men and two women, but had to escape through the back door and into the nearby woods, dragging his wife and seven children with him.[11]

Nicholas's brother, William, also had part of his house burned, as did another man named Granfield.[12]

Even the family of Magistrate Power had to abandon their home, despite the fact that Power was a known reformer and had acted calmly and impartially throughout the campaign.[13]

News of the escalating hostilities in Conception Bay prompted a nervous Governor Prescott to recall the Executive Council on December 9 in order to reassess the appeal for military aid. The magistrates' latest reports, containing details of the terrible proceedings, and Ridley's uncertain health, finally stirred the sluggish Council to action.[14]

This time the appeal was granted, and 100 troops were ordered to Harbour Grace.

That night another frightening event occurred in Carbonear, when around midnight three men broke into the house of William Talbot, a schoolmaster, and beat him mercilessly with pickets for having supported Prendergast. His life was spared when his landlady showed up and threw herself between him and his attackers.

Meanwhile, in Harbour Grace hundreds of armed men paraded the streets, preparing to repel an imminent "invasion" by men from Carbonear. Though the invasion never materialized, and there was something suspicious about this rumour, the effect on the people of Harbour Grace was evident. Magistrates Danson and Stark sent another panic-filled letter to the governor, not knowing that Prescott had already called out the troops:

---

11. Ash and his family were awarded temporary shelter in the courthouse at Harbour Grace.

12. See Appendix 4 for Ash's petition to the governor. Similar petitions were sent from William Ash and Mr. Granfield (*Journal of the House of Assembly,*[1841]).

13. Magistrate Power, accompanied by Catholic priests, had helped quash a serious riot on December 7.

14. Ridley eventually recovered, and was elected to the Assembly in a much quieter election two years later.

The greatest alarm prevailed, and in the evening the inhabitants, to a man, armed themselves by preparing and loading their heavy sealing guns, in self-defense, and had the attack really been made, the survivors would have had to report to His Excellency the loss of hundreds of lives. We apprehend the alarm of last night was to throw the people here off their guard, and we fear that the threat of burning the merchant's stores and this town, by the Carbonear men, will yet be carried out, unless we are afforded military protection.

Her Majesty's troops, under the command of Major Law, finally sailed into Harbour Grace on December 11 aboard the brig *Margaret Parker*. Their arrival ushered in a relative peace that hadn't been seen for days. Solicitor General H.A. Emerson, who accompanied the troops, immediately began investigating the riots and arresting perpetrators. His initial confidence might have been due to sheer ignorance of the forces arrayed against him. By December 17, though, he was less optimistic: "up to last night there had been but six persons arrested who have been concerned in the late outrages at Carbonear, and these not the most prominent actors, as far as the present evidence against them goes. The guilty have fled in all directions." The next day, two suspects, William Harding and a man named Kiely, turned themselves in.[15]

Their statements and those of others convinced Emerson that the attack on Prendergast's men on the final day of polling had been premeditated. Others were arrested, and a hundred or more witnesses examined but, largely due to contradictory statements, most of those involved never answered for their crimes.

Newspaper editors who had watched intently since the election began expressed their outrage. Most conspicuous was R.J. Parsons, whose vehement condemnation of Father Cummings's political agitation, and Bishop Fleming's covert involvement, once again equalled Winton's:

---

15. This may have been the same William Harding who was arrested in 1836.

Whether the Rev. Gentleman acted on his own responsibility, or under authority higher than himself, we do not positively know, but it is only a fair inference to draw that if the Rev. Mr. Walsh was silenced for the honest and discrete avowal of his opinions, the proceedings of the Rev. Father Cummings were certainly directed by instructions from the same mysterious authority! The political course of the Rev. Father Cummings throughout the contest of Conception Bay, has plainly proven that the subversion of the freedom of election is the sole aim and object of him and his directors.

Parsons's editorial was essentially a ratification of the position held by most conservatives. Governor Prescott also had no qualms about blaming the Roman Catholic clergy for instigating the trouble. Even though he admitted that some priests had been seen walking among the crowd on December 8, trying to encourage peace, Prescott compared this to the arsonist who sets a fire and then tries to smother the flames.

The governor and the Newfoundland press were not alone in spewing irate comments. Lord Russell, on hearing the latest of the old colony's election debacles declared to Prescott that Carbonear "ought no longer to be a polling place." James Stephen, the Under-secretary of the Colonial Office in London, was malicious in his communication with Prescott, declaring that the Irish colonists of Carbonear were "a herd of wild people" who "approach the savage much more nearly than the civilized state." The outrage over Newfoundland's attraction towards political violence was becoming noticeably transatlantic, especially now since England's own Reformers were taking a lot of heat from their Conservative opposition on the state of Newfoundland's affairs.

The fallout from this latest violent episode had ramifications for the entire colony. When the legislature reopened on January 2, 1841, Prescott insisted that new laws were needed to preserve the peace in future elections. With another general election expected that fall, he made it abundantly clear that he had no intention of calling for one unless these necessary laws were passed. Gaining little support from members of the House, and not a lot from the Colonial Office in London, Governor Prescott then asked to be relieved of his position.

CHAPTER 20

INTRUDERS AND DELIVERERS

By the spring of 1841 British authorities had had enough of Newfoundland's shenanigans. The ruling party in England was under pressure from an increasingly powerful opposition to investigate the accusations made by influential merchants in England as well as in Newfoundland. The petitions were impossible to ignore. Repeated attempts to have the obstinate Bishop Fleming dislodged by authorities on both sides of the Atlantic, including those inside the Vatican, had failed. Complaints about declining property values and weakening profit margins, both the result of years of sectarian violence said the merchants, as well as the negative effects of a transient population, were even heard by the queen. Some of the original supporters of Newfoundland's constitution now had doubts.[1]

It was apparent that the colony was incapable of governing herself, at least according to the anti-reformers. It was time for drastic measures. In the spring of 1841 Lord Russell agreed to appoint a select committee, with members from both sides of the House of Commons, to inquire into Newfoundland's political affairs.

The inquiry did not last long. Before summer began, the committee had adjourned and was prepared to recommend to the House that Newfoundland's constitution be temporarily suspended. Though several former officials who opposed the constitution had been called as witnesses, including ex-Governor Thomas Cochrane, the small group of delegates sent from Newfoundland to defend her arrived after the adjournment, too late to be heard. One of only two voices of dissent heard from within the committee was that of Daniel

---

1. John Shea, by now living in England, was a notable within this group of distinguished people. Another was a Thomas Brooking, an English merchant who had lived in Newfoundland for fourteen years.

O'Connell, Fleming's friend and ally. He had been prepared to argue on the delegation's behalf. But, in the end, it was all for naught. Unable to remove Fleming, whom they still considered public enemy number one, the conservatives successfully removed his political arena.

In the meantime, the navy had called Captain Henry Prescott to his former life, his venture into colonial governorship no doubt having left him feeling maligned and unappreciated, not unlike his predecessor. He departed Newfoundland in May, 1841, satisfied to leave Newfoundland with all her idiosyncrasies and unmanageable characters. His replacement, Sir John Harvey, ruled the colony during a much-needed period of political peace. Though the proud Sir John might later think that this repose was due largely to his congenial nature and conciliatory skills, the temporary suspension of the 1832 charter, along with the introduction of new election rules, had left the residents with little reason for rioting.

After examining the committee's recommendations, British parliamentarians replaced Newfoundland's constitution with an "amalgamated assembly." This body was composed of twenty-five representatives, fifteen elected by the people, and ten appointed by the governor. Under modified electoral regulations, polling would be completed over a shorter period of time and done simultaneously in all districts. To satisfy critics of the old system like Henry Winton, who had always complained that the 1832 franchise was tantamount to universal suffrage, stricter qualifications for voters and candidates were put in place.[2]

Exercising the franchise was expected to become more genteel than that to which Newfoundlanders had become accustomed.

The amalgamated assembly was a step in the wrong direction, according to observers agitating for a *greater* independence from the home government. One of these observers was Ambrose Shea, whose

---

2. The concept of universal suffrage, to most people in early-nineteenth-century Great Britain, may have referred strictly to men. Yet, as early as 1851 a resolution in favour of the female franchise was placed before the House of Lords. Universal suffrage for men *and* women, however, was not granted until after World War I.

brother John had testified before the select committee. The Sheas occupied a unique position in Newfoundland society, for even though they were Roman Catholic, and liberal in their ideology, they were not supporters of the Irish-led reformers, nor of clerical involvement in politics. Shea may have been particularly opposed to the priests, having been present during that Sunday Mass in 1836 when Father Troy had unceremoniously evicted the Scanlan family. Nevertheless, Shea was a strong advocate of self-government and, as part owner/editor of *The Newfoundlander*, he was in a position to have his voice heard.

In 1842, as the first election under Newfoundland's new political contrivance drew near, Shea launched a series of scathing attacks on those whom he blamed for the suspension of representative government. The reformers were "unauthorized intruders" and an "unprincipled faction," he said. They "stand charged before the Country as the chief destroyers of the Constitution we possessed." This was an extraordinary display, since his criticisms were not aimed at English conservatives but at that body of mostly Irish politicians and clergy who had seized control of Newfoundland's reform movement. As a first-generation Newfoundlander, Shea was a staunch advocate of the Natives' Society and its mission to further the political ambitions of the native-born. He likely felt betrayed by those noble reform leaders who had promised so much since gaining power in the Assembly in '36. Words like liberty, freedom, and justice had rolled off their tongues, yet their actions often demonstrated their interest in undoing the English merchants rather than equality for the Irish. Shea, on the other hand, realized that progress and equality could only be obtained with wealthy allies, not wealthy enemies, and he saw no benefit in turning Newfoundland into a "Transatlantic Tipperary."[3]

In a relatively quiet election, 1842 marked the return of yet another reform majority, with Ambrose Shea throwing his support behind the conservatives. He was bitterly disappointed, however, with the defeat of St. John's candidates Walter Grieve, Charles Fox Bennett,

---

3. A phrase coined by Henry Winton in an editorial dated August 31, 1838.

and Patrick Kough. In an attempt at conciliation, Governor Harvey appointed seven Protestant conservatives to the House, along with three Catholic reformers, thus balancing the denominational representation. Complaints were still heard from both sides, however, most notably from Henry Winton and Robert J. Parsons, two individuals who were impossible to satisfy. For the most part, the arrangement was seen as a compromise, providing a much-needed break from the dirty politics of recent years.

From 1843 to 1847 Newfoundlanders lived in relative peace under the amalgamated assembly. Like it or not, the new system had been thrust on them as a somewhat punitive measure, and the elected officials had to learn to live with it. The bull-headed Dr. Carson probably took the constitutional suspension harder than anyone. He had been the original agitator for an elected house of representatives, long before the current reformers had even immigrated to Newfoundland, and its loss was a bitter disappointment for him. Watching his life's work being trashed was probably the stimulus which brought about his demise.

By 1843 Carson's aging body could no longer keep up with the rigours of Newfoundland politics, and the end came on February 26. Many of his opponents said that his passing was expedited by the long-awaited Privy Council's ruling in the Kielley v. Carson affair, a decision with the potential to ruin Carson financially. On his deathbed he urged his longtime friend and ally, Robert J. Parsons, to continue the fight for a return of representative government—a reformer to the end. He would have been pleased to know that Parsons already had bigger and better things in mind.

Inside the amalgamated House of Assembly the two factions eyed each other uncomfortably. Several developments in the mid-1840s, however, eased the tension between the elected and appointed representatives, even briefly uniting them. The first of these was a near crisis along the French Shore during the summer of 1843, when a British naval officer shot and killed a St. Pierre fisherman who had been caught inside English waters. Subsequent demands from the French, and the concessions offered by the English, made Newfoundlanders of all denominations and political stripes react loudly. The debate over French fishing rights would not be settled for another sixty years, and in 1843 Britain was more concerned with appeasing her old foe than protecting the rights of her oldest colony. Already angered with an unfair bounty granted by France to her fishermen, many of Her Majesty's loyal subjects in Newfoundland justifiably felt betrayed by the mother country.

A second event that punished Newfoundlanders indiscriminately was the St. John's fire of 1846. Even though this terrible conflagration could have had a unifying effect on all classes and denominations, the actions of the recently arrived Church of England bishop caused an uproar that was widely criticized, and interpreted by many Catholics as confirmation that Anglicans often received preferential treatment.[4]

In the aftermath of a disaster that left 12,000 citizens homeless, aid poured in from Britain, the United States, and neighbouring colonies. This relief fund eventually surpassed £100,000, £17,500 of which was given to Bishop Edward Feild to replace St. John the Baptist Church with a grand cathedral—a substantial cut from a fund that was intended to aid fire sufferers. Demonstrating that he did not like to play favourites when it came to castigating offenders, Henry Winton loudly editorialized his disapproval of the bishop's actions. But the new leader of the Church of England was not one to be pushed around, and, unlike his predecessor, Aubrey Spencer, neither was he shy of public scrutiny. He had no qualms about using the money to assist with the construction of a new cathedral, arguing that huge grants of public property had been ceded to Fleming for his project several years earlier.[5]

The new cleric's bold Anglicanism won him many friends, as well as no shortage of enemies, a characteristic that made him a worthy opponent of his Roman Catholic counterpart in the coming decades.

By 1847 the experiment with the amalgamated assembly had ended. It was, after all, a temporary replacement for Newfoundland's

---

4. Bishop Edward Feild had arrived in 1844.

5. An investigation by the House of Assembly, headed by R.J. Parsons, later uncovered no wrongdoing in the fire fund allocations.

suspended constitution. In truth, many British politicians were as anxious as Newfoundland's reformers to have the colony manage her own affairs. The mother country had other problems to contend with, as major developments occurring throughout eastern Europe would soon mean war.[6]

The restoration of the 1832 charter came with conditions, most importantly revised election rules coupled with amended qualifications for candidates.

But diehard reformers in Newfoundland were not satisfied with this return to the old system—not when their colonial neighbours were being granted the latest form of democracy in the British parliamentary system, that of responsible government. Parsons had agitated for this ever since getting himself elected in place of his old friend, Carson. Under responsible government, the elected body of representatives, the Assembly, would be granted more authority to make laws than it had under the old system. The most significant change, however, would be in the selection of members for the Executive Council. In the responsible system these were chosen from the ruling party within the Assembly and not appointed by the governor at his pleasure. In essence, both the Assembly *and* the Council would be composed of elected officials. There would also be a considerable reduction in the governor's authority, something that appealed immensely to R.J. Parsons and the newcomer, Phillip Francis Little. Voices of dissent were still heard.

Although the struggle for representative government during the late 1820s had been largely a unified movement taken on by lobbyists from all classes and denominations, the fight for responsible government twenty years later was much different. Instead of unifying the population, this new political cause broadened a rift that had reappeared within Newfoundland society. Not surprisingly, Roman Catholic politicians, closely supported by their clergy, were leaders in this crusade. On the other hand, Protestant conservatives, especially the merchants, were naturally distrustful of any system that had the poten-

---

6. The Crimean War lasted from 1853 to 1856.

tial to create a Catholic legislative monopoly. They had seen how a Catholic-dominated House of Assembly acted when there was an *appointed* Council to keep them in check. The possibility of Catholic control of both chambers perturbed the conservatives, and they consequently opposed the measure. Nevertheless, before any discussion over the granting of responsible government could take place, a restoration of the original charter had to occur, and an election was called for November, 1848.

This polling was peaceful, demonstrating that the new election rules were performing as they should. The contest was another success for the reformers, who by this time were known as Liberals. The biggest news coming out of this election was the introduction of Phillip Little and Hugh Hoyles into Newfoundland politics. Little, a Roman Catholic Liberal from Prince Edward Island, and Hoyles, a Conservative from St. John's, would play leadership roles for their respective parties over the coming years, Little as a strong advocate for responsible government, and Hoyles an avowed opponent. The laborious debate over the new form of elected government dominated the next several sessions of the legislature, with both sides sending off delegates to London to argue their case. The battle was often like a game of chess, with one side challenging and the other countering. However, a new age was dawning throughout much of British North America, and in 1854 Henry Clinton, the Secretary of State for War and the Colonies, advised the Colonial Office to grant Newfoundland the right of responsible government. The Liberals under their new leader prevailed, while Hoyles and the Conservatives became unwilling participants in a different game, one more open, but no less dangerous.

Politico-sectarian rivalries dormant during the co-operative years of the amalgamated assembly re-emerged during the fight for responsible government. They were fuelled by the energetic exertions of Newfoundland's two highest-ranking clergymen, Bishop Feild and the new Roman Catholic bishop, John Thomas Mullock.

The deeply loved, but equally despised, and always controversial, Dr. Michael Anthony Fleming, had passed away in 1850, after years of failing health. The stress and toil of twenty years as leader of

Newfoundland's largest church had finally worn him out. His final Mass was said inside the beautiful Cathedral of St. John the Baptist, the object of his passion and determination for so many years, on January 6. It was said that during the final days he had attempted to make peace with his enemies, even being seen in public with his old nemesis, Henry Winton, conversing about matters that at the time may have seemed much more important than their longstanding political differences.[7]

Whatever Fleming's deathbed wishes may have been, by 1860 party spirit and renewed sectarian animosities reached a level not witnessed since the notorious general election of '36. Several circumstances foreshadowed more disturbing events.

Protestant Conservatives had grown exceedingly tired of Catholic domination in the house of representatives. They had learned to depend upon the governor and his appointed councillors to advance their concerns, but the need for equal representation in this new assembly was becoming more evident. With the governor's position significantly weakened, the Conservatives could no longer depend upon that individual to shoulder their responsibilities.

Secondly, responsible government had not noticeably improved the island's condition as its promoters had promised. Even though the late 1850s had been years of relative prosperity, by Newfoundland standards, starvation, epidemics, and failures in the fishery had re-emerged by 1860. Notably absent from the political scene by this time was the Natives' Society, the organization which had held such promise for unification. By 1860 it was mostly inoperative, a victim of internal squabbling, external pressures, and ill winds. (The Society's new building had literally blown down during a gale in September, 1846.)

The most critical malfunction of responsible government, as far as the Conservatives were concerned, was that it had not alleviated electioneering violence and intimidation nor lessened Catholic clerical interference in political campaigns. The 1859 general election, in

---

7. See Appendix 6.

essence a comprehensive review of the first four years of responsible government under the Liberals, marked a return to the nastiness of the pre-amalgamated assembly years. To make matters worse, in some constituencies the Roman Catholic clergy were not the only ones interfering. In Burin, for example, Liberal electors and candidates complained of the active campaigning of Reverend Gathercole, an Anglican clergyman who even held political rallies at the parish manse.

The worst incidents occurred in Harbour Grace, where a mob broke into the four polling booths, stole the registration books, and destroyed property owned by candidate Robert Walsh. Though a Roman Catholic and a Liberal, Walsh was not supported by the head of the newly created Harbour Grace diocese, Bishop Dalton. The former independent Catholic, James Prendergast, now found clerical favour, having learned the hard way that independence was not in line with clerical thinking. Under protest, Walsh retired from the contest after his home was attacked and his family threatened.[8]

Even though this sort of electioneering was expected in Newfoundland, it raised the ire of the new governor, Alexander Bannerman, who immediately sent troops and ordered an investigation. Bannerman, who had once been a well-known radical in the British parliament, and a friend of Daniel O'Connell, had replaced Charles Darling in 1857. Ironically, the liberal-minded Bannerman quickly learned to distance himself from Newfoundland's Liberals. Even the radicals in Great Britain, it seems, were far more genteel than the Liberals here. Politics in London might have been boorish, but in Newfoundland it was downright brutal.

For some inexplicable reason, Liberal ministers withheld all details of the Harbour Grace election violence from the governor. This was frustrating enough in itself, but when Bannerman heard the opinion of one of the three men investigating the riots he must have been totally bewildered. Attorney General George Hogsett was completely at variance with his co-investigators. While Bennett and Simms reported that "a widespread feeling of intimidation and appre-

---

8. See Appendix 7.

hension," existed throughout the district, Hogsett dismissed these assertions as the "groundless fears of a few timid individuals." It was his contention that the Harbour Grace riots were nothing more than what are "occasionally to be witnessed in most countries having the privilege of representative institutions." Coming from the colony's leading attorney, this statement was nothing short of preposterous.

In 1858 Phillip Little retired while still riding high on a wave of popularity. Citing ill-health as his reason for stepping out of the political ring, he accepted a position as Supreme Court judge, a move that permitted John Kent to reclaim the Liberal leadership. With Catholic against Protestant and Liberal against Conservative, a developing rift between Kent and Bishop Mullock soon aroused a series of events that brought the colony close to civil war. Before this, however, a tragedy in Conception Bay ensured that Newfoundland society remained bitterly divided.

Chapter 21

Mummers, and the Murder of Isaac Mercer

Bay Roberts is becoming quite a notorious place in the Conception Bay district of our island.

The Public Ledger
February 12, 1861

Christmas, 1860, probably began as a time of celebration and happiness, just like any other. It was, after all, a time for people to put aside their differences, to celebrate the season, to wish friends and strangers alike all the best for the coming year. Age-old traditions were resurrected, and new customs introduced, such as decorating the Christmas tree, a holiday tradition brought to England by Prince Albert from his German homeland. The smell of rum cake and raisin duff greeted visitors in most households, while richer citizens also enjoyed the scent of smoked salmon and glazed ham. Sleigh bells jingled and horses whinnied. Throughout the island, in small outports and large towns, in poor homes and wealthy mansions, the celebration of Christ's birth was eagerly anticipated.

But the cheerful images that appeared on mid-nineteenth-century Christmas cards, another recently acquired tradition, did not accurately depict 1860 Newfoundland. For years, despite their common hardships, religion, ethnicity, and politics had divided the people inhabiting this island. After the introduction of responsible government this had not changed. If the vaunted Natives' Society had not brought the two sides together, it was very doubtful that pretty ornaments and a blanket

---

1. Mummering is an old Yuletide tradition from England and Ireland. Participants dress up in disguises and go about the community knocking on doors. Once inside, they perform songs, dances, and recitations, and then are given food and drink, usually alcoholic.

of white snow would. Still, many people in 1860 probably did not expect a significant disturbance to occur during the Christmas season while everyone enjoyed another ancient custom, mummering.[1]

During the first half of the nineteenth century, in addition to troops of mummers visiting from door to door, mummers' parades were also common. Dozens of mummers marched through the streets of all major towns, including St. John's, some playing musical instruments, others cavorting about with "weapons" made from inflated pigs' bladders tied to sticks. These frolics often turned ugly when mummers used the opportunity to clobber a spectator with whom they had some personal grievance. In 1860, one such incident sparked a hail of protest from the more "sober" element of St. John's society, many of whom had petitioned for years for an end to the annual tradition. The frenzied antics of mummers grew to alarming heights in many communities, particularly Carbonear and Harbour Grace, where riots and assaults continued unabated. The worst incident, which eventually led the Newfoundland legislature to legally ban mummering, was the murder of a young man in Bay Roberts on December 28, 1860.

Twenty-two-year-old Isaac Mercer had been married just two weeks to Miss Elizabeth Brown on the day of the fatal assault. Having spent several hours in the woods, he had stopped at his mother-in-law's house on the return home, not just for a much-needed rest but also to seek the companionship of his brother-in-law, John. In a later examination before Judge Carter, John testified that Isaac feared the "jannies" that were known to be searching for him.[2]

A little before 6:00 p.m., Isaac, John, and a third man named Russell left Mrs. Brown's and headed down the harbour. As they neared an intersection known locally as Wilcox's Corner, they were approached by six men dressed as mummers brandishing heavy sticks. The attack was swift and brutal. One mummer grabbed the axe that Mercer carried over his shoulder, and, with the butt end of the blade, struck him a solid blow across the right temple. As Mercer crumbled to the ground, the attackers fled into a nearby grove of trees.

---

2. In the Conception Bay North area "jannies" was another name for mummers.

Slow to gain their full senses, Brown and Russell, when they realized the seriousness of Isaac's injuries, cautiously lifted him to his feet, and headed to his house, nearly a mile away. With only rudimentary medical attention available at the time, Mercer drifted into unconsciousness and died the next day.

News of the murder spread quickly throughout the colony, and a frantic search for the six perpetrators got under way immediately. The new Attorney General, Robert Lilly, and the Superintendent of Police, Timothy Mitchell, travelled to Bay Roberts to personally conduct the investigation. The names of several Roman Catholic men were soon freely, and perhaps unfairly, circulated throughout the community by those claiming to seek justice. It was said that these men "had it in for Mercer," presumably because of a ruckus during the recent election. The suspects—John Dawson, Stephen Dawson, James Hedderson, Denis Walsh, James Fleming, and Patrick Fleming—were questioned by Lilly and Mitchell.

Rowdy behaviour continued to make the news in the capital city, as well, despite a proclamation published in the wake of the latest mummers' parade in St. John's, exemplified by this January 4 report from *The Public Ledger*:

The fools have been out the last three days in pretty considerable force, to the great annoyance of the shopkeepers, several of whom were obliged to preserve their glass by putting up their shop shutters. A proclamation was issued forbidding this sort of thing, but no attention seems to have been paid to it.

The peace of the festive season was also mocked in Carbonear and Harbour Grace, as reports of disturbances by mummers there also flooded the newspapers. One particular incident warranted a detailed narrative in *The Ledger*: an attack on Henry Moore, the vice-president of the local British Society, by a large group of men armed with pickets. Moore, who had been brandishing a pistol, fired at his attackers without hitting anyone, but escaped to the shelter of a nearby store. He suffered some frightful injuries, including a small hole in his head caused by a nail that was still attached to a picket. Though no arrests were made, the editor of *The Public Ledger* assured his readers that the culprits were "Roman Catholic blackguards."[3]

Another event at Bay Roberts on New Year's Eve further elevated the ire of Protestants, and bolstered the accusations about Catholics being responsible for Mercer's death. The Protestant schoolmaster, Mr. Blackmore, had posted notices of the recently announced £100 reward for information that might lead to the arrest of the guilty parties. During the night of December 31, the Protestant school was broken into, ransacked, and copies of the King James Bible thrown into the harbour. This incident provoked a furious reaction from Bishop Feild, who published a lengthy letter in several newspapers calling on the people "for Christ's sake, to make some effort to restore peace and order." He criticized the Liberal government for their apparent indifference to the state of lawlessness throughout much of the island, and issued a strong warning to those who had failed to co-operate in the Mercer investigation:

> *But blood cries from the ground; and however much such a feeling may be deplored and deprecated, it is feared that, if other means are not used to bring the offenders to justice, an opportunity will be taken by the young men in the Harbour to avenge Mercer's death.*

One week after the publication of this letter, Hedderson and the two Dawsons were again taken into custody and indicted for murder. But the timing of these arrests seemed too coincidental, too staged, and gave the impression of an action merely aimed at appeasing the powerful Anglican bishop. As before, there was little evidence with which to hold these men, so they were eventually released.[4]

Unfortunately, Bishop Feild's letter was probably misinterpreted by the Protestant men of Bay Roberts as justification for taking the

---

3. Since the controversial Henry Winton had passed away on January 8, 1855, by 1860 editorials for *The Public Ledger* were being written by Henry Winton Junior.

4. When the Grand Jury returned later in the spring, it decided that there was insufficient evidence to proceed to trial.

law into their own hands. It soon became dangerous for Catholics to leave their homes, as gangs of armed ruffians walked the streets. On the evening of March 2, one mob pursued a local Catholic man for some distance until he eventually sought shelter inside the premises of a Catholic storeowner named Hackett. Refusing to give the man up, Hackett and his assistant bravely faced the mob with a picket and a poker. Both men were quickly overwhelmed and severely beaten before they could crawl back inside the store, at which time the building itself became the target. Windows were smashed and shutters and doors were splintered by rocks, bricks, and any other potential missile. As rumours had spread around the community that Hackett was harbouring several of the men involved in Mercer's murder, the mob's complete intentions can only be a matter of conjecture. Sensing that they were close to having their revenge, many more Protestants joined the mob, now armed with everything from pickets and knives to sealing guns. According to eyewitnesses, the scene grew uglier by the minute, until several members of the "respectable portion" of the town showed up. Luckily for Hackett, these men defused the situation and convinced the mob to return to their homes.

Though emotions continued to run high in Bay Roberts, the days stretched into weeks with little progress made in the investigation. By late March people were increasingly occupied with the upcoming seal hunt and preparations for the summer fishery. Ironically, men who had been ready to slay one another would soon pan seals together. Catholics and Protestants would sleep in close proximity in filthy quarters onboard the sealing vessels that prowled the Front, sharing the dirty, dangerous work that paid them a few extra dollars each spring before heading to the Labrador, where they fished on common grounds.

As the case of Isaac Mercer's murder gradually grew cold, the authorities were subjected to much criticism for their inability to make any arrests. An unfolding political crisis, however, soon relegated the story to the back page. No further investigations were carried out by the authorities, who knew all too well the unlikelihood of gaining new information. The murder of Isaac Mercer became another unsolved mystery.

Mercer's tragic death had one impact on Newfoundland society: On June 25, 1861, having witnessed how the Christmas tradition of mummering could turn deadly, the Newfoundland Legislature bowed to the pressures of powerful lobbyists long opposed to the practice. An Act for the Prevention of Nuisances was passed, which read in part:

> *Any person who shall be found, at any Season of the Year, in any Town or Settlement in this colony dressed as a Mummer shall be deemed a Public Nuisance, and may be arrested by any Peace Officer, with or without a Warrant.*

Although mummering was now a legal misdemeanour, the new law could only be enforced in larger communities with a noticeable police presence. Even there, one could still mummer within the boundaries of the law by obtaining a "licence" from the local magistrate. Needless to say, many who wished to revel in the ancient custom either refused or neglected to obtain one of these legal permits. The penalty for being caught dressed as a mummer without the proper licence was a fine of 20 shillings or a week in jail.

Chapter 22
Attention! Make Ready!! Prime and Load!!!

But then we have the satisfaction of seeing thousands upon thousands of pounds distributed among our locust-like *officials. We pay heavy taxes, but get comparatively no return; almost all goes in salaries and pretended compensations, and I have no hesitation in saying that the collection of revenue under the present system is but* legalized robbery. *I am aware that my name has been made use of to prop up the supporters' of this system, but I consider it due to myself, and to those whose interests I advocate, to repudiate any connexion [sic] with a party who take care of themselves, but do nothing for the people.*

Bishop John Thomas Mullock
June, 1860

The words of the Roman Catholic bishop were unequivocal; he was intensely upset with the Liberal administration of Mr. Kent, and was rescinding his support for that party. That the prime minister had never enjoyed Bishop Mullock's complete approval was common knowledge, yet the condemnation now appearing in pro-Catholic newspapers probably surprised most Liberals, and a few Conservatives. Months of dissatisfaction were poured onto the pages for all Newfoundlanders to enjoy, or take exception to, depending upon their political and/or religious affiliation.

Mullock's latest demonstration was motivated by the government's refusal to honour his contract with the owners of a New York steamship. Incredibly, Mullock had negotiated on behalf of the Newfoundland government, without its knowledge, for the lease of a vessel to service the island's outports. It was a worthwhile venture to be sure, but hardly Mullock's responsibility, and an astonishing misuse of his position. Consequently, the government had every right to refuse ratification of the deal. The bishop showed his displeasure at the Liberal government by publishing a lengthy criticism.

Closely watching the conflict unfold between Mullock and Kent was Governor Bannerman. Since learning of his ministers' attempt at withholding information about the 1859 election riots, Bannerman had determined that his executive was not only inept but also corrupt, and that a change in government was warranted. Bannerman was well aware of the imprudence of dismissing them at that time, however, and had chosen to wait for the opportune moment. It came in February when Prime Minister Kent accused the governor of being influenced by members of the Opposition to defeat a currency bill which would reduce the salaries of some officials. Angered by what he felt was an insinuation of conspiracy, Bannerman demanded that Kent explain himself. When he refused to comply, the governor knew that his moment had come. Recalling Mullock's scathing criticism of the current administration, Bannerman felt confident that he would receive little or no opposition on that front. He immediately dismissed the Liberals from office and called on Hugh Hoyles, the leader of the Conservatives, to form a new government. This unprecedented move shocked and angered every Liberal in the colony. The scene inside the House of Assembly on the first day of the new administration was "reminiscent of the early French Revolution," according to *The Public Ledger*. In front of a howling gallery, the Liberals predictably called for a non-confidence motion, which was carried sixteen to twelve, thus forcing an election for early May.

The formation of a new government by the Protestant Hoyles placed Bishop Mullock in an awkward position. Though he had castigated Kent in June, Kent was still a Roman Catholic Liberal susceptible to his influence. With Hoyles in charge, at least for the present, Mullock found himself in unfamiliar territory without any political clout. Realizing his sudden loss of power, Mullock was forced to backpedal. In March, one month after the Liberals had been ousted, the bishop published a letter retracting his earlier condemnations and, with dire warnings of Catholic "enslavement" under a Protestant government, urged his people to vote Liberal in the forthcoming election.

Apparently wanting a share of the spotlight, the Anglican bishop published his own letter, calling on the electorate to support the Conservatives, even taking shots at Liberals who he said were "obliged to seek office for the emoluments." Feild, still fired up over the Bay Roberts affair, no doubt experienced some satisfaction with the dismissal of the Kent government. Now that the Liberals were outside looking in, Feild had no intention of letting them back inside, if he could help it.

With the powerful leaders of the two biggest churches openly opposed to one another, the gathering storm alarmed even the authorities in London. The Colonial Office knew that Bannerman did not have the authority to "dismiss" his executive as he had done, but merely to "suspend" it. New amendments were swiftly passed to cover the governor's oversight, and to avoid a potentially embarrassing situation. The greatest concern, however, was the likelihood of Kent's Liberals winning the election and regaining power. Bannerman would then have virtually no influence over his ministers, having already taken his best shot by banishing them in the first place. For many individuals, the stakes were high as they entered another possibly violent campaign. All eyes, as usual, were on the troublesome districts, particularly those of St. John's and Conception Bay.[1]

It did not take long for trouble to appear. Knowing well the tendency in Harbour Grace toward electoral violence, Bannerman dispatched troops there prior to nomination day, April 26. One hundred soldiers of the Royal Newfoundland Companies under the command of Captain Thomas Hanrahan arrived on April 23, and were quartered at Temperance Hall on Victoria Street. Three candidates vied for the two available seats in this district. The Liberal incumbent, James Prendergast, was expected to poll most of the Catholic vote, while Conservatives John Hayward and Henry Moore could count on the majority of the Protestant electors.[2]

There were also "independent" Catholics, not influenced nor

---

1. After 1855 St. John's became two districts: East and West; Conception Bay, five districts: Harbour Grace, Carbonear, Bay de Verde, Harbour Main, and Port de Grave.

2. In the two previous elections Hayward had been elected as a Liberal, but in 1861 he was running as a Conservative.

intimidated by their clergy who had backed Robert Walsh in '59. This group comprised the all-important swing vote that both Liberals and Conservatives wanted to entice.

Having finally learned that a show of force won elections in Newfoundland, on the morning of April 26 a mostly Protestant crowd, in excess of 1,000, paraded behind Hayward and Moore to the courthouse for the required nomination of candidates. Except for a minor scuffle with some of Prendergast's men, the proceedings were relatively quiet. The Conservatives then returned to Victoria Street, where both candidates addressed their supporters from the steps of Moore's house, complimenting them on their good behaviour and advising them to return to their homes. With no apparent reason for concern at this point, the crowd dispersed, many heading up the bay and others to Bears Cove in the east end of town. But the initial peace of nomination day did not last. Minutes later the first of a series of brutal clashes occurred.

While walking along Water Street, some Protestant men from Bears Cove encountered a large number of Prendergast supporters marching uptown. Naively expecting no trouble, the outnumbered Bears Cove men attempted to pass along the side of the street, when a shower of stones staggered them and compelled them to take flight. Watching the entire scene from a distance, Thomas Ridley sent a messenger to the magistrate in charge, Robert Pinsent, asking to use the military to quash any riot before it could start. A report of the encounter reached Hayward and Moore first, however, and minutes later hundreds of their supporters reassembled and ran to the scene. Now Prendergast's men were outnumbered and chased from the area. The Protestants then turned their aggression on the homes of Roman Catholics living along Water Street, including that of Prendergast himself, smashing windows and doors. After another brief encounter in which the Catholics retreated up LeMarchant Street, the Protestant crowd was approached by Ridley, who advised them to remain peaceful and to allow the military to do their job. But the crowd was unwilling to take the chance that Prendergast's men might get control of the town, so they split into smaller groups and commenced parading the streets.

Magistrate Pinsent was slow to react to the swiftly intensifying conditions. It is uncertain whether he believed that the early reports were exaggerated, or that he gravely feared his own role in the imminent uproar. It wasn't until Ridley approached him with a telegraph warning of several hundred Prendergast supporters on their way from Carbonear that Pinsent realized the desperateness of the situation. His poor judgment and unwillingness to use the force at his disposal later invoked much criticism from town leaders, Conservatives, and even the governor, who subsequently called an inquiry to fully investigate the magistrate's actions.[3]

On Ridley's advice, Pinsent led the troops under Captain Hanrahan to the intersection of Harvey Street and Carbonear Road in time to meet the invaders as they charged into town. The appearance of these men was unnerving, armed as they were with knives and bludgeons and carrying two flags, one green and the other white with a red Latin cross, the so-called "bishop's flag." Oblivious to the presence of the soldiers, they clamoured over fences and charged on past, as Pinsent stood in the street, pathetically reading the Riot Act. Those who bothered to pay the magistrate any attention declared they had come to protect the convent, as they had heard it was being attacked. Watching Pinsent's meek attempt at repelling these men, Ridley was flabbergasted, and quickly returned to his home to secure it from almost certain destruction.

Marching through the streets, the Carbonear men soon joined up with Prendergast's men, a total force that now numbered about 700 by some accounts. Minutes earlier a group of Prendergast supporters had threatened to pull down Moores's house on Victoria Street, but were driven off by troops under Corporal Francis Dooling. Dooling's decisive action was the only example of bravery and determination displayed by either the police or the soldiers during the

---

3. Pinsent claimed that Captain Hanrahan had been told to "only fire" on the rioters if called upon to act. Whether this meant that the soldiers were not permitted to assist in making any necessary arrests is unclear, but may have caused Pinsent to falter. Hanrahan's own testimony at the inquiry suggests that he would have acted more forcefully had Pinsent given the order.

entire confrontation. In the presence of a larger foe, the corporal had ordered his company to "load with ball," and told the mob to move on and do no mischief or he would be forced to fire on them. Faced with such bold conviction, the mob had obeyed.

A momentary lull in the action now provided the authorities ample time to re-evaluate their plans, and retake control of the town. Though the local police force was just six constables under the capable leadership of Luke Fallon, the support of 100 trained soldiers should have made this a relatively easy task. Yet, Pinsent again hesitated, continuing to demonstrate a demoralizing indecisiveness.

An hour or so later the opportunity had passed; the opposing sides again collided, this time at the foot of Victoria Street. After battering one another mercilessly with sticks and stones, Prendergast's men retreated up the hill, regrouping at the intersection of Harvey Street. Thinking quickly, Captain Hanrahan positioned his troops between the two mobs, and ordered his men to fix bayonets and load with ball. This was to be the moment of truth: back down, or be killed. With all sides apparently waiting for the other to make the first move, Pinsent stepped to the front and read the Riot Act yet again, a ridiculous and pointless repetition. The standoff did buy some time, however. With the troops armed and prepared to act, Pinsent convinced the Protestants to lay down their weapons. It was a mistake. As Pinsent and Hanrahan remonstrated with the mob leaders, Prendergast's men saw their opportunity. They charged past the block of unsuspecting soldiers and into the Protestants in a wild melee of blood and broken bones. Astoundingly, no orders to intervene were given.[4]

With nothing to deter them, Prendergast's men swarmed into Water Street, destroying the homes and property of known Conservatives, both Protestant and Catholic, followed by the lame military. A disgusted Sergeant Daniel McCartney later testified, "They (the mob) proceeded to other houses and we followed them from one

---

4. For reports of the Harbour Grace violence, see PANL, CO 194/165, beginning on page 174. One man, Lorenzo Pike, was so badly beaten that he would likely have died had not a Roman Catholic named Pumphrey lain down on him to ward off the blows.

place to another, halting while they attacked a house until they had it destroyed, and so we without making the slightest effort to prevent it." Pinsent's consistent unwillingness to act forcefully finally waned as the unrestrained vandals turned on Ridley's home. Probably fearing the powerful merchant more than the mob, Pinsent instructed Captain Hanrahan to fire if he thought necessary. At this opportune moment, as the soldiers brought their rifles to the ready position, a Roman Catholic priest appeared among the crowd, urging them to disperse.[5]

Once again the powers of the clergy were remarkably demonstrated, as the rampaging mob quickly abandoned the street, leaving in its wake a shattered town. Mercantile premises and private homes all along Water Street had been "dreadfully destroyed." It was a familiar scene to the law-abiding citizens of Harbour Grace.

Pinsent's only wise decision was to refuse to open the polls, knowing well the certainty of more violence and bloodshed if the election was allowed to continue. A disgraceful measure of the neglect with which the authorities had carried out their duties was the fact that not a single person was arrested for their involvement in the riot.

In the days following, the mood in Harbour Grace was reported as extremely tense, with "the inhabitants in great dread, one party as much as another, women and children running about seeking shelter." At a time when everyone should have been preparing for the lucrative Labrador fishery, the daily affairs and exchange of the community slowed considerably. Candidate Hayward even felt so threatened that he and his family took refuge in the military barracks.

The violence at Harbour Grace surprised no one, as there was a clearly established disposition for such. What infuriated most observers was Magistrate Pinsent's deplorable lack of leadership. Unlike previous

---

5. Some witnesses later claimed that the priest had been with the mob all along. Sergeant McCartney observed him "in the attitude of speaking to the crowd in a low tone, and tapping them encouragingly on the back." These reports are not substantiated, however. See *Journal of the House of Assembly* (1861).

governors who had often been criticized for not providing the means to repress rioting, Bannerman had equipped local authorities with ample support. He was so disturbed by the latest events that he ordered Pinsent temporarily relieved of his magisterial duties, and afterwards called for an investigative inquiry into the affair.[6]

Heightened anxieties instigated an immediate response in nearby communities, as well. In Spaniard's Bay dozens of people turned out with sealing guns to guard their town because of an alarming report that men from Riverhead were headed up the Bay, "murdering and destroying all Protestant life and property on the way." Even men from Bay Roberts were called on to aid their neighbours. The report was likely the overreaction of an anxious citizenry, however, and, after an uneventful night patrolling the streets, the following morning everyone returned to their homes. This story gained notoriety, though, when Bishop Mullock claimed that Denis O'Neil, a Roman Catholic of Spaniard's Bay, had his person and property threatened by the angry mob of Protestants. In an astonishing letter to Governor Bannerman, Mullock asserted that "a war of extermination against Her Majesty's Roman Catholic subjects" existed in Newfoundland, and warned that the priests might not be able to "restrain the feelings of their people." If the bishop was implying that Newfoundland's Roman Catholics were prepared for open revolt, then an audacious editorial in the ultra-conservative *Public Ledger* basically encouraged a Protestant uprising to counteract what *it* perceived as the Catholic threat:

> *A rally must be made. The Protestant men of Conception Bay must remember that the battle now being fought is openly and clearly admitted to be a battle between Protestants and Roman Catholics. It has been stirred up by Bishop Mullock himself - it has been admitted to by John Kent upon the hustings here; it must be fought upon those grounds, and the Protestants of Conception Bay are looked to*

---

6. As a result of Pinsent's weak performance, Magistrate Joseph Peters of Old Perlican was sent to replace him. Pinsent refused to recognize Peters's authority, and was subsequently removed from his post. Astonishingly, Pinsent was made a member of the Executive Council in 1862.

for a stern and unflinching determination to return their men - to defend and to maintain their rights and privileges come what may.

Both statements were extraordinary. At a time when restraint and compromise should have been called for, neither clerical leaders, politicians, nor journalists were promoting either. And things were about to get much worse, for nomination day violence also disrupted the proceedings in St. John's, merely previewing what was to come there.

In the electoral district of St. John's West, Kenneth McLea and an independent Roman Catholic named Barron were among five candidates seeking nomination for three available seats. Urged by their priests, local Catholics were pressured to vote Liberal. In a public pronouncement, the merchant supporters of McLea and Barron were declared "arbitrary oppressors" of the people. Posters nailed up throughout the city asked, "Will you patronize this cold, blood-thirsty crew, who have the blood of the *innocent Catholic electors on their guilty hands?*" The answer became clear during nomination, when dozens of stick-wielding men chased McLea's supporters from the hustings, then turned on his premises. In a desperate attempt to save the property from being destroyed, those sheltered inside warned they would open fire if attacked. Ignoring the angry shouts of the defenders, some of the excited mob scaled the gates and fences, while others hurled stones through windows and doors. The men inside made good their threat, and fired several pistol shots that wounded some of the mob. The scene, as ugly as it was, could have been much worse, had a company of troops from Fort William and two or three Catholic priests not arrived in the nick of time.

McLea had likely prepared his people for such an assault, for he clearly understood Newfoundland politics. Twenty years earlier he had been severely beaten during the campaign of his fellow Scotsman, James Douglas. Now a successful merchant with substantial holdings, he no doubt intended to protect his property. One Catholic newspaper, *The Record*, expressed its opinion that the actions of McLea's men had been premeditated. This accusation was followed with some inflammatory rhetoric: "Mr. McLea and his cowardly band of murderers have read for the people of St. John's a lesson which shall never be forgotten; blood is upon that cowardly band; that blood will be remembered!" The indiscriminate use of the word "murderers" by the editor, Thomas Talbot, when in truth no one had died in the incident, was abhorrent, and further incited the masses.

Surprisingly, the spark which propelled Newfoundland to the brink of civil war occurred in the normally quiet little outport of Cat's Cove, Conception Bay. Half a day's ride by carriage outside St. John's, this little village, populated by fewer than 300 Roman Catholic residents, might have seemed too insignificant to be of any consequence during the 1861 election.[7]

Protected from behind by high forested hills, the community offered visitors a scene of tranquility rather than turbulence, peace and harmony instead of rioting and bloodshed.

Four candidates contested the two seats in the district of Harbour Main, where Cat's Cove was located. All four were Liberal and Roman Catholic; however, George Hogsett, the former Attorney General, and Charles Furey had the support of the clergy, whereas Patrick Nowlan and Thomas Byrne were independent.[8]

Cat's Cove voters were partial to Nowlan and Byrne, a preference that greatly displeased Father Kyran Walsh from Harbour Main, whose coercive canvassing did nothing to alleviate the increasing unrest in the area.[9]

---

7. Cat's Cove would later change its name to Conception Harbour. According to the 1836 census, the population of the Cove was about 250 residents.

8. According to the *Dictionary of Canadian Biography*, George Hogsett was born and raised an Anglican, but converted to Catholicism probably in the early 1850s (s.vs "Hogsett, George James").

9. The testimony of David Kenny was somewhat typical: "It was because my Pastor advised me that I intended to vote for Hogsett and Furey. My Pastor advised me to go back on my word, which I had given to Nowlan and Byrne."

Trouble was inevitable when it became known that voters from Salmon Cove, a nearby community that was throwing its support behind Hogsett and Furey, were informed they had to cast their votes at Cat's Cove.[10]

Nasty words were exchanged following Mass one Sunday when Walsh announced he would lead the Salmon Cove voters. Several Cat's Cove men took exception to this, and made it clear they were not intimidated by Father Walsh. One of the more assertive leaders, Thomas St. John, even warned the priest that if a mob attempted to enter his community, the people would "throw them over the cliff." Most Roman Catholic priests in Newfoundland were not accustomed to being spoken to in such a disrespectful manner. Those loyal to Walsh apparently felt the same insult for, in the days prior to the election, several skirmishes broke out, the most serious occurring at Harbour Main. While returning from a meeting one night, Nowlan and several of his supporters were attacked, even shot at, by unknown parties. Added to the commotion were accusations that the chief returning officer, Patrick Strapp, was partial to Nowlan and Byrne, a nasty little rumour that resulted in Strapp's fence being torn down and his house slathered with tar.

When polling day arrived, no one questioned *if* there would be serious trouble; it was a certainty. For this reason, Tom St. John and five others drew up a letter and forwarded it to Father Walsh, via the local constable.

To the Very Rev. K. Walsh -
Cat's Cove, Harbour Main,
May 1st, 1861.

The people of Cat's Cove have been told that you intend to bring a mob to this place on the polling day, for the purpose of beating and intimidating the voters here. If such be your intention, we fear some-

---

10. This is not the same Salmon Cove where John Snow had been murdered. The community referred to here is further up the bay, and is today called Avondale.

thing bad may take place, for of course we must be prepared to defend ourselves, and would do so fearlessly, at the same time we wish you to understand that we are disposed to carry out the election peacefully, therefore if your party would allow our voters to go to the poll at Harbour Main and Holyrood, we will not interrupt your voters at this booth. We wish an answer to this note by the bearer.
We remain faithfully,

Maurice Mahoney	*Thomas St. John*
James Buck	*Thomas Connell*
Thomas Trickey	*Edward Bryan*

Clearly, this letter held a dual purpose. First, it left no doubt about the resolve of the Cat's Cove men to protect themselves and their property. But, it was also somewhat conciliatory, stating that the Cat's Cove men would allow the Salmon Cove voters to proceed unmolested into their community to cast their votes. From the accounts of several witnesses, Walsh chose to ignore this attempt at compromise, a decision that triggered an irreversible series of tragic events.

Shortly after dawn on polling day, shots were fired from Furey's wharf in Harbour Main, a predetermined signal for all supporters of Hogsett and Furey to assemble. In the semi-darkness they came, no doubt each aware of the potential repercussions of their plan. At 6:00 a.m. Walsh led about 250 men toward Cat's Cove, including the candidate Charles Furey, and his cousin George. Within this crowd were thirty-six voters from Salmon Cove.

The signal shots were heard by others that morning, as well. Patrick Strapp immediately recognized their significance, and watched from his front yard as the men gathered. These were his neighbours, his fellow Catholics. Some were longtime friends. Recent events, however, had demonstrated that politics often turned friends against one another. An unfortunate misjudgment on Strapp's part had antagonized his neighbours even more. Running the only boarding house in Harbour Main, he had opened it up to Nowlan and Byrne while they campaigned in the area, convincing the townspeople of Strapp's political inclinations. Friends had turned into enemies overnight, and they were not slow to show their disapproval, most likely with the blessing of Father Walsh. As Strapp walked past this assemblage of men on his way to open the nearest polling station, their bahs, hisses, and groans proved he had reason to fear for his personal safety. But the crowd had other aspirations, and their hostility toward Strapp was at this time only a minor distraction.

Men on both sides later offered differing accounts of what happened during the next several hours. Some claimed that during the march to Cat's Cove the mob was loud and unruly, smashing property belonging to supporters of Nowlan and Byrne along the way. Others claimed that the mob was no mob at all, just an assembly of men who walked peaceably in support of the Salmon Cove voters, and who displayed no tendency toward violence. Nevertheless, when the crowd rounded a bend in the road, about a mile from the hustings, they faced a barricade of fence posts and tree limbs. Some distance behind the barricade stood fifty or sixty men and women from Cat's Cove, determined, as promised, to turn back the intruders. Even though the defenders were armed with sticks and stones, and ready to fight, it was not immediately obvious to Father Walsh's crowd that some carried black powder sealing guns. Knowing well that they would be outnumbered, the Cat's Cove people had evened out their disadvantage.

Ordering his men to remain still, Walsh walked forward by himself, boldly defying his adversaries, who exhorted him, "Don't come! Don't come!" As he threw aside the barricade longers, two men from Cat's Cove acting as liaisons, Maurice Wade and John Keating, advanced in an apparent attempt to negotiate. These men suggested that if Walsh turned his people around, the Salmon Cove voters would be permitted to proceed to the hustings to vote.

Walsh's version of this interaction conflicted greatly with that of Wade and Keating, however. Walsh claimed that the only man he spoke with was Edward Bryan, and that it was Walsh himself who suggested the Salmon Cove voters be allowed to proceed if the others turned back. But his claim to have attempted a compromise is dubious: first, it seems unlikely that Walsh would have the rest of his crowd backtrack, after marching that distance to ensure the Salmon Cove men cast their votes without interference; and, second, the Cat's Cove letter that Walsh had chosen to ignore.

Either way, at this point another discrepancy is inherent in the various versions of the story. Cat's Cove men claimed that Walsh signalled his entire crowd to advance; Walsh himself claimed to have urged only the Salmon Cove voters to come forward. Whatever the priest's true intentions were, his people must have understood that the wave of his hand meant for them all to move. Almost immediately his men ripped down fences along the roadside, obviously intending to surround the defenders. The Cat's Cove men were quick to understand what was happening, but for a brief moment some uncertainty and panic probably surfaced. They had hoped that this show of force would deter Walsh's crowd, and that violence and bloodshed might be avoided. But as more of Walsh's men poured into the fields along the road, the Cat's Cove men could see they were about to be overrun. Unwilling to be chased from their own ground, several fired their weapons. About twenty of Walsh's party bravely responded with stones, but the general effect was a hasty retreat. Several Cat's Cove men gave chase, some firing as they ran. The count is uncertain, but some witnesses later claimed to have heard seven shots, others ten. When the smoke cleared, George Furey lay dead, and as many as ten others were wounded. It was over in a matter of minutes, and an uncomfortable silence immediately descended on the scene.

After the shooting the Cat's Cove contingent likely experienced a brief period of mixed emotions as they realized they had just killed at least one man, and possibly others. There was probably some degree of guilt, as well as fear. But there may also have been a sense of satisfaction at having turned away a hostile mob grossly superior in number. For the most part they remained convinced that theirs was the right cause. This defiance was exemplified by the fact that some men immediately returned to the hustings to cast their votes for Nowlan and Byrne. But, for the people of this normally quiet little outport, the story was unfortunately not over and, as they would later discover, peace and tranquility would not return for a long time.

In the meantime, deputy returning officers farther up the bay were having troubles of their own. At Kelligrews a mob of Hogsett and Furey supporters, reinforced with men from as far away as St. John's, brandished sticks and knives to intimidate their opponents and turn them from the poll. Anyone intending to vote for Nowlan and Byrne could not get near the door, even with the protection of the special constables, some of whom eventually abandoned their duty rather than risk their lives. Literally dozens of electors were denied the right to vote. On the other hand, George Hogsett and his people later claimed that their opponents had *their* own outsiders brought in to intimidate and coerce. For many voters, exercising the franchise had become largely an exercise in futility.

Around 3:00 p.m., the first of Father Walsh's defeated host straggled back into their respective communities. Some of the wounded were in bad shape, stumbling, bleeding heavily, and needing immediate medical assistance. By now the shock of being fired on had worn off, replaced by feelings of anger and calls for revenge. The reaction of onlookers watching this parade of vanquished was that of complete disbelief, especially when it became known that George Furey was dead.

Upon learning of the Cat's Cove riot, George Hogsett accompanied the thirty-six men from Salmon Cove straight to Strapp's polling station, and ordered the returning officer to accept their votes. This was the first Strapp had heard of the riot, though he was probably not surprised. Knowing that electors had to cast their votes at the polling station where they were registered, he was hesitant to comply with Hogsett's demand, at which point Hogsett scribbled some lines on a piece of paper and thrust it into his hand. The furious faces that surrounded him, along with muffled threats from several of those present, left Strapp with little choice but to do as he was told. As a precaution, though, in case the names should be questioned later on, he wisely jotted them down on a separate sheet of paper.

His compliance, reluctant as it was, was not enough to convince some doubters of his neutrality, for later that evening two men came to his door with an ominous warning. Supporters of Hogsett and Furey were determined to make him pay for his alleged favouritism, and were meeting at that moment to decide his fate. Around 9:00

p.m. there were more bad tidings, when two deputy returning officers showed up to inform Strapp, that the poll books from Topsail and Lance Cove had been stolen, and those from Colliers, Kelligrews, and Cat's Cove were missing. One of these officers, Strapp's own son Tom, had been mugged while transporting the poll books, and was bleeding from a broken nose. Later still, as the Strapp family lay in bed, large beach rocks were hurtled through their windows. The warnings were unmistakable. Patrick Strapp was a marked man.

The following morning a terrible feeling of dread permeated Conception Bay. Some of the wounded men had lain awake nearly the entire night, their families whispering prayers for their recovery in one breath and uttering pledges of revenge in another. It was early when George Hogsett knocked on Strapp's door, inquiring whether or not Patrick had all the poll books, and suggesting that Tom go in search of them. He did not stay long, but his appearance at such an hour, and his *coincidental* inquiry, should have aroused suspicion. Yet Strapp naively agreed to send Tom in pursuit of the missing books.

At around 9:00 or 9:30 p.m. that night Strapp received another strange visitor, this one bearing an urgent message for him to meet with Father Walsh. Clearly understanding that this was not a friendly invitation, Strapp hurried to the priest's residence, where he was ushered into the drawing room. During the course of Walsh's interview, which was basically a furtive attempt to convince Strapp of the wisdom in declaring for Hogsett and Furey, a group of people came to the door and engaged in hushed conversation with the priest. Re-entering the drawing room, Walsh sombrely advised Strapp that he ought to keep his son in better order, but did not elaborate. As Tom had not yet returned home, the priest's warning was especially ominous.

On Saturday, May 4, two days after the Cat's Cove riot, Hogsett again showed up at Strapp's home, this time with fifteen or twenty men. All were clearly displeased with Strapp for the delay in announcing the victorious candidates, a declaration they should have known would be challenged because the poll books had yet to be recovered. A written document that essentially declared Hogsett and Furey elected was then thrust upon Strapp, and he was advised that it was in his best interests to sign it. Under such duress Strapp agreed, but not before insisting that Hogsett write the following guarantee:

> *I, George Hogsett, hereby undertake to protect Mr. Strapp, Returning Officer for the Southern District of Conception Bay, in the discharge of his duty in legally declaring the Polls for the said Election.*

Strapp may have had several reasons for desiring Hogsett to draw up this note. He was certainly doubtful about the legality of the thirty-six Salmon Cove votes, so he may have been hoping that Hogsett's promise would aid him in the event of prosecution. There was also the likelihood of violent retribution from one side or the other, no matter which candidates he declared elected. It is unlikely, though, that Hogsett could have afforded much protection, if, in fact, he had any intention of keeping his word.

Strapp's tribulations were only beginning, for two days later Magistrate Charles Simms, on orders from the government, sailed into Harbour Main with a contingent of soldiers under the command of Colonel Grant. They caused quite a stir as they marched directly to the returning officer's house, with young boys and curious onlookers in tow. Simms, an impatient, no-nonsense individual with a reputation for quick, decisive action, announced that he was in Harbour Main to protect Strapp in carrying out his duty. He then handed over three of the missing poll books, which he had acquired from a man named Power in Brigus. It is unclear how Power had obtained these books, but presumably he had been too alarmed with all the violence to return them earlier.

Strapp was in a dilemma. The new books clearly indicated that, without the thirty-six Salmon Cove votes, Nowlan and Byrne were the winners. With this proof Strapp's position became even more precarious, and he expressed his reservations to the magistrate. If he changed his earlier declaration, and returned Nowlan and Byrne in place of Hogsett and Furey, he would undoubtedly face the wrath of hundreds of vengeful voters. Making Strapp's decision even more difficult was the unexpected appearance of Father Walsh. The priest initially maintained that he would see no harm come to the distraught man should he be compelled to make a new declaration. This was likely a ruse for the magistrate's benefit, for when Strapp appeared willing to overturn the election Walsh strongly intimated that he might not guarantee protection after all. This sudden repeal provoked Magistrate Simms to issue a stern warning of his own. "If any injury happened to Mr. Strapp's house, or person, or family, the moral, if not the legal responsibility, would attach to you."

The returning officer, visibly shaken by Walsh's veiled threat, then retired to an adjoining room with the poll books, and motioned for Simms to follow him. He repeated his fears to the magistrate but, after some urging, agreed to sign a writ that declared Nowlan and Byrne the elected members for the district of Harbour Main. In so doing, Strapp knew that he was carrying out his sworn duty, but also inviting serious repercussions upon his household.

The general election of 1861 eventually concluded with the Conservatives winning a narrow margin of just two seats. It was by no means an overwhelming endorsement of the Hoyles party. Instead, Liberals throughout the colony protested, particularly as four candidates still claimed victory in Harbour Main, and no return was allowed for Harbour Grace. Though the Tories had the majority, it was a tenuous lead at best. In the wake of all the violence, no right-minded individual on the island expected a gentle return to government, now that a map of the Avalon Peninsula looked like a military campaign chart.

Amid much anxiety, therefore, the new House of Assembly was set to open on May 13. The word was that the two ousted candidates from Harbour Main would take their seats in defiance of the returning officer's decision, and a crowd of about 2,000 had gathered beneath the steps of the Colonial Building to ensure that they be allowed to do so. Present also were two of the St. John's magistrates, Peter Carter and Thomas Bennett, along with scores of special constables sworn in earlier, as well as a detachment of soldiers under Colonel Grant.

The crowd appeared menacing from the start. Fuelled with a

dangerous sense of righteous indignation, they had not come just to demonstrate. Bishop Mullock's earlier warning of a "war of extermination" rang loudly in the ears of many Catholics, and the outcome of the election was regarded as proof of the devious lengths to which Protestant leaders would go to eliminate their enemies.

Just after 1:00 p.m. men within the front ranks of the mob made an attempt to break through the main door of the Colonial Building. As the constables were barely able to contain them, Justice Carter read the Riot Act, issuing warnings that he would use whatever force necessary to clear the steps. But the crowd grew in strength, their increasing numbers unperturbed by the magistrate's words, the constabulary, or, for that matter, the soldiers lining Military Road. They cursed and taunted the defenders, goading them to act on their threats, and exhibited signs of becoming more violent. Most of the mob had heard of the soldiers' anaemic defence of Harbour Grace, and probably felt confident that their presence that day would be equally unassertive. Carter, however, was not a timid Pinsent. Seeing that this crowd was not easily intimidated, Carter turned to Colonel Grant and instructed him to disperse the crowd. The troops were then ordered to load their weapons.

Inside, Hogsett and Furey had taken their seats, as promised, only to be ordered out of the building when they refused to relinquish them. It took cajoling from the prime minister before Furey eventually realized the absurdity of this demonstration, and agreed to leave. Hogsett, clearly the more stubborn of the pair, had to be carried from the chamber and out onto the front steps. The appearance of their champion being so rudely manhandled stirred the crowd even more, many of whom then hoisted the former attorney general into the air and hustled him back inside the building.

The attention of many protestors was detracted at this time by the sight of Governor Bannerman exiting the building from a side door. But the governor's honour guard was prepared to intervene, and kept the crowd at a safe distance. Nevertheless, rocks and yells of contempt pelted his carriage as it sped by, transporting Sir Alexander to the relative safety of nearby Government House.

Taking advantage of this distraction, three government members attempted their own getaway, but someone in the crowd observed them. Two were chased back inside, while the unfortunate Kenneth McLea was pursued up Military Road. Pummelled with sticks and stones, he finally found refuge inside the home of his rival, R.J. Parsons. The crowd remaining in front of the Colonial Building then turned their wrath upon the building itself, smashing windows and attempting to pull doors from their hinges.

Riot Acts and loaded weapons could not deter this crowd, but maybe the arrival of three Roman Catholic priests could. In order to give the priests the opportunity to converse with their people the troops held their positions, and their fire. Although there was a noticeable cooling of tempers as a result of the priests' efforts, it still took a promise that Hogsett would address the crowd from the Cathedral steps before they agreed to leave the premises. At about 5:00 p.m., with the crisis temporarily averted, Colonel Grant marched most of his troops back to Fort William, leaving a small body under Captain Hanrahan to guard the Colonial Building.

But the furore had not been satiated, merely relocated.

Within an hour, Magistrate Bennett again called on Grant to assist the civil authorities, this time in Water Street, where the mob had reassembled and were attacking property owned by supporters of Nowlan and Byrne. Grant immediately sent a detachment of about eighty soldiers under the command of Lieutenant Quill, promising to be there himself shortly.

By the time Grant joined his men, several merchant premises had been ransacked, and the troops were being harassed by a huge crowd numbering in the thousands.[11]

A fearful noise arose from the debris-ridden street, as shouts of anger and alarm mixed with the sound of crashing glass and splintering wood. As Grant sat astride his horse and gauged the devastation before him, he too became the target of insults and projectiles.

The size of the mob and the magnitude of their fervour intimated an uprising, not merely a political riot. Several priests moved through

---

11. Grant estimated the crowd at about 10,000; this may have been an exaggeration.

the crowd, frantically exhorting them to disband, but with little effect. After a while, Grant was approached by one of the priests who suggested that he retire his men some distance to the east, as their presence probably added to the crowd's agitation. Grant initially refused, stating that his men were present because of a requisition for assistance from the civil authorities, and he could not retreat even if he wished. As the crowd showed no signs of dispersing, and, in fact, were increasing in number, Magistrate Bennett agreed to allow the troops to be moved away so that the priests might more easily convince their people to go home in peace.

Unfortunately, this movement did not have the desired effect. The unrestrained mob ignored the pleas of their clergy, and followed the retreating soldiers, hurling stones from behind and along the sides. When the troops were adjacent to the Market House, Grant could see that his withdrawal had not calmed the crowd at all, but had exposed his men to more harassment. He therefore ordered the troops to halt and turn to face their tormentors. At this point they were under tremendous pressure to maintain an orderly front, having already endured over an hour of abuse. Watching from his store across the street, Thomas Mabin wondered at their fortitude, later commenting, "It was a bitter sight to see the soldiers pelted so." Blood and bruises appeared on the faces of many, including Colonel Grant, but the soldiers held fast.

Suddenly, in a moment of reckless bravado, one individual attempted to pull Grant from his horse. The alarmed animal reared and lashed out with its hooves, forcing Grant to wrestle with the reins in order to maintain control. A constable standing nearby saw Grant's predicament and moved swiftly to give assistance, only to be assaulted by several other men himself. The front line of soldiers then rushed forward. More stones rained down. The noise and confusion increased.

The original offender was finally apprehended and secured within the ranks, but Grant now had to contend with a new threat from the street above. Having observed a vantage point on the hill next to the Market House, several hundred rioters had climbed there, and were pounding the soldiers below. Many, emboldened by the soldier's reticence, taunted them to "Fire! Fire!"

Grant realized that his men were now in a most adverse position—almost surrounded by an extremely hostile crowd. Fearful of the outcome of this prolonged confrontation, and weary of the continuous stoning of his men, Grant turned to Magistrate Bennett and in desperation hollered, "Am I to fire?"

Probably realizing the necessity of deadly force at this point, but still not willing to commit himself, Bennett replied, "Well sir, you must use whatever measures you think necessary."

Bennet's words were hardly out of his mouth, when suddenly a shot rang out from the hill. The bullet apparently ricocheted off Sergeant Patrick Matthews's sword, breaking it, but causing no other harm. Men near Matthews thought he was seriously wounded, though, as blood ran from a cut on his head. They cried now in desperation, "Colonel, they are firing on us!"

After several hours of insult, humiliation, and injury, Grant was not prepared to watch his men being murdered in the street. He then gave Lieutenant Quill instructions to clear the hill. But even at this point the officers were uncertain over the amount of force to use, with Quill desiring to know his orders should the column be directly attacked by the crowd. Grant's response was noncommittal: "You will receive orders."

Frustrated, Quill led his eighty-four men up the sloping ground, possibly hoping that the crowd would give way. But instead of retreating, the crowd met Quill's advance with another barrage of stones, their bold determination intensifying. Marching along the flank of the leading section, Quill was keenly aware of his men's desire to retaliate, but calmly urged them on. As more and more stones found their mark, it became increasingly difficult for the soldiers to hold their fire. Several bled profusely from head and facial wounds. Others favoured a leg or an arm as they marched.

Then came the defining moment, the incident which would be debated and talked about for months, even years. The leading section of troops halted, and fired at the crowd on the summit. It was a ragged volley, not a uniform discharge of weapons like that delivered by a trained body of soldiers, thus indicating that some of the men may not have heard the order to fire. In fact, both Quill and Grant later denied giving the order. Seeing the deadly effect of the guns, both officers charged to the front of their men and demanded they cease firing. The crowd had temporarily retreated, but within a few minutes reassembled. When another shot rang out from the hill, several soldiers returned fire, creating even more confusion and hostility, and making it tremendously difficult for Grant and Quill to regain control. Eventually though, despite more rocks and insults, the troops were reorganized and led back down the hill. In their wake they left three men dead, and twenty wounded. Numbered within the latter group was a priest named O'Donnell, who had been exhorting the people to disband.

After some delay, a decision was made to march the soldiers back to Fort Townshend, though it was clear that the mob was undaunted by the military's considerable show of force. The authorities likely felt at this point that to continue the confrontation would only result in a greater effusion of blood on both sides. But the march back was not an easy one. As the troops climbed Prescott Street, dozens of rioters attacked the column from alleyways and side streets, hurling stones and injuring more soldiers. Without orders, some in the column fired back at their tormentors; these men were later reprimanded, and one, James Thompson, was even placed under arrest.

Suddenly, the bells of the Roman Catholic Cathedral rang loudly over the city, beckoning people from the dreadful scene of carnage and turmoil. The crowd's immediate response was yet another extraordinary example of obedience to their church. By the thousands, men dropped their weapons and walked up the hill and through the great doors of the Cathedral to hear the words of their clerical leader. By this act, Bishop Mullock almost single-handedly ended the riot, a feat for which he later took full credit. However, while many applauded Mullock's action, others pointed out correctly that if he had known he possessed such authority, he should have summoned his people long before they lay dying in the street.[12]

The peace and quietness that prevailed over the city in the hours immediately afterwards was not indicative of the emotions of its citizens. Most people remained inside their homes contemplating the tragic events of the day, but some troublemakers were not content with the degree of chaos that St. John's had witnessed. Later that evening, Bishop Feild was returning home, when he was pelted with a shower of stones. Though his injuries were only slight, Anglicans viewed this as a dastardly and unjustified attack on a man of the cloth. Hours later, Field's stable was set on fire, as was Judge Robinson's. Though Feild's building was saved, due to the timely response of close neighbours, Robinson's stable and its contents were completely destroyed.

It was obvious that any attempt to return to normalcy would not be easy following May 13. Although the city of St. John's had an established history of politico-sectarian riots, recent events had elevated the emotions of its citizens to alarming new heights. Animosity and fear were paramount, and accusations of blame were hurled from partisans on both sides. After May 13 it was impossible to avoid confrontation. Enemies inevitably crossed paths as people went about their daily business and, as a result, reports of assault became common. On May 15 arsonists burned Prime Minister Hoyles's summer cottage. Three days later, Thomas Talbot of *The Record* printed a fiery editorial about the shootings at the McLea premises on nomination day.

These assassins are walking daily in the public streets before our eyes, while the victims of their murderous onslaught, honest, patriotic, and noble-hearted young men, are writhing in pain and anguish upon

---

12. In a letter to the Duke of Newcastle, August 14, Governor Bannerman insinuated that Mullock may actually have conspired with the leaders of the mob: "Regular signals were passing between Water Street and the Cathedral, and if there had been any great desire to prevent mischief the Cathedral bells would have been tolled two hours before they were" (CO 194/166, 281).

*their beds from all but mortal wounds inflicted upon them by these
base, cowardly, and demoniac assassins.*

As proponents contemplated these impassioned words, 200 soldiers
of Her Majesty's 62nd Regiment arrived from Halifax, in response to a
request by Governor Bannerman, who saw the colony's military presence
as terribly inadequate. He would later petition the Home Government
for a permanent increase in the garrison, including a battery of artillery.

As the soldiers disembarked in St. John's, more trouble
unfolded in Harbour Main. Patrick Strapp had been keeping a low
profile since his controversial return. But the locals were not about
to forgive and forget. On May 18 a vengeful mob of no less than
200 descended on his property, and pulled his house, his stable,
and other outbuildings to the ground. Strapp barely escaped with
his life, but his horses and cattle were either run off or killed. Most
alarming of all, though, was the disappearance of a little seven-year-
old girl, who fled into the nearby woods during the attack. For the
anti-clerics, a report that Father Walsh had witnessed most of the
destruction but did nothing to stop it was more proof that Roman
Catholic priests were encouraging civil disobedience.[13]

Strapp himself found shelter in Brigus, while his family stayed
with friends at Harbour Main. Terrorized, and immensely upset with
the absence of security provided for him and his family, he sent off a
telegram to Prime Minister Hoyles two days later:

*Our lives in danger. Are you prepared to send protection or not -
answer quickly. Awaiting your answer since Saturday.*

Strapp did not know that Bannerman had already ordered fifty
soldiers to proceed to Harbour Main under the cover of darkness
to round up as many of the mob as they could. Late at night, in a
well-coordinated surprise manoeuvre, five of the ringleaders were
arrested as they lay sleeping in their beds, and were hustled to the

---

13. In a letter to the Duke of Newcastle, June 4, 1861, Bannerman refers
to this report, but does not name the witness.

St. John's jail. Unaware of the soldiers' presence, the rest of the community slept, offering no resistance. It was a small, but not insignificant, sign that the authorities remained in control.

Amid this ever-present threat of violence, the Conservatives attempted to govern the embattled colony. Their first order of business was to set up committees to investigate the recent troubles, and to determine the true representatives for Harbour Main.[14]

There was also the issue of a necessary by-election at Harbour Grace, since that town could not continue indefinitely without representation. With the Conservatives still holding onto a frail majority, Hoyles understood the significance of these outcomes. But if anyone had more to worry about than Hoyles, it was undoubtedly Governor Bannerman. He had, after all, engineered the fall of the former government, causing the whole mess in the first place. Whether or not his actions had been justified, the fact remained that if the Liberals returned to power, especially after all that had happened, Bannerman was finished. On the other hand, if the Conservatives maintained a majority, it would be perceived as an endorsement of Bannerman's actions.

On May 23 a large funeral Mass was held for the three men killed during the St. John's riot. Examination of the bodies by the coroner, as well as a prolonged period of grieving, apparently delayed the interment.[15]

Tremendous excitement surrounded the event, but the people's emotions were this time kept in check by Bishop Mullock. The liberal media, however, when reporting on the ceremony, offered no such restraint in their condemnation of the military:

It must be discovered who gave the order for the troops to fire with ball-loaded rifles upon the unarmed and flying multitudes. The necessity for such a murderous, cowardly order must be made apparent.

---

14. For the testimonies made during this inquiry, see *Journal of the House of Assembly* (1861).

15. Only two of the bodies were examined by a coroner. The family of the third man refused to allow the authorities to touch his body, even threatening to murder the surgeons.

For what could be conceived more murderous and cowardly than for an armed body of men to fire upon an indiscriminate crowd of unarmed men, women, and children![16]

In the meantime, circumstances in Conception Bay remained perilous. On May 21 and 25 *The Public Ledger* reported two more assaults on Protestant clergy. At Southern Gut,[17] the Anglican Reverend Blackman was recuperating after being stoned by unknown individuals, and two men in Harbour Grace were in jail after Reverend Jones had been "grossly insulted." Ever since April 26, residents of all the major towns walked cautiously about their business, or stayed home, thus prompting a lengthy and detailed letter to Bannerman from the district's leading merchants. Magistrate Peters's telegraph to Hoyles was succinct:

Considerable excitement, frequent assaults, houses injured, and angry threats alarmingly prevalent. Military protection very much needed. Please reply.

His plea had gotten through just in time, for shortly afterwards the telegraph lines in several communities were severed, ensuring that messages to and from the capital would now depend on the packet boats, slowing the means of communication considerably.

On April 30, mob violence broke out again at Carbonear and Harbour Grace. In Carbonear, dozens of men took to the streets after dark, smashing windows, breaking doors, and stealing whatever they could. They met with considerable resistance, however, when a second mob attacked the first with a liberal application of sticks and stones. Firearms were then employed. Numerous individuals were severely wounded. Several hours later, with the desire to fight finally expended, everyone hobbled back to what remained of their homes. Harbour Grace police had been unable to lend assistance as they had to contend

---

16. *The Patriot and Terra Nova Herald*, formerly known as *The Newfoundland Patriot*, May 27, 1861.

17. Called South River today.

with problems of their own. In the evening, a mob had taken over the police station, beaten the officers, then freed one of their own who had been arrested earlier for assaulting Benjamin Sweetland. Though the identities of some in the crowd were known to the authorities, these men were never made to answer for their crime, largely because the police force was so few in number it was unable to guarantee that another assault on the jail would be repelled.

Against such a violent backdrop it is surprising that any investigation could be carried out at all. By June the select committee looking into the Harbour Main election, composed of both Conservatives *and* Liberals, had interviewed dozens of witnesses. A clear image of intimidation and election-tampering swiftly formed. Members of this committee were not surprised to learn, however, that some of the witnesses had been threatened prior to testifying. The returning officer at Holyrood, William Holden, for example, refused to answer his summons after receiving a particularly shocking letter:

> *Now, Mr. Holden, a few words with you. I send you this letter to inform you that you ought never to be tired giving thanks to God for preserving you from our clutches when you were in St. John's last week. We were looking for you when you were here, but we could not make you out; but as sure as God is in Heaven, if we had happened to catch you, you would never go home alive, you two-faced Tory w—eson.*[18]

Despite the considerable interference, the committee completed its mandate, and by the end of June had decided that Nowlan and Byrne were the legitimate winners. No one was surprised with the immediate backlash from Liberals, both in- and outside the House. However, these complaints of partiality were countered by committee members themselves, who agreed that there had been a complete and objective examination of the evidence.

There was more bad news for Hogsett and Furey when the committee investigating the May 13 riot released its report. The general

---

18. See Appendix 10 for the complete letter (*Journal of the House of Assembly* [1861]).

consensus was that the military had endured great provocation on that day, and had acted within reason. Hogsett and some of his supporters responded with a petition signed by 8,000 people, accusing Governor Bannerman and Prime Minister Hoyles of setting up a "Reign of Terror, Tyranny, and Fraud," and calling for both to be removed. *The Record*'s highly invective editorials somehow appeared in sympathetic newspapers on the other side of the Atlantic. Champions of the liberal cause in Ireland, such as *The Vindicator* of Galway, published their distaste for the "Orange conspiracy" in Newfoundland. But in London, the Duke of Newcastle, who had been on tenterhooks since Bannerman had thrown out the Kent government in March, expressed tremendous relief with the outcome of the investigations, and sent a letter of approval to Bannerman.

Though the committee's findings were good news for the Conservatives, neither Prime Minister Hoyles nor Governor Bannerman were very optimistic, knowing that the Harbour Grace by-election still loomed. The Liberals could easily return two candidates in this notoriously violent district, and probably regain control of the House. But for a few brief months, a relative peace settled over the colony as men from every Conception Bay community fished on the Labrador. Elections or no elections, people still had to eat, and the annual migration north had already been delayed.

This left the media, the clergy, and the politicians to keep the fires of contention burning. *The Record*, for example, encouraged its readers to "celebrate the butchery and slaughter of the people of St. John's committed by the Orange party" at a public meeting set for August 13. Subsequent issues accused Bannerman of being an "Orangeman and an arch-Tory," allegations that likely confounded him, in view of his previous association with Daniel O'Connell and other Liberals inside the British parliament. Bishop Mullock himself did little to alleviate the tension, with conspicuous warnings of "long dark nights" on the return of the fishermen.[19]

---

19. The bishop's insinuation of more trouble was made at his residence when he was entertaining the French consul and several naval officers.

Bannerman sent the evidence to the Duke of Newcastle as justification for his continued requests for an increase in the island's military. He had already determined that Harbour Grace would be afforded a greater degree of protection during the impending November by-election, and his intentions were public knowledge. In October, almost as the first of the Labrador schooners re-entered the harbours, *The Record* published its most disturbing editorial yet—a challenge to the governor:

> *Will the Catholics and Protestants of that district [Harbour Grace] cut each other's throats for the special gratification and profit of his Excellence and His Excellency's little contemptible Orange faction of St. John's? Will they do this we ask? Never: be assured, never. But, says somebody, Sir Alexander will repeat his former experiment, and send Queen's troops to force compliance with his wishes. We challenge him to do it. His Excellency cannot dare do it. The first moment he moved a body of troops against the constitutional independence of the people - that moment a civil war was proclaimed, his allegiance to the Crown became forfeited, he stood before the country a traitor to his Sovereign; and as a traitor should have to be dealt with by the people. Repeat this experiment! Ah, such an experiment cannot afford a repetition. Try it, Sir Alexander - if you dare.*

And there it was: the unveiled threat of civil war. A "treasonable threat," in the words of Governor Bannerman, and one he would not let pass. It was clear that *The Record* did not speak for all Roman Catholic citizens, nor for all Roman Catholic priests, but these words in print were unnerving. Civil disobedience was one thing, civil war another. Yet Bannerman was undeterred, and in response to a petition from the Harbour Grace magistrates he reiterated his assurances that the town would have more than adequate protection during its by-election. A revival of hostilities there, and especially the murder of a police officer in late October, emphasized the importance of Bannerman's commitment.[20]

---

20. On the night of October 22, Constable Jeremiah Dunn was struck on the head with a stone as he and other officers attempted to make an arrest. He died five days later, having never regained consciousness.

As the by-election drew near, all eyes were on Harbour Grace.

Then, just days from the reopening of the polls, Bishop Mullock had a change of heart, or at least a reconsideration of priorities. Knowing well that he influenced his congregation on secular as well as clerical matters, Mullock now desired to lead his people away from what was clearly a path with serious ramifications. He likely saw the direction in which the colony was headed, with talk of civil war and challenges issued to the queen's representative. He undoubtedly realized that Bannerman would not, could not, retreat from such a blatant threat. Therefore, in a pastoral letter published on November 1, he called for peace and goodwill during the forthcoming campaign. Communicating with Bannerman, Mullock gave assurances that he would assist Bishop Dalton of Harbour Grace to prevent a reoccurrence of the recent violence. Mullock stated his intention to penalize by excommunication any of his people using firearms, stones, or other deadly weapons with the intent to kill or injure, or anyone caught maliciously burning, wrecking, or destroying houses or property. After months of almost continuous threats, here finally was the guidance and support that Bannerman had sought from Mullock. In all likelihood, though, Bannerman was not convinced, for his plan to send troops to Harbour Grace remained unaltered.

On November 20, Bannerman kept his word. Not only was there a military detachment present as Harbour Grace electors went to the polls, but also two warships rode at anchor just offshore. In a strange sense, the long-anticipated, much-dreaded by-election was anti-climatic: "Throughout the day not a gun was fired, not a sword drawn, nor even a policeman's staff called into action." More than 1300 people cast their votes in an unusually quiet contest, which resulted in the return of the two Conservative candidates, Hayward and Moore. Given that they had polled more than double the votes for Prendergast, it seems clear that many Roman Catholics may have reversed their political allegiances or, without clerical pressure, felt free to vote as they wished.

The results ensured the House majority required for the Hoyles party to carry on as the government and, in no small sense, vindicated

Bannerman's course of action since dismissing Kent's Liberals. But, more significantly, the successful preservation of the Conservative government provided an opportunity for Prime Minister Hoyles to heal Newfoundland society. In the wake of all the rioting and bloodshed, most people were of the opinion that this was almost an impossibility. To the surprise of many, at the next opening of the Legislature Hoyles offered cabinet positions to both John Kent and Ambrose Shea. It was a noble gesture, sensitive to the will and needs of the Roman Catholic population. But Kent and Shea refused, probably feeling that their people required more time to reflect and heal before such an offer would be acceptable. Hoyles was undeterred. Clearly understanding the danger of religious involvement in politics, he determined that to weaken this influence he had to eliminate one of the most prevalent motives for conflict, that of unequal sharing of government patronage.[21]

Concurrently, another drama unfolded at the Supreme Court as four separate trials for those arrested during the various disturbances got underway. Chief Justice Francis Brady, a Roman Catholic respected by all classes and denominations, expressed his concern that personal or sectarian feelings were often carried into the jury box, resulting in improper verdicts. His apprehension would soon be justified, as the first two cases saw the acquittal of everyone involved in the St. John's nomination day violence, and the charges against George Hogsett for allegedly leading the mob on May 13, thrown out.

In the third case, the Cat's Cove men charged with the murder of George Furey selected a Protestant-only jury, as they had no faith in the supposed impartiality of their co-religionists. Although the defendants were found guilty, the Protestant jury recommended the judge's leniency. Apparently bothered by the actions of Father Walsh on May 13, Brady asserted that the march on Cat's Cove had been "far worse than silly or foolish," and that the defendants had been provoked. He then ordered sentences of less than two years, inclusive of the time already spent in jail.

---

21. Both Conservatives and Liberals had been guilty of this.

The fourth case was against the men who had destroyed Strapp's property on May 18. During the trial none of the terrified Strapp family gave adequate testimony regarding the attack on their household, thus frustrating the Crown's case and resulting in the charges being dropped. Commenting on the Strapp case, the editor of *The Public Ledger* was rigid: "The only explanation suggested for this conduct is that the witnesses are Roman Catholics, and that ghostly terrors have been brought to bear on them - they being under the spiritual rule of the same priest who led the mob."

Bishop Mullock eyed the Supreme Court proceedings as closely as anyone. Upset by Brady's censure of Father Walsh, and displeased by the light sentences handed out to the Cat's Cove men, Mullock expressed his opinion that there was no justice on the Bench, even when it was occupied by one of his own faith. Then, in *partially* fulfilling his earlier commitment to Bannerman, Mullock instructed his clergy to pronounce the Church's sentence of excommunication on any person "using firearms with the unlawful intention of killing or wounding." Notably excluded from these instructions, either by intention or oversight, was the bishop's earlier condemnation of anyone caught using sticks or other deadly weapons for the same purpose.

If he had been angered by Brady's leniency towards the Cat's Cove men, Mullock must have been irate when he learned that Bannerman, on closely examining the extenuating circumstances of their case, had decided to release them. The presentation of a convincing petition, signed by hundreds who sympathized with the incarcerated men, motivated his decision. The backlash from *The Record* was swift and predictable. Catholics who had signed this petition were berated and scorned. The original crime, it said, was nothing short of murder, a transgression for which the guilty should pay. Thus, if the Cat's Cove men had been counting on a pleasant trip home, they were in for quite a shock. A public celebration given in honour of their renewed freedom, complete with music and dancing, was considered by Mullock as a personal affront to his authority, and he spitefully pronounced the following decree:

Having made the necessary enquiries we have been convinced of the truth of an outrage on Religion and humanity, perpetrated in Cat's Cove, by public rejoicing and hoisting Flags, not only in the Harbour, but at the place where George Furey was murdered, on the return of the "Convicts from the St. John's Jail." Brutal and savage as that act was, this last outrage shows that the perpetrators are a disgrace to human nature and that the place they inhabit is branded with the curse of Cain. Therefore invoking the Holy Name of God, etc., we ordain that no Mass be said, no Station held, and no Sacrament, unless to the dying (and Baptism in the case of extreme necessity) be administered in Cat's Cove, for the next twelve months, from this date. The Church will remain closed for the same time. We pray that God may enlighten the darkened understanding, and soften the stony hearts of these people, that by sincere repentance they may escape the awful judgement which His judgement holds over them.

With this oppressive enunciation Mullock's bias against dissident members of his own church was abundantly clear. Even though he severely chastised the people of Cat's Cove for conduct he deemed outrageous, he chose to ignore a similar celebration in Harbour Main on behalf of the five liberated men from that community. His discrimination was not lost on Bannerman, who considered Mullock's decree "worthy of the Dark Ages of the Church," an opinion silently shared by many Roman Catholics.

Bannerman grew increasingly satisfied with one unforeseen development: the decline of the Catholic Church's influence in matters of local politics. There was clearly a split between those who steadfastly adhered to the wishes of their spiritual leaders, and those who desired to make their own choices at the polls. The debacle at Harbour Main was evidence that this emerging schism could pit Catholic against Catholic in a dispute just as nasty as any row with Protestants. This realignment of Catholic ideology, if it could be called that, was confirmed when clerical influence failed to reinstate George Hogsett at another by-election at St. John's later that year. His opponent was an independent Catholic, a fact demonstrating that "the great political-ecclesiastical confederacy"[22] in which the Roman Catholic Liberal party dominated Newfoundland's House of Assembly for almost thirty years, had ended.

By the mid-1860s an entirely new issue, one that spanned the borders of religious affiliation, stirred up emotions: a controversial debate over confederation with the rest of British North America. Proponents for and against came from all denominations and classes. The new Catholic champion, Ambrose Shea, for example, along with such Protestant stalwarts as Frederic Carter, was strongly in favour of confederation. The greatest irony was undoubtedly that, in their opposition to confederation, most of the colony's merchants forged an allegiance with the majority of its Roman Catholic citizens. Under the leadership of a staunch Anglican, Charles Fox Bennett, the anti-confederates eventually succeeded in rejecting the infamous Canadian wolf in 1869.

The extraordinary events of 1861 had long-lasting positive effects for Newfoundland. Politicians, clergymen, merchants, and newspapermen finally realized the treacherous state into which Newfoundland politics had slipped, and a willingness to co-operate slowly developed among the leaders of various institutions. Following 1861, the so-called "denominational compromise" settled the claims of discrimination previously declared by Roman Catholics, and, in effect, eliminated the political interference of the clergy. The compromise, which had been part of Prime Minister Hoyles's mission, guaranteed equal opportunities for *all* denominations to government patronage and jobs. Even though this new policy helped to maintain a relative peace among the citizens of Newfoundland, it would be an exaggeration to state that they now lived in harmony. Thirty years later, the words of former Governor Thomas Cochrane were still true. There would be more violence yet, terrible incidents that would shake the roots of Newfoundland society, but at least the outrageous scenes of the past would not be repeated during future political campaigns.

---

22. Coined by Henry Winton Jr. in his *Chronicles of 1861*; quoted in Gertrude Gunn, *The Political History of Newfoundland, 1832 to 1864* (Toronto: University of Toronto Press, 1966).

Any examination of the turbulent 1861 election raises several concerns that should be at least briefly addressed. Prominent among these is the *alleged* threat of civil war, alluded to by Talbot in *The Record* on May 18. Was there any *real* threat, or were Talbot's words simply an exaggeration to further a political agenda? We have, after all, seen how biased and unethical the media could be in Newfoundland during this period. Maybe Talbot's editorial was merely an honest misinterpretation of civil disorders, which were serious but not a step toward actual rebellion. If any politicians thought as Talbot did, they did not express it in the House of Assembly, the proper venue for discussing matters of such consequence. It would, however, be negligent to ignore or minimize Talbot's remarks. If we consider the fact that Talbot was a great admirer of Bishop Mullock, the man responsible for placing him as editor at *The Record*, and was, in all likelihood, privy to some of the prelate's personal observances and opinions, we might understand the motivation behind Talbot's editorial. It was common knowledge within a circle of confidants that Mullock desired to see Great Britain at war with France and America, and, in consequence, relegated to a third-rate power.[23]

By itself this statement would probably be insignificant, and though unpatriotic, hardly treasonous. But when the editor of *The Record* railed of Great Britain's losing "the key to the St. Lawrence," there likely was some nervous shuffling of feet in the chambers of the Colonial Building.

Others in Newfoundland also commented on the rebellious nature of the recent riots. In his address to the Grand Jury on November 20, Chief Justice Brady spoke of the "existence of a civil or intestine warfare raging" in certain parts of the island. His references to the "unhappy condition of society" and the "angry feelings which contested elections have most unfortunately generated amongst the people of this country, ever since the earliest concession of representative institutions" may have merely stated the obvious, but they were

---

23. Ibid. This declaration is from a confidential exchange between Bannerman and Newcastle, July 31, 1861 (CO 194/166).

only now being acknowledged by high-ranking Roman Catholics. Brady's assertions were likely shared by many others.

Since this book tells only the story of Irish Catholic/English Protestant relations in Newfoundland, we will not dwell on a lengthy analysis of our *brush* with civil warfare, though further study may indeed be warranted. It may be enough to say here that the old colony had her issues. Interestingly, three years after the rioting, in a letter to Newcastle's successor, Governor Bannerman expressed his belief that he had averted an "actual rebellion" in 1861. He may have been right.

CONCLUSION

*I would here in conclusion, respectfully give it as my opinion, that it was
and is no political contest, but purely a religious one - Roman Catholic
against Protestant.*

Magistrate John Rorke
Carbonear, 1861

At this point a clear understanding of why our English and Irish ancestors did not get along may be called for; however, such in-depth study
is probably better left for a graduate thesis. Nevertheless, the issue
requires some small commentary here in these closing paragraphs in
order to appreciate the roots of this rivalry, which for too long has
been excluded from polite conversation.

There were numerous incidents of political interference by
Roman Catholic priests from that first election of 1832 when Bishop
Fleming publicly declared whose corner he stood in, to the 1861
debacle, which culminated in Bishop Mullock's censure of his own
people at Cat's Cove. Supported by politically active priests like Troy,
Walsh, and Cummings, the Roman Catholic leadership controlled
the Conservatives, and often through the use of questionable tactics
kept the reformers/Liberals in power. Unlike their opponents, the
Conservatives could never seem to unite against the "common foe."
Protestants tended to vote Conservative, but except for strongly opinionated newspapermen like Henry Winton, they did not to have the
same degree of moral support that the Catholics had in their clergy.

Although clerical interference certainly did escalate and coarsen
the tensions between the two ethnic groups, this was not the only
factor. Long before Newfoundland was granted self-government, Irish
Roman Catholics were treated worse than second-class citizens. The
humiliation and degradation they endured throughout the latter 1700s
fostered a culture of animosity and distrust that was periodically mani-

fested through some horrendous crimes, and, on one occasion, even an attempted mutiny, thus in turn fuelling English distrust. Even considering such conditions, it would be untrue to say that the trouble all began because of the social, political, and economic status of the Irish here in Newfoundland, for the seeds of this feud were planted long before Newfoundland was colonized, and were set deep in the soil of the Old Country. As one historian notes, "In retrospect, one sees Newfoundland in the first three decades of representative government as an embittered little Ireland, for conditions in the new land fostered memories of wrongs in the old."[1]

The Irish indeed had some serious issues as they entered that first House of Assembly in 1832, and they were, understandably, spoiling for a fight. The pity is that some of their leaders, secular as well as clerical, antagonized and offended many prominent English who might otherwise have been sympathetic. Nor was it just the English who were offended. Beginning in 1832 with Timothy Hogan and Patrick Kough, a line of disenchanted Irish Catholics, labelled "mad dogs" by their co-religionists, can be traced all the way to Nowlan and Byrne.

Political campaigns became much more civilized after the bedlam of 1861, but not necessarily quieter. The debate over confederation with Canada raged for years, until the issue was finally settled in 1949. It raised its head several times before that, however. Usually when Newfoundland stumbled through a particularly gruelling economic downturn some confederate would toss the subject about as a viable solution to the island's woes. But these were only half-hearted attempts, for the most part, and confederation really did not become election fodder again until Joseph Smallwood arrived eighty years after the initial debate.[2]

While politicians of different stripes forged some very unprecedented, some people would have said very unorthodox, alliances, the general population still suffered under the same virulent animosities

---

1. Gunn, *The Political History of Newfoundland.*
2. There were negotiations in 1895, in the wake of the Bank Crash, but neither side appeared particularly serious.

as before. The wounds were cut way too deep for this to change overnight. The bitterness had become more than just ethnic, political, or even religious; it was also personal. Irish Catholic Liberals might live on the same street as English Protestant Conservatives but, for the most part, both avoided each other when possible, or fought when the opportunity presented itself, as it often did during periods of little work. Just months after the deadly election riots of 1861, for example, the town of Carbonear erupted again in one of the most destructive, and certainly most protracted, ethno-religious riots the island ever experienced.

It began on Old Christmas Day when a parade of Roman Catholic mummers clashed with Protestants living in the area of Harbour Rock Hill in the east end. It lasted for five days; dozens of people were wounded by cudgels and firearms, Water Street became a field of debris, and it was finally quelled by a significant military force from St. John's. This became infamously known as the Mummers' Riot. The media's reaction was harsh, though biased, as exemplified by the January 10 *Public Ledger* editorial: "The town of Carbonear has long enjoyed an unenviable notoriety for festering scamps and rowdies of the worst description, who were as easily picked out from amongst a crowd as if they were specially decorated with distinguishing badges." The more peaceable citizens of Carbonear were greatly disturbed by what one letter writer called "our war troubles." However, with so many participants, and both sides relating differing versions of what instigated the riot, the subsequent investigation, like so many others before, was futile.

It must have appeared to many leading citizens in Newfoundland that a peaceful coexistence between the religions was not possible. Despite the redirected efforts of numerous politicians and clergy, Newfoundland was now reaping what decades of clerical electioneering had sown, a community made up of mostly fishermen trying to eke out a living in an often inhospitable environment, where half the population hated and distrusted the other half. Years after the introduction of self-government, Roman Catholics still thought Protestants had an advantage in society, and Protestants, after over twenty years of Liberal rule, saw Catholics wanting their own way in politics. But the 1861 election had taught Protestants that a united front could defeat the Catholic clerical hegemony at the hustings. Having known the bitter taste of defeat for so long, Protestants now found that they liked the taste of victory. This new political confidence further united the general Protestant population, and may have instigated the appearance of that fraternal brotherhood which had been condemned by Roman Catholic leaders for years, the Loyal Orange Association (LOA).

Despite the early scare tactics used by reform (later Liberal) politicians, clergy, and media, there were no Orangemen in Newfoundland until 1863, when Dr. Thomas Leeming of Prince Edward Island encouraged ten prominent St. John's citizens to start Royal Oak Loyal Orange Lodge.[3]

A decade later there were thirteen lodges scattered throughout most of the larger towns on the Avalon and Bonavista Peninsulas. The appearance of the LOA in Newfoundland was probably inevitable, largely because of the presence of strong English loyalties, but also because it was well established in the rest of British North America. The rapid expansion of the LOA in Newfoundland undoubtedly had many Roman Catholics, and some Protestants, worried. What did its emergence mean? How could it be possible to "fix" Newfoundland society when an increasing number of the Protestant population was being initiated into this potentially dangerous anti-Catholic society? With the rapid decline of Roman Catholic clerical influence after 1861, the opportunity was ripe for Orange ascendancy. But it could not happen without a violent Catholic response.

In 1875 the first major disturbance involving the LOA broke out aboard the sealing vessel *Greenland* in St. John's harbour. Orangemen from Bay Roberts were implicated in what was initially a fistfight with crewmen from St. John's, but which quickly spread out into the nearby street. According to one press report, "sticks, gaffs, and knives [were in] speedy requisition, and cuts and blows freely exchanged between

---

3. One of whom was David Smallwood, grandfather of J.R. Smallwood.

the combatants, who were in a state of fury little short of madness." Dozens of police officers and magistrates responded, along with clergymen, to quell a disturbance that threatened to become another full-scale riot.[4]

Thus, the Orange Order began a new chapter in the history of Protestant/Catholic relations in Newfoundland, ensuring that, while politics might make for strange bedfellows, religion was much more discriminatory.

The ensuing years would clearly demonstrate this curious anomaly, as Catholics and Protestants united for some important matters, such as the decision on confederation and the French Shore question. The latter issue may have been especially effective in helping Newfoundlanders of all creeds to see the benefits of collaboration, since French fishing rights were considered by *all* as an infringement on their sovereignty. Catholics and Protestants, merchants and fishermen, clergymen and politicians were universally opposed to this ongoing international oppression. Yet, in the background lurked the spectre of past conflicts and prejudices. We *could* unite against a common foe, but in daily transactions Catholics and Protestants still preferred to remain segregated. Organizations such as the Orange Lodge and the Benevolent Irish Society ensured that this social order remained firmly in place.

---

4. See Appendix 11 (from *The Newfoundland Express*).

Appendices

#1
The Riot Act

Our Sovereign Lady the Queen chargeth and commandeth all persons, being assembled, immediately to disperse themselves, and peaceably to depart to their habitations, or to their lawful business, upon pains contained in the Act, made in the first year of King George, for preventing tumults and riotous assemblies. God Save the Queen.

I am, &c.
James Crowdy, Secretary

#2
Instructions to the magistrates at Harbour Grace for the cutting down of the trees on the sides of the road from that place to Carbonear

Gentlemen,
It having been represented to the Governor that it is very desirable that the wood on each side of the road from Harbour Grace to Carbonear shall be cut down to the extent of at least 50 yards from the center in order to prevent the recurrence of such atrocious attacks as that made on Mr. Winton, I am directed by His Excellency to request you will have this service performed in the most economical manner and with the least possible delay, and on your transmitting to me a certified statement of the expense incurred the amount will be immediately paid.

#3

Extract from Bishop Fleming's response to the Pope's censure,
February 28, 1841

My heart is pierced by an indescribable pain at the mere thought
that His Holiness may have been able to believe for a moment
that I did not follow the instructions given me by the Sacred
Congregation. But the fact is that I have not received, neither
directly nor indirectly, such an order or instruction from the
Sacred Congregation with regard to the present case; neither
have I the least idea (even at this moment) of the time and the
manner in which this instruction was communicated, and so I
believe myself guiltless of any accusation in this regard.

#4

Petition of Nicholas Ash of Carbonear, Planter, January 21, 1841

To His Excellency, Henry Prescott

The petitioner was induced from conscientious motives to take
an interest in the late election. That he felt himself bound, on
various accounts, to give his unbiased vote in favour of Mr.
James L. Prendergast, notwithstanding the repeated attempts at
intimidation with which he had been repeatedly assailed.

That on the evening of the 8th December he was obliged
to return to his house in consequence of the violence of the
mob that had sided with the opposite party, and that now threatened to visit with immediate punishment all those who had
voted against them.

That having witnessed the relentless cruelty of the said mob
towards a number of individuals but a few hours before, he felt
himself compelled to use every lawful precaution for the preservation of his own life, as well as that of his wife and little ones.

That between the hours of 7 and 8 o'clock in the evening
aforesaid, petitioner's house was assailed in the most furious

manner by a large number of persons, who commenced throwing large stones at the windows, battering in the doors, and in fact demolishing the house and property, and placing the lives of its inmates in the greatest jeopardy. That at this crisis, hearing the groans and screams of his wife and children, succeeded by savage yells of the mob, who now were on the point of entering, petitioner after warning them of the consequences, caught up a gun, and fired a load of small shot among the foremost of the assailants.

That the crowd becoming more dense and furious, after again warning them to desist, he repeated the act, which seemed only to increase their rage and determination, upon which petitioner was obliged secretly to quit the house to save himself from immediate destruction.

That very shortly after this the house was set fire to, and the whole building with its contents was speedily reduced to ashes. That the value of the property thus destroyed must have been at its lowest estimate value at 500 pounds sterling, the loss of which in all probability has made a poor man of petitioner for the rest of his days.

That under these afflicting circumstances, and in accordance with the advice and wishes of many of his friends, petitioner now craves to the liberty of laying this brief statement of his case under your Excellency's notice, petitioner being encouraged with the hope that your Excellency will take its peculiar merits into your Excellency's gracious consideration, and that your Excellency will be pleased to direct that some public measure be taken in order that petitioner may be remunerated for his otherwise irreparable loss. And as in duty bound will ever pray.

Nicholas Ash

#5

Complaint made by Mary Barron against Father Troy's refusal to give spiritual assistance to her dying husband, July 4, 1837

On Sunday night the 21st November my husband, the late Lawrence Barron being dangerously ill, and desirous of seeing one of the Roman Catholic clergymen, two of my neighbours, Lawrence Maccassey and Mrs. Ansack, went to see one, and on learning where the clergymen were they repaired to the house where they had been spending the evening. On seeing them and on communicating their business, one of the clergymen the Reverend Mr. Waldron expressed his willingness to come and prepare my husband for death but was prevented by the Reverend Mr. Troy who is the superior, and who said that no priest should prepare him, and that is the way in which all Mad Dogs should die - that there would not be one of them alive in five years. On being repeatedly solicited he still refused, and further stated that if Mr. Waldron should prepare him, or administer any Sacrament to him, he would have his vestments taken off him in the morning. In less than an hour afterwards Mr. Maccassey came into my house and said to my dying husband that one of the priests would attend him, if he would write an apology for having ever acted in any manner against the will or opinion of the clergy, and of his determination to act in every respect in future as they should direct. My husband well knowing he had never committed any offence against his religion or its clergy and indignant at such treatment, got pen and paper and commenced writing. Mr. Maccassey who saw what he was writing said that won't do, but as Father Waldron is now in my house, I'll step over and get him to write the paper and you will have nothing to do but sign it. On this Maccassey retired and shortly after returned with a paper - he read it in my presence - it contained an expression of sorrow for having acted against the will of the clergy - for having associated with those who were opposed to their views, and above all for having dined at the Factory on the Festival of St. Patrick. It contained a great deal more which I do not remember. My husband neither did nor would sign it - he was then very ill, he said he would look at it in the morning. He died that night without having been prepared, and they refused on being sent for to attend at the graveyard at his interment.

Mary Barron

#6

Extract from Bishop Fleming's obituary in *The Public Ledger* for July 16, 1850

DIED - On Sunday night the 14th inst. at twenty minutes past ten o'clock, at the Franciscan Monastery of this city, the Right Rev. Michael Anthony Fleming, D.D., Roman Catholic Bishop of Newfoundland, after a prolonged illness of nearly two years, borne in a spirit of Christian fortitude and resignation. Dr. Fleming lived not for himself but for his people; for their advantage he put forth every energy; all his exertions were devoted to the amelioration of their moral, their religious, and their social condition.

#7

Part of Robert Walsh's testimony regarding the assault upon his house during the Harbour Grace election of 1859

In Callahan's and French's there was a good deal of property destroyed by the mob; fearing another attack, I put my father in the cellar for safety; in about half an hour the same crowd returned; I went to the upper part of the building for safety and to avoid them, they forced the door and entered, the only weapon I had to defend myself was a knife, I called on my son to bring it to me, he was prevented by my wife; heard someone say "Pull the b——r out"; my wife stood on the stairs; the mob forced their way up; she said I was not in; they left without finding me; they forced in the shop door, my wife went in and ordered them out.

#8

Extracts from Henry Winton's obituary in *The Public Ledger*, January 16, 1855

He was a man of unbounded hospitality - a fair specimen in this respect of the good old English gentleman.

Not that he was at all intolerant where religious opinions and convictions were concerned; but he strongly deprecated the interference of ecclesiastics in political questions, and their assumption of any influence beyond those associated with their sacred calling.

It requires a heart of steel and nerves of brass to withstand the ebulitions [sic] of the discordant elements of those troublesome times - and he was admirably adapted for the work, and performed the duty with a consistency and integrity which earned for him the admiration of his friends and the respect of his enemies.

#9

Henry Winton's obituary in *The Patriot*, January 29th, 1855

The editor of *The Ledger* lived long enough to see the utter prostration of the politics he advocated so stoutly but so insincerely and the party he defended so boldly. Let him rest!

#10

Threatening letter received by William Holden, Returning Officer at Holyrood

Holden, I think you ought to make much of your time in Harbour Main now, for I think you have not long to live there. Another thing, you won't have anything to live in, for before two months is at an end, you will not have a stick or a stump in Harbour Main. You bloody informer - you bugger, it was you who informed on the liberal men that hauled down Strapp's house, although the Harbour Main people did not hear it yet, but they will not be long so, for it will be proved before this day's week. Ah Holden! I would not be in your place for 1000 pounds. You are nearly as bad as that murderer Nowlan - You are after depriving them men of their summer's earnings for their poor families. What will the Harbour Main people say when they hear all that? Oh Holden! God forgive you, you Tory Rascal of Hell. There is no one to be pitied as your *"Liberal wife," and that she is to the back bone*, and her house full of children. Oh God help you, you foolish man.

Holden, before two weeks is at an end, your house and all in it will be no more. You Tory vagabond - you informer on rum and men.

Now, Mr. Holden, a few words with you. I send you this letter, to inform you that you ought never to be tired giving thanks to God for preserving you from our clutches when you were in St. John's last week. We were looking for you when you were here, but we could not make you out; but as sure as God is in Heaven, if we had happened to catch you, you would never go home alive, you two-faced Tory w—eson. We were not told where you resided until you were gone. If we knew you were at Walsh's house, we would not leave a stick of it standing, you bloody Nowlan supporter. You tried *underhand*, with your sneaking ways, to get him in, you scamp. Only for you were afraid to do it in noonday, you would speak for Nowlan and

Byrne on the hustings. You bloody informer, you went and signed a number of names to a petition, and sent it to Byrne, the *"old humbug"*, to come and oppose Furey, but we know the reason - you were opposed to Furey because he had a shop in opposition to you, and was beginning to take a *little* of the call from you. Do you mind the time you informed on the poor people that had not license for selling rum, you selfish Tory? Ah! Holden my boy, if you don't mind yourself, you will rue the day. Faith, if we ever get hold of you in St. John's again, you will never get the better of it. We know where you stop now. You were afraid to stop at Mrs. Brennan's. I don't think you stirred out, on the time you were here. You Tory villain, if you meddle or go against a Liberal candidate again, we will not wait to catch you here, the distance is not far to Harbour Main. It was you, you cursed informer, that wrote a list of the names of the men, and got them taken, that tore down Strapp's house, although there is not many know it, you villain, but we never intend to make it public, you Nowlan bigot.

#11
The Newfoundland Express, Monday, March 15, 1875

A row of a very serious character took place in Water street about midday last Wednesday, between a number of Bay Roberts men composing the crews of the steamers *Greenland* and *Iceland* on one side, and some St. John's men on the other. It originated, as often happens, between two of opposing parties, but soon became general. The opening scene was on Messers Stabbs' premises, but the prompt presence and active exertions of Inspector Carty and a body of police, served to repress the riot there. It quickly broke out, however, in other places, and was continued on the ice, sticks, gaffs, and knives being in speedy requisition, and cuts and blows freely exchanged between the combatants, who were in a state of fury little short of madness. For an hour or two the whole town was in a state of alarm, as it was impossible to say to what an extent the disturbance might reach; fortunately, however, though severe bodily injuries were inflicted in several instances, nothing worse resulted. The steamer *Greenland* sustained much damage from the violence of some men who forced their way on board.

His Excellency the Governor, and Chief Justice Hoyles were present for some time, and did good service in preventing further mischief. The Reverend Fathers Forristal, McGrath, and Scott exerted themselves with marked effect in restoring peace, and the two Captains Jackman and Dawe gave judicious and valuable assistance. Inspector Carty and his men deserve high praise for their conduct on the occasion - no management could have been better than that with which they met the emergency. Those amongst us who have underrated the mounted Police could have seen on Wednesday what ought to be enough to satisfy them of the efficient service this force can render in breaking up knots of rioters.

What the special cause of this fray was, we do not know, but something will probably be learned of it in inquiries now going on before the Police Court.

BIBLIOGRAPHY

<u>Books</u>

Andrews, Gerald. *Heritage of a Newfoundland Outport: The Story of Port de Grave.* St. John's: Jesperson Publishing, 1997.

Darcy, Brother J.B. *Fire Upon the Earth: The Life and Times of Bishop Michael Anthony Fleming.* St. John's: Creative Publishers, 2003.

Galgay, Frank. *Life and Times Sir of Ambrose Shea: Father of Confederation.* St. John's, NL: Harry Cuff Publications, 1986.

Greene, John. *Between Damnation and Starvation: Priests and Merchants in Newfoundland Politics, 1745-1855.* Montreal: McGill-Queen's University Press, 1999.

Gunn, Gertrude. *The Political History of Newfoundland 1832 to 1864.* Toronto: University of Toronto Press, 1966.

Horwood, Harold. *Newfoundland.* Toronto: MacMillan of Canada, 1969.

Matthews, Keith. *Lectures on the History of Newfoundland: 1500-1830.* St. John's, NL: Breakwater Books, 1988.

Moyles, R.G. *"Complaints is Many and Various, but the Odd Divil Likes It." Nineteenth Century Views of Newfoundland.* Toronto: Peter Martin and Associates, 1975.

McCarthy, Michael. *The Irish in Newfoundland: 1600-1900: Their Trials, Tribulations, and Triumphs.* St. John's, NL: Creative Publishers, 1999.

Noel, S.J.R. *Politics in Newfoundland.* Toronto: University of Toronto Press, 1971.

O'Flaherty, Patrick. *Old Newfoundland: A History to 1843.* St. John's: Long Beach Press, 1999.

O'Flaherty, Patrick. *Lost Country: The Rise and Fall of Newfoundland, 1843-1933.* St. John's, NL: Long Beach Press, 2005.

O'Neill, Paul. *A Seaport Legacy.* Erin, ON: Press Porcepic, 1976.

O'Neill, Paul. *The Oldest City: The Story of St. John's, Newfoundland.* Portugal Cove-St. Philip's, NL: Boulder Publications, 2003.

Prowse, Daniel. *A History of Newfoundland.* Portugal Cove-St. Philip's: Boulder Publications, 2002.

Rowe, Frederick. *A History of Newfoundland and Labrador.* Toronto: McGraw-Hill-Ryerson, 1980.

Ryan, Shannon. *Newfoundland-Spanish Saltfish Trade: 1814-1918.* St. John's: Harry Cuff Publications, 1983.

Smallwood, J.R. *Dr. William Carson, The Great Newfoundland Reformer; His Life and Times.* St. John's: Newfoundland Book Publishers (1967) Limited, 1978.

Articles

Byrne, Cyril. "Some Comments on the Social Circumstances of Mummering in Conception Bay and St. John's in the Nineteenth Century." *Newfoundland Quarterly* (Winter 1981).

Darcy, J.B. "Out of the Past: Father Edward Troy (1797-1872)," *The Monitor.*

Dunne, Ben. "In Search of the Masterless Men." *East Coast Trail Association News* (Fall 1997).

Fraser, Joy. "Newfoundland Mumming," *Shima: The International Journal of Research into Island Cultures* 3.2 (2009).

Fleming, Michael Anthony. "The Catholic Mission in Newfoundland," *The London and Dublin Orthodox Journal* (September 10, 1836).

Gough, Rev. T.J. "Reverend James Duffy's Well – RIP." *Newfoundland Quarterly* (December 1926).

Harrington, Michael. "Flaming History." In *Book of Newfoundland.* Ed. J.R. Smallwood. Vol. 2, St. John's Book Publishers, St. John's, 1937.

Hooper, Tom. "The St. John's Gibbett." *National Historic Parks and Sites, Manuscript Number 107.* June, 1968.

Horwood, Harold. "The Masterless Men of the Butter Pot Barrens." *Newfoundland Quarterly* (November 1966).

Moyles, R.G. "Fire, Frost, and Famine: St. John's in 1817." *Newfoundland Quarterly* (June 1970).

McCarthy, Michael J. "The Irish in Early Newfoundland." *Newfoundland Quarterly* (Winter 1988).

O'Flaherty, Patrick. "The Road to Saddle Hill." *Newfoundland Quarterly* (July 1995).

O'Flaherty Patrick. "The Newfoundland Irish." *Newfoundland Quarterly* (October 1990).

O'Hara, Aiden. "'The Entire Island is United." *History Ireland* 8 (Spring 2000).

O'Neill, Paul. "Father Duffy: Parts I, II, and III." *The Monitor* (April 1980).

Parsons, Richard A. "Our Former Constitution." *Book of Newfoundland.* Volume I. St. John's Book Publishers, St. John's, 1937.

Wakeham, P.J. "The City That Refused to Die." *The Atlantic Advocate* (July 1967).

Archival Sources

PANL
CO 194, 1817-18; CO 194/87, ff52-4, 60-83, 106-11; CO 194/88, ff 21-9, 55-9; CO 194/89, ff376-8; CO 194/90, 1835; CO 194/94, ff45 - 73, 63-66, 72, 318; CO 194/95, ff206-93,310-32, 368; CO 194/97, 1836; CO 194/108, May, 1840; CO 194/109, ff13-40, 284-90; CO 194/110, ff44-52; CO 192/111, ff4-22; CO 194/161, ff 44-55; CO 194/165; CO 194/166; GN 1/1, Governor Prescott's Despatches 1836-37.; GN 2/1/A, Volumes 1-4, and Volume 32; GN 2/2, January-August, 1834; May, 1840; GN 5/2/A/1, 1820-21; GN 170, Court Records Collection

<u>The Journals of the House of Assembly</u>
1833-41, 1843, 1854, 1859-61.

<u>Archives of the Roman Catholic Archdiocese of St John's, The Basilica</u>
Bishop Michael Anthony Fleming's papers

<u>Newspapers</u>

The Harbour Grace Standard, The Mercantile Journal, The Newfoundlander, The Newfoundland Express, The Newfoundland Patriot, The Public Ledger, The Star and Conception Bay Journal, The Times

<u>Internet Sites</u>

www.heritage.nf.ca

www.stjohnsarchdiocese.nf.ca
"History of the Basilica of St. John the Baptist"
"Fools and Mummers"
"Apostolic Priests"

www.ucs.mun.ca/~melbaker/1815-48.htm

www.books.google.ca, "A Chapter in the History of Newfoundland for the year 1861," Henry Winton (Jr.).

www.genweb.ca/nf

<u>Interviews</u>

Hynes-Lawlor, Tammy. April 1, 1998.
Strapp, Mr. and Mrs. Michael. July 5, 2010.

INDEX

David Dawe was born in Bay Roberts and currently resides there with his wife, Corinne, and two teenaged children, Meagan and Aaron. He is an educator at Holy Redeemer School in Spaniard's Bay, teaching elementary and junior high students who say they enjoy his classes for the stories he relates. This is entirely in line with his philosophy of teaching his greatest love, history, which is "to tell the human stories, not just to regurgitate the facts."

Mr. Dawe's fascination with history was born when he was a youth, listening to the war stories of his grandfather, a veteran of World War I and Mr. Dawe's personal hero. There have been other inspirations as well, including colourful local characters, entertaining writers, and engaging university professors.

As he gets closer to retirement, Mr. Dawe hopes to spend more time researching and writing Newfoundland history.

Québec, Canada

2011

Printed on Silva Enviro 100% post-consumer EcoLogo certified paper, processed chlorine free and manufactured using biogas energy.